A radical history of development studies

UMA KOTHARI | editor

A radical history of development studies

Individuals, institutions and ideologies

David Philip
CAPE TOWN

Zed Books
LONDON | NEW YORK

For Tim, Jay and Kim

A radical history of development studies: individuals, institutions and ideologies
was first published by Zed Books Ltd, 7 Cynthia Street, London N1 9JF, UK
and Room 400, 175 Fifth Avenue, New York, NY 10010, USA in 2005

www.zedbooks.co.uk

First published in Southern Africa in 2005 by David Philip (an imprint of New
Africa Books), 99 Garfield Road, Claremont 7700, South Africa

Cover designed by Andrew Corbett
Set in Arnhem and Futura Bold by Ewan Smith, London
Index: ed.emery@britishlibrary.net
Printed in Great Britain by the MPG Books Group, Bodmin and King's Lynn

Distributed in the USA exclusively by Palgrave Macmillan, a division of
St Martin's Press, LLC, 175 Fifth Avenue, New York, NY 10010.

A catalogue record for this book is available from the British Library.
US CIP data are available from the Library of Congress.

ISBN 978 1 84277 524 0 hb
ISBN 978 1 84277 525 7 pb

Contents

Acknowledgements

Although it seems a while ago now, the origins of this book lie in a research project funded by the University of Manchester entitled 'From Colonialism to Development'. I am grateful to those who shared with me their life stories, experiences and understandings of the history of development in the course of this endeavour. These include: Derek Belshaw, Robert Chambers, Bill Dodd, Colin Fuller, Tommy Gee, Dick Grove, Margaret Harwood, Richard Jolly, Anthony Kirk-Greene, Hans Singer and Terry Spens. I would also like to thank my friend and colleague Martin Minogue, with whom I first began to develop these ideas on the genealogy of development studies. Over the years I have benefited greatly from discussions with students at the Institute for Development Policy and Management, University of Manchester (IDPM), particularly those on the Social Policy and Social Development programme, about their experiences of studying and doing development.

Earlier versions of some of the chapters in this volume were presented at a conference on 'A Radical History of Development Studies' at IDPM in November 2002. I would like to thank Debra Whitehead, whose administrative expertise ensured that this over-subscribed event went smoothly, and David Hulme and Phil Woodhouse for their encouragement and support. The conference provided a space for thought-provoking and stimulating discussions for which I thank the paper presenters and participants. I am grateful to the contributors to this volume, Karen Hunt for her part in putting together the final manuscript, and to my editor at Zed Books, Robert Molteno.

Numerous friends and colleagues have offered invaluable advice and intellectual support during the production of this book, and I would particularly like to thank Jo Beall, Tony Bebbington, Sarah Bracking, Andries du Toit, Tim Jacoby, Nina Laurie, Cameron McCarthy and Hulya Ulku. A special note of appreciation to Sam Hickey, who provides intellectual as well as moral support, and ensures that work does not get in the way of tea breaks. Thanks also to family and friends, especially Izzat Darwazeh, Sue Hay, Lopa and Avani Kothari and Leti Volpp. And finally, love and respect to Tim Edensor, who continues to draw my attention to new and exciting perspectives.

1 | A radical history of development studies: individuals, institutions and ideologies

UMA KOTHARI

Why a radical history of development studies?

This book provides radical, historically informed readings of the emergence, trajectories and interpretations of international development. It presents a critical genealogy of development studies through exploring changes in discourses about development and examining the contested evolution and role of development institutions by focusing upon the recollections of those who teach, research and practise development. These accounts challenge the dominant, modernist narrative that posits a singular, unilinear trajectory and present alternative versions of ideas and institutions, and the people that embody them. The book shows how the work of individuals and institutions engaged in contemporary development studies cannot be properly understood without adequate historical contextualization. Accordingly, the chapters presented in this volume will attempt to understand why and how international development, generally, and development studies, specifically, have evolved.

This is a radical chronicle because it includes plural conceptions of development history and adopts a critical perspective towards, and engagement with, orthodoxies of development theory and practice. Each chapter, moreover, is radical in at least one of two other senses – first, by highlighting those concealed, critical discourses that have been written out of conventional stories of development or marginalized in mainstream accounts of ideas that have influenced contemporary understandings of development thought; second, in that their critique of ideas and practices of development is founded upon, and emerged out of, thinking from the 'left'. In this book these radical interpretations are represented by, for example, Marxist, post-colonial and feminist perspectives and analyses.

With a few notable exceptions the history often rehearsed in development research and teaching has tended towards a compartmentalization of clearly bounded, successive periods characterized by specific theoretical hegemonies that articulate a singular theoretical genealogy. Typically, the story commences with economic growth and modernization theories, moves on to discuss theories of 'underdevelopment', and culminates in neo-liberalism and the Washington Consensus (see Hettne 1995; Preston 1996). This periodization, moreover, is mapped on to particular events and processes, most notably with the reification of 1945 as the key year in which development was initiated owing to the establishment of the World Bank and other Bretton Woods institutions. Recent critical explorations, from post-colonial, postmodern and feminist perspectives, have undoubtedly provided important challenges to orthodox development chronologies but they have to varying degrees continued to conform to the same periodization (Marchand and Parpart 1995; Rist 1997; Kothari and Minogue 2001), as have those that present alternative visions of development (Munck and O'Hearn 1999; Rahnema and Bawtree 1997). To counter these trends and develop the longer historical perspectives and alternative readings of the origins and evolution of development taken by Jonathan Crush (1995) and Cowen and Shenton (1996), the chapters in this book highlight how bounded classifications and epochal historicizations not only obscure a longer genealogy of development but also undermine attempts to demonstrate historical continuities and divergences in the theory and practice of development, compounding the concealment of ongoing critiques. They underscore how this limited analysis reveals the largely unreflexive nature of the field of study, partly engendered through the imperative to achieve development goals and targets.

By providing different understandings of the growth of development studies, this book subverts a mainstream unilinear history and moves beyond a periodization of theoretical positions. More broadly, by using development studies as a case study, some of the chapters challenge ideas about discourse and power by questioning particular notions of what constitutes development and the 'Third World', and interrogate our understandings of the interrelationship between what Stuart Hall (1996) refers to as the 'West and the Rest'. In critiquing orthodox ideas, challenging normative representations and highlighting both continuities and divergences over time and across space, they disrupt the projection of a singular record of the past. These understandings are essential to identify how the present is informed by the past and to further recognize that history can enable a (re)visioning of future strategies for change.

While the importance of reflexively tracing the evolution of their disciplines has recently been acknowledged by some within, for example, anthropology and geography, understanding the implications of the past is not a mainstream preoccupation within development studies. This volume represents an attempt at exploring the history of development studies as a multi-disciplinary subject that emerged in the post-war era of decolonization, but was also informed by antecedent influences. It takes a multi-methodological and holistic approach by weaving together different narratives, including personal recollections of working in development studies, histories of particular themes, such as gender, social development and natural resources within development studies, and genealogies of development institutions such as the World Bank. Some of the chapters redirect attention towards ideas, ideologies and concepts in a field that for some time has been characterized by more practical and technical concerns. The insistence on the link between past and present, and adopting a radical appreciation of a range of perspectives, will (it is hoped) mark a significant moment in the critical reconfiguration of development studies.

Understanding development studies

Understandings of the nature and concept of development studies are as varied, multiple and contentious as definitions of what constitutes development itself. Indeed, particular perceptions of what constitutes development studies are linked to, and often embedded in, particular notions about what development is.

That development studies is open to varying and contesting interpretations is evident from ongoing discussions among those in relevant academic departments, institutions and associations. There are diverse views concerning what development studies is or should be, ranging from opinions as to whether it is primarily about academic research or more concerned with policy and practical relevance, whether it possesses a specific epistemology and methodology, and the extent to which it is multi-disciplinary, inter-disciplinary or cross-disciplinary. These contesting points of view reflect competing understandings about the purpose of development and the nature of the relationship between theories and ideologies, policies and practices. Furthermore, they highlight the various insights into, and perspectives on, the genealogy of development.

Significantly, these issues have cohered around debates on the distinctiveness of development studies as a field of academic study. There is general agreement that development studies cannot claim to be a distinct and separate academic discipline in the same way as, for instance, economics or geography, partly because it is a relatively new field of study. Rather it is cross-disciplinary, engaging with different bodies of theory, conceptual and methodological frameworks, and understandings of policy relevance and practical implications. It is this borrowing and application of ideas from different disciplines that to some extent provides the distinctive characteristics of development studies. A series of articles in *World Development* (2002) explores this issue of cross-disciplinarity, a generic term relating to forms of analysis that are substantially based on theories, concepts and methods of

3

more than one discipline (see Kanbur 2002). Inter-disciplinary partnerships have proved difficult to achieve, however, and development studies can be more accurately described as multi-disciplinary. Although various disciplines are brought together in development studies and share the same academic space, and despite attempts to identify its epistemological and methodological distinctiveness (see Sumner and Tribe 2004), there has been limited success in producing truly hybrid theories, methodologies or practices.

While development studies cannot be identified as a discrete academic discipline there is a broad convergence among those in the 'community' on shared concerns and objectives. For example, there is some agreement about what the object/subject of study should be and what foundational theories and concepts students of development should be familiar with. Most commonly, development studies is seen to be concerned with processes of change in so-called 'Third World' or 'developing countries', and more recently this has been widened to encompass transitional economies. For some, there is also a narrowing of focus on studies of poverty and poverty alleviation while others have become increasingly concerned with socio-economic dimensions of global inequities and exclusionary processes. There remains, however, an ongoing debate as to the overwhelming importance of practice in relation to theory. In a paper on the irrelevance of development studies, Michael Edwards (1989) directly addresses this issue and argues that research within development studies is often abstract and divorced from development in practice and the realities of poor people. Thus, he contends, to understand development problems requires being involved in the process of development itself, thereby strengthening the links between research and action. The continuing relevance of this debate about research and practice is, in part, engendered by the legacy of the original context of post-independence development studies. When many development studies institutes were first established, those involved were primarily concerned with policy formulation and the technical and practical measures required to implement economic and social change, and accordingly spent much of their time overseas. This theory/practice divide, or what Sumner and Tribe (2004) refer to as the divergence between 'discourse-related' and 'instrumental/empirical-oriented' categories of development studies, has become exacerbated as alternative strands in development studies are increasingly uneasy with what is seen as the over-emphasis on planning change without significant identification and critique of the ideologies that underpin these standard policies and practices.

To clarify these points, Alan Thomas (2004) suggests that as the definition of 'development' adopted varies, so does the viewpoint concerning what development studies is *about* or *for*. His typology of the relationship between ideas

4

about development and ensuing definitions of development studies, which is presented below, explores further this issue of what should be studied and from what viewpoint.

Development as:	Development studies is:
Visions or measures of progressive change	*About* development: debating what is desirable or progressive for society; understanding human needs; measuring dimensions of poverty and 'development' (philosophy, psychology, economics, statistics, etc.).
Historical change process	*About* development: knowing about lives, livelihoods, social relations, etc., in different parts of the world and how they have changed; understanding, debating and applying theories of social change at local and global levels (history, sociology, political science, economics and anthropology).
Deliberate efforts at progress	*About* development: knowing about types of development agent, concepts of trusteeship, accountability; understanding the architecture of policy and governance locally and globally (social policy, organization studies, political science).
	For development: building skills and competencies for development policy and management (management, public administration, policy studies); empowering through study; building attitudes and skills of participation, lobbying and activism (development education, organization development, community development).

Source: Thomas (2004)

It is the interrelationship between theories, ideas and histories of development policy and practice which makes the identity of development as a subject of study so complicated and contested. There are those who feel that the study of development is most closely connected to ideas about social, economic and political change, while others are informed by a more instrumental goal of shaping policy and a practical concern with the implementation and evaluation of development interventions. Thus, there is disagreement as to where development studies should be located along a continuum from intellectual analyses and interpretations of processes of change to 'doing development'

5

utilizing the practical skills and techniques associated with transformation on the ground. Those who draw a parallel with the emergence of social policy as an academic discipline suggest that influencing, formulating and implementing policy must guide development studies. For example, Raymond Apthorpe suggests that development studies should be thought of as poverty or policy studies, and that 'changing from Development Studies to Poverty Studies offers an opportunity to incorporate ideas and methodologies from other disciplines into the social analysis of poverty' (1999: 535). These reflections on analysing and doing development – or *about* and *for* development – are at the heart of attempts to define development studies.

Michael Burawoy's (2004a) thought-provoking article on the disciplinary division of labour in sociology is particularly useful to those wrestling with the dilemmas involved in identifying coherent yet diverse development studies. Burawoy identifies four interdependent sociologies – policy, professional, critical and public – and makes the case that these are not 'alternatives but necessary complements'. He constructs a disciplinary matrix, reproduced below, while acknowledging that the boundaries between the different fields are often blurred, individuals can have multiple interests, and priorities vary between academic institutions, and over time.

	Academic audience	Extra-academic audience
Instrumental knowledge	Professional	Policy
Reflexive knowledge	Critical	Public

Source: Burawoy (2004b)

Burawoy (2004b) contrasts different audiences and different forms of knowledge and suggests that professional and policy work are primarily instrumental forms of knowledge 'inasmuch as they are concerned with orienting means to given ends, namely puzzle solving in professional research that takes for granted the presumptions of a given research program, and problem solving in the policy arena that takes for granted the goals and interests of the client'. He envisages critical and public fields as reflexive forms of knowledge that are oriented 'to a dialogue about assumptions, values, premises' among those in the discipline and with the public.

Applying this sort of disciplinary matrix to development studies could provide a useful starting point for identifying and appreciating the interconnectedness of the diverse range of activities, and perspectives, that come under its rubric. A discussion of this kind is imperative given the shifting local and global context in which development currently takes place. The chapters in this book, in various ways, contribute to this debate by demonstrating, for example, that development studies is not only about describing and understanding planned interventions but also about analysing discourses of development and seriously interrogating processes of socio-economic, political and institutional change. Not all contributors see their research as having direct policy and practical relevance but rather as providing the very necessary critiques and analyses of them. Development studies must, therefore, create opportunities to carry out policy-relevant research and devise methodologies and practical tools for development interventions, as well as a space for critical and radical academic investigation of ideas and histories.

Some of the authors challenge the dichotomies between 'studying' and 'doing' development that have been alluded to above, while others reaffirm these dualisms by emphasizing the distinct roles of theory and practice. Whatever their position, however, collectively these chapters provide further evidence for the importance of historically analysing the nature of development studies and exploring the ways in which development works both in and against its past. Despite their different and occasionally divergent conceptions of development studies, they provide a critique of, and challenge to, mainstream and orthodox notions of development and versions of its history.

What the book says

The histories of the institutions, ideas and individuals associated with development provide the focus for the analysis of development studies presented in this book. It is through these interconnected subjects that a radical and critical history of development is mapped out, continuities and divergences recognized and parallel histories remembered. This radical take on the archaeology and genealogy of development draws upon readings, from a range of viewpoints, that challenge established accounts of how development studies emerged, its priorities and ideological basis. The chapters link micro and macro levels of analyses, demonstrate how the past and present are imbricated and explore the relationship between personal experience, ideas and institutions of development. Some of the authors effectively weave their own personal narratives into the history of development studies as they map their individual trajectories on the development landscape. Producing stories of travel, networks, flows and relationships forged and maintained over time and space, they highlight the interconnectedness of ideologies, institutions and individuals that is arguably peculiar to development studies.

The authors who have contributed to this volume are, or have been, variously involved in a range of activities that include policy advice and technical assistance for non-governmental and governmental agencies, secondments to bilateral and multilateral organizations, consultancy work and funded academic research or that supported by bilateral donors. Some are first and foremost academics, involved in teaching and researching in development studies, while others see themselves primarily as advocates, practitioners and activists. Despite the variety of the forms of our engagement with the development industry, most of us are based in, or affiliated to, academic institutions. Although our academic backgrounds are located within the more traditional social science disciplines, we now work in multi-disciplinary departments or institutes of development studies. The increasing focus on research and teaching and the reduction in long periods of secondment overseas have changed the nature of development studies, and this is reflected in some of the histories presented in the book.

That this book is overwhelmingly UK focused is itself a reflection of the origins of development studies and particularly a colonial legacy of ideas concerning progress, modernity and trusteeship. In North America and much of western Europe studies of development in the main take place either within traditional social science disciplines or in area studies. In the UK, there were numerous sub-fields of, for example, development economics, the sociology of development, anthropology and development and development geography, and although these are still evident there has, since the late 1980s, been a tendency for development studies to be concentrated in specialized multi-disciplinary centres. While the case for highlighting the beginnings in the UK justifies the focus, we hope that this book opens the door for subsequent critical histories of development studies, especially from those located in parts of the world that have for long been the subject of the (Western) development gaze, yet are also significant agents of change and critics of development.

The body of the book is divided into two parts. The first presents personal recollections of working in development studies which highlight the emergence of development institutions and changes in the theory and practice of development over time. The colonial legacy of development is explored in this section, together with the political and personal tensions of working for development agencies. The second part begins with histories of radical ideologies of development, informed by Marxist critiques, that present parallel histories to those rehearsed in mainstream accounts. Other chapters in this section trace the path of ideas and ideologies of discourses on gender and development, natural resources and environmentalism, and non-governmental organizations, uncovering when and how they emerged and have transformed over time.

The book begins with a chapter by John Harriss, who describes and evaluates key trends in the history of development studies, combining his personal history as the 'first student of development studies' with a history of the people and ideas that have shaped the nature of the 'discipline'. He divides the history of development studies into three moments, those of promise, hubris and recovery, arguing that while development studies began with high ambitions, these were crushed in the 1980s with the onslaught of economic liberalism. Amid the hubris of that period, however, there were the roots of a recovery, though one that is not yet quite certain. The essay concludes with some assessment of the present paths of development studies, arguing that the challenge now lies not so much in resisting the critiques that derive from postmodernism as in renewing the discipline's relevance through improved historical understanding of development, and of the moral and practical requirements of global justice.

Although John Harriss's version of the history of development studies focuses primarily on the post-war period, he does acknowledge the legacy of colonialism, a theme that is developed in the following two chapters by Uma Kothari and Robert Chambers. Uma Kothari is concerned with a colonialism that 'survives the demise of empires' (Nandy 1998) and provides a postcolonial analysis of continuities and divergences over time. More specifically, the chapter focuses on the transition from colonialism to development and is, in part, based on the personal narratives of individuals whose experiences bridge and overlap this historical shift. These interviews with former colonial officers who subsequently worked in development studies institutes of higher education provide one historical method for uncovering and understanding the varied articulations of the transition from 'colonialism' to 'development cooperation', and the ongoing relationship between colonial forms of rule and governance and the purpose and practice of development. The chapter argues that mainstream development studies tends to conceal its colonial past and thus, perhaps unwittingly, creates a dichotomy between a colonialism that is 'bad', exploitative, extractive and oppressive and a development that is 'good', moralistic, philanthropic and humanitarian. In this way the apparent 'goodness' that inheres in development goes unquestioned.

Robert Chambers presents a personal history which begins with a period overseas as part of the Colonial Service. He reflects on his experiences as a colonial administrator and his involvement in former colonies after independence while based at the Institute for Development Studies at the University of Sussex. He describes how he has always felt on the margins of mainstream

9

development as an 'undisciplined non-economist'. He uses his experiences to reflect on what we do and how we do it in development studies, while recognizing that his story presents an idiosyncratic view. He concludes with a radical agenda for the future of development studies, advocating greater methodological awareness and critical reflexivity. In the final analysis Chambers argues that those working in development studies should become more nomadic 'to avoid the traps of isolation, insulation and complacency' and develop a greater facility for analysing the powerful and their actions.

Teresa Hayter, in Chapter 5, offers another personal story, but this time one that is connected with development institutions. The chapter reflects tensions and conflict as she narrates her attempts to challenge the World Bank and expose the divergence between what it says it is doing and what it actually does. The chapter focuses on her experiences of carrying out research on, and with, the World Bank from the 1960s to the 1980s, and some of the difficulties associated with publicizing her findings.

The second part of the book presents a history of ideas about development. Some chapters provide alternative versions while others invoke forgotten or marginalized histories. The section begins with a chapter by Henry Bernstein that considers the relationship between development studies and Marxism and some of the tensions that each brings to their encounters. These are sketched in terms of two conjunctures and the passage between them. The first incorporates the founding moment of development studies as an academic specialism in the 1950s and 1960s, a time of intense political and intellectual contestation additionally fuelled by the strong revival and development of Marxism in universities in the 1960s and 1970s. The second proposes some paradoxes about development studies from the 1980s with the ascendancy, then hegemony, of neo-liberal ideas. The first paradox is that whereby less (interventionism) prescribed by development doctrine becomes more (expanding political, social and cultural conditions for markets to work effectively); the second that whereby more, that is an expanding agenda, becomes less owing to the intellectual and political constraints of neo-liberal hegemony. The chapter argues that this second conjuncture also incorporates the challenges to Marxism presented by the demise of any extant examples of socialist development and other manifestations of political defeat in a period of apparently untrammelled globalization of capital.

John Cameron also invokes Marxism, in the following chapter, as he explores studies of poverty through his research publications over a period of thirty years. He suggests that the early 1970s were a high point in neo-Marxian development research, partly because this agenda could engage with the emerging basic-needs approaches that marked the key shift in development discourse during this period. The reassertion and dominance of neo-liberal principles and practices in the 1980s, however, demanded defensive reviews of ideas and principles associated with pro-poor research. This led to an uneasy engagement with post-structural and critical realist thinking in the 1990s which remains unresolved, although they could stimulate development thinking beyond simplistic anti-neo-liberalism. This journey is traced through the author's publications accompanied by reflections on what links them in terms of their ontological, epistemological and teleological coherence.

The following three chapters trace the intellectual history of particular fields of development: gender and development, natural resource management and environmentalism and the rise of NGOs. Ruth Pearson's chapter on the rise of gender and development traces the history of the discourse from its institutional and academic beginnings to its widespread positioning in contemporary development studies. This journey begins with an understanding of gender and development as a critical intervention into a predominantly masculinist discourse and ends with the mainstreaming of gender into development policy and practice. The author highlights some of the difficulties in moving gender and development studies forward which are posed by the recent postmodern and post-development turn in some academic writing in the field, as well as the institutional pressures to dissolve gender within more generalized categories of (in)equality and exclusion. The chapter concludes that in spite of its apparent success in terms of institutional development practice, radical gender analysis has yet to be acknowledged in key sites of development analysis and policy within the global context of development.

Phil Woodhouse and Admos Chimhowu's chapter similarly follows the origins and genealogy of a global issue that has become increasingly significant in development studies. Drawing on the authors' experience in southern and West Africa, the chapter traces the discourse of natural resource management and environmentalism. It begins by considering how a colonial discourse on nature continued to influence environmental thinking at the time development studies was emerging in the 1950s and 1960s. The chapter traces the crisis of modernization since the 1970s, and the rise of environmentalism that culminated in international consensus on the need for sustainable development in the 1990s, opening spaces for a variety of environmentally informed narratives of development. It argues that the contested meanings of sustainable development reflect continuing struggles over the control of natural resources of all kinds, in which environmental narratives are used to legitimize particular agendas of social and economic change.

The final chapter, by David Lewis, takes a personal look at the startling growth of writings within development studies on non-governmental organizations (NGOs), which began in the late 1980s. As he argues, however, NGOs were not new, but were 'discovered' by policy-makers and researchers during this period, in a process that tended to obscure a two-hundred-year history of international non-governmental public action. Furthermore, this period saw the rise of 'non-governmentalism', in which a set of unproven assumptions and often unrealistic expectations about NGOs became prevalent, driven by new policy imperatives concerning privatization and non-state actors within the wider context of neo-liberal ascendancy. The chapter contends that while valuable writings on NGOs emerged, some important problems with the 'NGO literature' resulted from all this, including normative bias, an emphasis on managerialism and a low theoretical content. NGOs remain, however, important actors in development, and the chapter concludes with some suggestions for a way forward for a critical NGO research agenda.

Taken together, the chapters in this volume challenge orthodoxies through personal histories and individual narratives to construct different, radical histories of intellectual origins, drawing upon traditions and debates that have been sidelined in mainstream international development discourse. Consequently, invoking Burawoy's matrix described above, these chapters can be located within the sphere of reflexive knowledge, which is both critical and public. They demonstrate that notwithstanding the co-optation of potentially radical discourses within a neo-liberal hegemony, which has dramatically reduced spaces of dissent and contestation, and as is evident from the writings in this volume, there remain critical voices.

References

Apthorpe, R. (1999) 'Development studies and policy studies: in the short run we are all dead', *Journal of International Development*, 11: 535–46

Burawoy, M. (2004a) 'Public sociologies: contradictions, dilemmas and possibilities', *Social Forces*, 82(4): 1603–18

— (2004b) 'The world needs public sociology', *Sosiologisk tidsskrift (Journal of Sociology*, Norway), 3

Cowen, M. and R. Shenton (1996) *Doctrines of Development*, London: Routledge

Crush, J. (1995) *Power of Development*, London: Routledge

Edwards, M. (1989) 'The irrelevance of development studies', *Third World Quarterly*, 11: 116–35

Hall, S. (1996) 'The West and the rest: discourse and power', in S. Hall, D. Held, D. Hubert and K. Thompson (eds), *Modernity: An Introduction to Modern Societies*, Oxford: Blackwell, pp. 39–47

Hettne, B. (1995) *Development Theory and the Three Worlds*, London: Longman

Kanbur, R. (2002) 'Economics, social science and development', *World Development*, 30(3): 477–86

Kothari, U. and M. Minogue (eds) (2001) *Development Theory and Practice: Critical Perspectives*, Basingstoke: Palgrave

Marchand, H. and J. Parpart (1995) *Feminism, Postmodernism Development*, London: Routledge

Munck, R. and D. O'Hearn (1999) *Critical Development Theory: Contributions to a New Paradigm*, London: Zed Books

Nandy, A. (1998) *The Intimate Enemy: Loss and Recovery of Self under Colonialism*, Delhi: Oxford University Press

Open University (1992) *Development Series*, Oxford: Oxford University Press

Preston, P. W. (1996) *Development Theory*, Oxford: Blackwell

Rahnema, M. and V. Bawtree (eds) (1997) *The Post-development Reader*, London: Zed Books

Rist, G. (1997) *The History of Development: From Western Origins to Global Faith*, London: Zed Books

Sumner, A. and M. Tribe (2004) 'The nature of epistemology and methodology in development studies: what do we mean by rigour?', Paper presented for session on the 'Nature of Development Studies', Development Studies Association Conference, London

Thomas, A. (2004) 'The study of development', Paper presented for session on the 'Concept of Development Studies', Development Studies Association Conference, London

Individuals, institutions and ideologies

ONE | Individuals and institutions

2 | Great promise, hubris and recovery: a participant's history of development studies[1]

JOHN HARRISS

The origins of theorizing, analysing and studying the social processes that are involved in bringing about the great changes in societies that can be described in terms of 'development' may be sought in the work of the Enlightenment philosophers, and in that of the great social theorists of the nineteenth century. Theirs was a grand vision of great processes of historical change. There were other scholars, too, such as Friedrich List, who developed more limited theories about how it may be possible for countries that have started their economic development after others to 'catch up'. Subsequently, in the twentieth century, Marxists and socialists and some progressive colonial administrators developed ideas and projects for bringing about social change. It is a matter of history that much that was implemented in the name of development policy after the end of colonialism reproduced ideas and projects that had already been initiated by colonial administrations. Quite when 'development studies' began, therefore, may be a matter for debate.

In this chapter, however, I will refer expressly to development studies as a self-defined field of academic and practical research and study that emerged, as I explain below, in a particular intellectual and political context in the 1960s.[2] 'Development studies', thus constituted, is a cross-disciplinary field of enquiry, concerned with analysing and understanding processes of social change (by 'social change' I mean to refer to 'society' in all its economic, political and cultural complexity). But development studies, even more than is usually the case in the social sciences, is also centrally concerned with studying how and why people act in particular ways, through 'policy interventions' or through political action, to change the *structure* of the social world. Much of social science is concerned with change, but development studies is concerned specifically with structural and institutional change, in contexts where countries are engaged in transformations towards an 'image of their own future' drawn from models usually provided by the experience of 'first comers'. It has, therefore, a normative dimension: the field is concerned with evaluating the ways in which people act to bring about change and sometimes with addressing the question of 'what is to be/should be done'. The history of development studies has involved, therefore, work on all these planes: that of the positive, historical analysis of how and why the social world is constituted as it is; that of the positive analysis, specifically, of intervention intended to bring about 'development' – study, that is, of what may be described as 'the development project' that was initiated after the Second World War; and the normative one. Work across the field has often been driven by problems in the 'real world', though there have also been moments when it has been driven perhaps too much by questions generated from within particular literatures, or from development 'practice' itself. Thus, for example, there was a moment in the later 1970s when some scholars in development studies were so preoccupied with their own particular concerns, deriving from theory or from particular policy engagements, that they were less aware than they might have been of the way in which the world was changing as the whole global regime of capital accumulation was undergoing radical transformation.

Development studies has been, *institutionally*, a distinctively British and to a lesser extent other European field of study. This is not to say that scholars from developing countries have not themselves made fundamental contributions, because of course there have been many of these made by Latin American, Asian and African writers such as Raul Prebisch, Mahmood Mamdani and numbers of Indian economists.[3] Similarly, immensely important contributions have been made by American or USA-based scholars. Here I am thinking of the work, for instance, of Robert Bates, Sarah Berry, Peter Evans, Merilee Grindle, Gillian Hart, James Scott and Michael Watts.[4] Among economists there is the work of, for example, Pranab Bardhan, Jagdish Bhagwati, Dani Rodrik and Joseph Stiglitz; and from an earlier generation of scholars that of Almond and Coleman, Clifford Geertz, Samuel Huntingon and Walt Rostow.[5] They have not, however, usually worked in specifically cross-disciplinary departments or institutes.

In this chapter I aim to describe and to evaluate important trends in development studies historically. Development studies began with high ambition but saw those ambitions crushed for a time by the onslaught of economic liberalism in the 1980s. Amid the hubris of that period, however, there were the roots of a recovery, though one that is not yet quite certain. I conclude with some assessment of the present trajectory of development studies in a context in which there are those who speak of 'post-development', which might be taken to imply the eclipse of development studies. This is rather a personal history, by a participant, so it inevitably involves distinct biases. Mine relate to the fact that I am not an economist, and that I have been devoted for a good deal of my professional life to empirical field research (where 'field' has often been taken literally), and to a particular region of the world (South Asia). With the advantage of hindsight I think that my own trajectory through development studies, like that of a good many others, has not involved anything like enough study of, or concern with, questions of international political economy. I do not regret my long engagement with grounded, local research and with one particular region of the world, and I believe that a strong defence can and should be made for area studies, unfashionable though they now are. But our 'areas' have to be placed in their context of international political economy and international relations in a way that they have often not been.

Rather mixing metaphors, I see the history of development studies as involving three movements, those of Promise, Hubris and Recovery, which have played themselves out through a drama in five acts:

Act I   Prolegomenon: the era of the positivist orthodoxy
Act II   Time of promise (c.1965–80)
Act III Hubris in the 1980s?
Act IV   Reinvention in the 1990s
Act V   'Post-development' in the twenty-first century: recovery or decline?

I entered into the drama myself at a critical stage, at about the end of Act I, when many of the principal players themselves recognized the existence of a 'crisis' in the prevailing orthodoxy. It was in the context of that sense of crisis that academic 'development studies' took off. Act V has just begun with a renewed sense of crisis, reflected perhaps in the recent advertisement (in late 2002) by a leading British university for a chair in *Post*-development Studies (though an appointment was not made). But 'crisis' once again contains the seeds of regeneration, and there is the possibility now of the recovery of that high ambition of the 1960s.

Prologomenon: the era of the 'positivist orthodoxy'

The 'positivist orthodoxy' is Colin Leys' term for the development theory of the late 1940s and 1950s, the heyday of development economics and of the idea of economic planning as an exercise of applied science. As Leys wrote, 'the goal of development was growth: the agent of development was the state and the means of development were national economic planning in the context of the macro-policy instruments established at Bretton Woods. These were the taken-for-granted presumptions of "development theory" as it evolved from the 1950s onwards' (Leys 1995: 7). The positivist orthodoxy implied that technocrats should analyse the problems of bringing about economic growth, and that good 'scientific' analysis would generate 'right answers' to the question of what should be done through planning.[6]

India was perhaps the paradigmatic case, as I have argued elsewhere (Harriss 1998). We should not forget the significant achievements of Indian planning in the 1950s and early 1960s, when in pursuit of the economic modernization that had been one of the principal drivers of Indian nationalism, the industrial structure of the economy was completely transformed and rates of industrial growth were achieved which have hardly ever been surpassed subsequently. But by the middle of the 1960s the whole planning effort had started to break down, foundering ultimately because of the compromise of power between the big bourgeoisie and the rural elite, and the consequent inability of the state to raise the revenues that were necessary to sustain the effort of planning (Corbridge and Harriss 2000). There was a 'crisis of Indian planning', recognized at the time in the eponymous title of Streeten and Lipton's book of 1968.

That book, and some others, such as Dudley Seers' and Mike Faber's book (Faber and Seers 1972) on the more general crisis of planning and of development economics, published later but stemming from a conference held at around the same time, helped to lay out the agenda for development studies. Another important contribution was made by Gunnar Myrdal's magisterial *Asian Drama*, also published in 1968. Now largely forgotten, Myrdal's *magnum opus* anticipated themes in the political economy of development which have subsequently been recognized as being of major importance, and his idea of the 'soft state', for instance, stands in many ways counterposed to that of the 'developmental state' coined later by Chalmers Johnson (1982). In this work there was an explicit recognition of the need to take much more serious account of social and political factors than had been the case hitherto, and hence that theorizing about development must involve more than mainstream economics and, on the part of some scholars, more than positivistic sociology and political science too. With the advantage of hindsight it is possible to see that the mission taken up by the editors of the new *Journal of Development Studies*, first published in October 1964, was being surpassed even as it was being written. In a short statement, Edith Penrose, Alec Nove and Kurt Martin, the editors of the new journal (the title of which helped to identify the new field of study), made it clear that the studies that they had in mind were generally expected to be those of development economists, though they also referred to the need, as they saw it, for more studies of political development. Well before the end of the 1960s the idea that studies of development certainly had to be multi-disciplinary, and perhaps most desirably should be inter-disciplinary, was very well established.[7] Those who were involved in the formation of academic development studies in Britain, economists such as Dudley Seers, Leonard Joy, Mike Faber, Richard Jolly, Hans Singer and Michael Lipton, some of whom had been active in development planning in the later colonial period in Africa (and who, according to an account once given to me by Hans Singer, dreamed up the idea of the Institute of Development Studies somewhere in East Africa), were all in some way (though maybe only implicitly) responding to the crisis of the positivistic orthodoxy, abetted by some influential non-economists such as Ron Dore and Colin Leys himself.[8]

The further aspect of the context in which development studies took self-conscious shape was that of the culmination of liberation struggles in the colonial world, with the securing of independence by most, if not quite all, of the African colonies at the beginning of the 1960s. There was certainly a sense in which academic development studies provided a means whereby those who had started their careers as academics or as government servants in African colonies could continue to dedicate themselves to the tasks that they had taken up. 'Crisis of planning' there may have been, but new ways of intervening to bring about progressive social change could surely be found.

At much the same time the most important radical critique of the positivist orthodoxy was being marshalled by Andre Gunder Frank, building on the work of Paul Baran and the economists of the Economic Commission for Latin America, notably Raul Prebisch (see Booth 1975). Frank's *Capitalism and Underdevelopment in Latin America* was first published in 1967. Perhaps even more influential than the book, however, in establishing dependency theory, which had, as Teddy Brett says (see note 8), such a dramatic impact among social scientists concerned with development, was Frank's essay on 'The development of underdevelopment or the underdevelopment of sociology' (Frank 1966). In part this was a swingeing critique of Walt Rostow's conceptualization of development in terms of 'stages of growth' which had been offered up, for example, as the basis for such teaching as there was on development in the geography department of Cambridge University in the mid-1960s[9] (see Rostow 1960).

In 1971, then, when I entered the scene, as the first ever student of development studies, as I have sometimes claimed,[10] at the University of East Anglia, the field was being defined from these two directions. On the one hand there was the response by some development economists to their own perception of the failure of their discipline, and on the other there was the 'external critique' articulated by the dependency theorists. I myself was influenced more to begin with by the first of these currents. As I entered the field of development studies with the intention of doing research on agrarian change in India in the context of the 'green revolution', a topic that had excited me from the experience of witnessing a little of the transformation of agriculture in Punjab on a visit to

21

India in 1969, I was influenced by some of the ideas coming out of the Village Studies Programme (VSP) at the Institute for Development Studies (IDS). This was Michael Lipton's attempt to construct a new, multi-disciplinary theory of development, based on systematic comparison of micro-studies (see Lipton's article on interdisciplinary development studies in the *Journal of Development Studies* in 1970). I was influenced, too (as was the VSP), by Lipton's fieldwork-based study of peasant agriculture in 'The theory of the optimising peasant' (1968). I started off with a commitment to micro-level, fieldwork-based research, stimulated by my reading of Lipton and encouraged in this by my mentor at Cambridge, Benny Farmer, who was a reader in the Geography of South Asia and a long-time observer of agricultural development in Ceylon/Sri Lanka, and who had a strong commitment himself as a researcher to 'getting mud on his boots'. These influences were moderated or modified in my year of MSc study at UEA in 1971/72 when I created my own programme in 'development studies', embracing anthropology, sociological theory and agricultural economics. Especially important for me was the teaching of David Feldman, who was an extremely good conventional agricultural economist, but also a Marxist, who had undertaken research in Tanzania, a country that then seemed to many of us to be some sort of a 'model' of development. David introduced me to both Lenin's *Development of Capitalism in Russia* and Chayanov's *Theory of Peasant Economy*, and also to David Mitrany's *Marx against the Peasant*. In the same year Teodor Shanin's *Awkward Class* and his Penguin Reader on *Peasants and Peasant Society* were published. So by the time I went to India to begin my fieldwork at the end of 1972 I had a research plan in which I anticipated studying the adoption of new agricultural technologies and their social impact by means of anthropological methods, influenced by Lipton's theory of the optimizing peasant, but also expecting to analyse the differentiation of the peasantry and the process of rural capital accumulation. I also had in my mind the work on the anthropology of India of Andre Beteille, in particular, and his analysis on Weberian lines of the coming apart of 'caste', 'class' and 'power' in a southern Indian village (Beteille 1965). So I expected, also, to examine the relations of caste and class and power in the course of my fieldwork in Tamil Nadu and Sri Lanka, which was to be part of one of several quite large fieldwork-based research projects conducted in the early 1970s, involving young scholars from different disciplines. In South Asia, in addition to our 'Cambridge Project on Agrarian Change' (see Farmer 1977), my later friends and colleagues in the School of Development Studies (DEV) at UEA were studying the political economy of Nepal by means of intensive field studies around Pokhara in west central Nepal (see Blaikie et al. 1980), and Clive Bell, Steven

Biggs, Edward Clay, Gerry Rodgers and Geof Wood were writing up the results of the IDS-based Purnea Project (see Joy and Everitt 1976).

What was missing in my own rather haphazard formation at this time, and what I think was generally under-emphasized in teaching in development studies as it took off in the 1970s and 1980s, was international political economy. The significance of the dismantling of the Bretton Woods system in the early 1970s for the way in which the whole international economy worked (see Wade 2000) passed me by, as it did, I suspect, very many others among the early students of development studies.

The promise of development studies

I have already located the origins of development studies, in the responses of a number of mainly British development economists and of a few specialists from other social science disciplines, in the crisis of the positivist orthodoxy in the 1960s and in the critique of that orthodoxy by dependency theorists. This was in that historically remarkable and, in retrospect, very brief period of (fairly) generously funded expansion in higher education in Britain following the Robbins Report of the early 1960s. The new universities were going 'to do different', and all of them in one way or another set out to encourage multi-disciplinary or inter-disciplinary studies. Development studies fitted in well into this context. The Institute of Development Studies (IDS) was established at the University of Sussex (in 1966) and benefited from the interests of that university in multi-disciplinary African and Asian studies. And the School of Development Studies, which set up the first ever undergraduate teaching programme in development studies, was established at the University of East Anglia (UEA) in 1973. The School was based, however, on the Overseas Development Group, set up by Athole Mackintosh, which had already been in existence for five or six years in the School of Social Studies.

My own perception of the flourishing of development studies in the 1970s is inevitably influenced by the UEA experience. DEV was a very exciting place to be in the late 1970s. Our students were not always in the top flight academically, but most were very highly motivated and they shared our excitement about the creation of a new field of study. DEV really did 'do different' in its teaching, and we and our students had a very strong sense of our distinct identity within the university, and in relation to teaching in the mainstream social science disciplines. In the core course in development studies that we taught in the students' first four terms we tried to teach the history of the development of capitalism and of the development of thought within the social sciences in the context of that substantive history. It was extremely ambitious. At one point we gave as many as four lectures a week in 'core', as well as seminars. We had a self-conscious project of restoring the unity of social science, around a broadly Marxist perspective.

But by now the two sources of development studies that I have distinguished had come into conflict with each other within the School and, I believe, much more widely among the development studies 'community'. There were those on the one hand who still sought to maintain the positivist orthodoxy, albeit within a multi-disciplinary context, and who often worked in multi-disciplinary teams within the likes of Integrated Rural Development Programmes; and, on the other, those who had moved from an interest in the critiques of the early orthodox development theory from within dependency theory to Marxist positions. The latter were taken up at UEA, for notable example, by John Cameron, Piers Blaikie and David Seddon in their extensive work on Nepal, and by John Cameron (again), Ken Cole and Chris Edwards in their teaching of economics through a comparative approach, though one that sought in the end to extend the claims of Marxian economics (see Cole et al. 1983). The radicals were divided, in turn, between those whose Marxism strongly stressed economic determinism, and those who were inclined to look more for political determinations and to reject what we saw as the reductionist views of our colleagues regarding ideology. Some of us (perhaps most notably Gavin Williams at Durham and later at Oxford) sought to marry the insights of Marx and Weber.

At UEA, the first group, the practitioners of multi-disciplinary orthodoxy, were happy within the Overseas Development Group and valued Athole Mackintosh's invention of the DEV/ODG arrangement, whereby all faculty members were expected to spend up to a third of their time working in development outside the university. The significance of this arrangement was very different then from what it became later, when consultancy work started to underwrite departmental budgets. Mackintosh's idea was, simply, that those teaching and doing research on development should continually renew their practical experience. The radicals on the other hand often had difficulty in reconciling their critiques of the then prevailing orthodoxies of development policy and practice with the need to take on development consultancy projects. Their work, in turn, was sometimes castigated as being 'prescriptively sterile' by those of the first camp. But these were only local echoes of a much wider debate in development studies.

The practical orthodoxy of development studies: redistribution with growth
Some of the first practitioners or advocates of multi-disciplinary development studies, most of them from the IDS at Sussex, had by this time produced a

collective volume that laid out the state of art, as they saw it. This was the book *Development in a Divided World*, edited by Dudley Seers and Leonard Joy (1971). Reviewing this text almost thirty-five years later reveals a remarkably contemporary ring to it. The introduction states, for example, that:

> A great deal of the discussion of development has been vitiated by the failure to take account of the world's economic and political structure. Unless one is fully aware of the context within which governments have been trying to develop their countries, it is easy to fall into the trap of assuming, usually implicitly, that analyses and prescriptions derived from the experience of rich countries are also applicable to countries which are not merely poor, but poor in a very unequal world ... (Seers and Joy 1971: 8)

This is a statement that appears remarkably appropriate to the present (of 2004). The influence of 'the world's economic and political structure' is still not recognized sufficiently in policy advice, while Ha-Joon Chang has recently reminded us that the now rich countries did not make their way by pursuing the kinds of policies that they enjoin upon poor countries (Chang 2002). The last words of the book, written by Dudley Seers, similarly fit the present remarkably well:

> What we have really been talking about ... is the need for a world-wide system of co-ordinated policies, national and international, in many different fields, to tackle the problems of world poverty, which become increasingly repulsive as the rich – which now includes virtually the whole population of the industrial countries – become richer. Aid does have a function, but treating it as the *central* policy issue provides, for some people, a way of evading the realities of a divided world. (Seers and Joy 1971: 347)

Except for those who subscribe to the Panglossian views of writers such as Martin Wolf of the *Financial Times*, who argues that globalization over the last decade or so of the twentieth century has brought greater equality as well as a very significant reduction in poverty, we now confront a world that is even more divided than that which Seers and Joy contemplated, and one in which the problems of poverty are even more 'repulsive'.[11]

The 'world-wide system of co-ordinated policies' that Dudley Seers and his co-authors had looked for were laid out at the end of the decade in the Brandt Report of 1980. It is a matter of history that the whole approach reflected by Brandt was already being comprehensively rejected with the resurgence of economic liberalism, and it is only now being rediscovered as individuals and agencies search for alternatives to contemporary neo-liberalism (see, for example, the recent report of the World Commission on the Social Dimension of Globalization 2004). Before the publication of Brandt, however, some of the ideas current in IDS at the beginning of the 1970s were clearly reflected in the text that more than any other defined the policy approach of the time, *Redistribution with Growth* (RwG) (Chenery et al. 1974), produced by a group based mainly in the research division of the World Bank and by IDS scholars. It was recognized that the high rates of economic growth that had been achieved in many if not all of the developing countries had not resulted in improved living standards for very many of their peoples. Attention had started to be focused on the problem of poverty that had been already flagged up by *Development in a Divided World*,[12] and the approach advocated was indicated in the title of the book. The aim was to achieve redistribution with economic growth by focusing interventions on specified 'target groups' of poor people, and in such a way as to improve their productive capacity. The approach was picked up in the World Bank's *Rural Development* Sector Paper of 1975, which defined 'rural development' as a strategy for the alleviation of poverty, and encouraged investment in programmes for 'integrated rural development' that would enhance productivity and incomes in rural economies through the strategic allocation of credit for individuals and appropriate infrastructural improvement. The solution to poverty, which was seen as being primarily a rural problem, lay in the integration of rural producers into markets. These programmes were intended to benefit especially the small and marginal farmers who constituted the most important of the target groups identified in RwG. At around the same time both John Mellor in the United States and Michael Lipton in Britain published books both of which, in their somewhat different ways, laid out powerful criticism of the primary focus on industrialization in the old positivist orthodoxy of development economics, and advocated a 'food and agriculture first' approach to economic growth. This was Mellor's *New Economics of Growth*, published in 1976. Lipton, controversially, identified 'urban bias' as the root cause for, in the title of his book, *Why Poor People Stay Poor* (1977), and similarly advocated an approach to development based on what he saw as the relative efficiency of small-scale agriculture. It was an argument that he had sketched first in a seminal essay on Indian agriculture, published in *Crisis of Indian Planning* (Streeten and Lipton 1968) and then in an important paper on land reform (Lipton 1974).

Another of the target groups for RwG were those poor people employed in what by now was known as the urban 'informal sector', following the recognition of this concept as a result of ethnographic research on employment in a slum of Accra, in Ghana, by Keith Hart (1973). The idea, first expounded at a conference held at the IDS in September 1971, resonated strongly with a policy discourse influenced by Lipton's arguments about the possible efficiency of small-scale production and its significance for poverty alleviation. So it took off in the policy sphere even before Hart published his paper. It was the central idea in the report produced on employment and incomes in Kenya by a team working for the International Labour Office led by Hans Singer and Richard Jolly from IDS. Recognizing that very many people found employment and the means of livelihood only in the informal sector, the report advocated policies to improve the productivity of informal sector activities in the way that was recommended a year or so later in RwG. Similar reasoning led the ILO, through the World Employment Programme, to undertake an extensive research programme on the informal sector (see Sethuraman 1981). This was an important part of a programme that was based around the idea of the satisfaction of the 'basic needs' of poor people as being what development must centrally be about. This was the ILO's version of ideas coming out of the World Bank and the IDS (see ILO 1977). There were certain overlaps and some complementarity, too, in arguments about 'intermediate technology' that were advocated in the influential book *Small Is Beautiful*, by E. F. Schumacher (1973). At one point in the 1970s *Small Is Beautiful* was, as I recall, found to be the book that was most widely read among British MPs.

It is very important to note that the influence of the ideas contained in RwG persists to the present, for small (including 'informal') business development, and poverty-focused service delivery, are intrinsic to many contemporary Poverty Reduction Strategy Papers. The particular focus on small-scale or peasant agriculture, too, is once again returning to the agenda of development with the recognition of the existence of crisis in the rural economies of poor countries, especially perhaps in India and China.

Against populism and dependency: the attack from the left A significant minority of those working in what were by now defined as institutes or departments of development studies stood out against these powerful normative thrusts.[13] Set against *Development in a Divided World*, championing the views of those inspired rather by a critical perspective, were Bob Sutcliffe's *Industry and Underdevelopment* (1971) and a little later the Penguin Reader on *Underdevelopment and Development: The Third World Today*, edited by Henry Bernstein (1973), which was guided by what the editor described as a 'radical' approach to development. This, Bernstein conceded in later editions of the book, had an *'ideological* rather than theoretical character' (his emphasis 1973 [1976]: 9), and the book was not in fact, in many ways, so very different from *Development in a Divided World*. Michael Lipton, incidentally, appears as an

27

author in both books. Bernstein championed, however, a historical social science. And this was the kind of social science taken up by critics of the 'green revolution', notably Keith Griffin in his book *The Political Economy of Agrarian Change* (1974) and Terry Byres in an early review of research done in India (1972). They were implicitly or explicitly critical of policy arguments in favour of rural development, pointing out, in effect, that the increased integration into markets which the strategy entailed could lead to impoverishment just as easily as to higher incomes. This, it was argued, is an inherent aspect of the process of capital accumulation. The critics of the green revolution were sceptical, too, about the feasibility of the 'food and agriculture first' approach to growth, certainly in the absence of either collectivist or redistributive land reform. The debate over the green revolution partly stimulated, and certainly fed into, and from, a wave of interest in the idea of 'peasant economy' and in peasant studies. This was driven at least in part by the recognition of the role of peasants in twentieth-century revolutions, studied by Hamza Alavi (1965) and by Eric Wolf (1971), as well as of their contemporary role in confronting the power of the United States in Vietnam. The emergence of 'peasant studies' as a vibrant field of research was reflected especially in the publication of Shanin's Penguin Reader, *Peasants and Peasant Societies* (1971), and then in the foundation of the *Journal of Peasant Studies* by Terry Byres, in 1973.[14] In this literature the old Russian debate over the nature and tendencies of peasant agriculture, between those who took the view expounded by Lenin in his *Development of Capitalism in Russia* that this development required the deepening of class differentiation among peasant producers, and, on the other hand, the populists who held that there is a distinctive 'peasant economy' which persists even in the context of capitalism, an argument expressed most articulately by Chayanov (1966), was revived and explored in a variety of contexts.[15] The work of Michael Lipton, whose arguments about the efficiency of small-scale production in agriculture were so influential in the formulation of RwG, was subjected to stringent criticism as being 'populist' (see, for instance, Byres 1979; Kitching 1982). 'Peasant studies' in America, meanwhile, remained focused more, in the vein of Eric Wolf, on the politics of peasantries, in work exemplified best by James Scott's *Moral Economy of the Peasantry* (1976). This drew a striking response from a rational choice perspective by Samuel Popkin (1979), although the Scott–Popkin debate attracted less attention in Britain than in the United States.

Like the critics of the green revolution, some researchers who worked on the urban 'informal sector' were strongly critical of the normative arguments in the ILO's approach, and of RwG. They argued that what was described as informal sector activity should rather be analysed in terms of the concept of petty commodity production, and this as inherently subject to the dominance of larger-scale capitalist production (see Gerry 1978; Moser 1978). These scholars were critical methodologically, too, of the descriptive, cross-sectional approach that was taken in the ILO studies of the informal 'sectors' of a number of major cities, and they argued instead for studies of industrial branches in which the relationships between different scales and types of enterprises would be studied. They also sought to show that policies for the 'development' of the informal sector, as of small-scale 'peasant' agriculture, involved inevitable contradictions. Gavin Kitching's little book on *Development and Underdevelopment in Historical Perspective* (1982) encapsulated a big argument exposing the limitations of the inherently populist character of much of the development policy of the time.

These empirical studies of agrarian change and of urban petty commodity production drew their theoretical inspiration from a rich vein of literature exploring the application of Marxist theory to development, in the work of writers such as Geoffrey Kay (1975) who re-examined Marx's arguments about the role of merchant capital, or those who argued over modes of production and their articulation (see Taylor 1979; Wolpe 1980). These scholars were often responding to their sense of the weaknesses of dependency theory, and they were all explicitly or implicitly critical of the 'world systems' theory associated especially with Immanuel Wallerstein (1974), which inspired a group of followers but without really exercising widespread influence. The most powerful single critique of Frankian dependency theory and Wallersteinian world systems theorizing was that of Robert Brenner (1978), who described them in terms of 'neo-Smithian marxism'.[16] Meanwhile, early on in this first period of development studies, Roger Owen and Bob Sutcliffe had edited an important collection of studies on *Theories of Imperialism* (1972), which together offered a classical perspective on the relations between imperialist powers and their empires, and the end of the decade of the 1970s saw a major restatement of a classical Marxian perspective with Bill Warren's *Imperialism: Pioneer of Capitalism* (1980). The key contribution made by Brenner and by Warren was to emphasize the positive nature of capitalism for development, cutting the ground from the negative and rather sterile dependency critique. This line of argument might be seen as having culminated more recently in Meghnad Desai's book *Marx's Revenge* (2001).

In regard to the relations between countries and the international context of development, the idea of 'unequal exchange' was hotly disputed (see Kitching 1982). But still, I think, with the advantage of hindsight, many of us did not engage enough with the international political economy of development, for most of us were also area specialists. A great deal of my own work, for instance, was firmly within South Asian area studies, and many of my colleagues, not only at UEA, were equally clearly 'East Africanists', 'West Africanists' or 'Latin Americanists'. More of us were inclined towards 'micro' studies rather than towards the macro, and though we often sought to analyse the linkages between societal levels, such as the mutual determinations of local and national politics, too few of us examined trends in the global economy and their implications, except at the level of generality of much of the work in the dependency and world systems theoretic traditions.[17] The distinctly Marxist literature was focused far too much on abstract, and abstracted, debates such as that on the mode of production in Indian agriculture and not nearly enough on the actual processes of capital accumulation in the contemporary world. A notable exception was provided by Teddy Brett's work on precisely this subject (Brett 1983, 1985). Thus it was that 'real world' development, in the early 1980s, took academic development studies by surprise.

Hubris in the 1980s?

Just as the foundation and flourishing of development studies were strongly influenced by the expansion of British universities in the later 1960s and early 1970s, and by the continuing enthusiasm for development planning, especially in Africa, with the support of aid from the richer countries, so the faltering of the still-new field in the 1980s was influenced by external events. In Britain, the golden age of universities made possible by the Robbins Report was over, and in many departments, as in DEV at UEA, hardly any new appointments were made through the decade, under the onslaught of Thatcherism. There came to be a 'missing generation', not just of development researchers but of social scientists generally in British universities. The first flagship of development studies, the IDS at Sussex, was threatened with closure, and its core funding from the British government began to be cut. The new climate in the universities affected students as well as staff, and much of the excitement and the various radical enthusiasms of the 1970s were overlain by uncertainties about the future. Radicalism was understandably diverted into the cause of opposing nuclear weapons in Europe. But students also became more anxious about finding jobs, and more came into development studies with the hope of finding jobs in such fields as international finance. It started to become possible to distinguish between those students who were interested in 'how economies (and perhaps me, too) get rich' and those whose concerns remained with such problems as those of poverty and environmental degradation.

The onslaught of economic liberalism and the retreat of development studies
Meanwhile, in the world of development policy and practice, the ascendancy
of so-called 'neo'-liberal thinking (it was really just classic liberalism) des-
troyed a great deal of what the pursuers of orthodoxy via multi-disciplinary
approaches had sought to achieve. For many of those who had been committed to the ideas of the 1970s it appeared that in the 1980s development went
into reverse. A marker of the new thinking was the 'Berg Report' of 1981 on
Accelerated Development for Sub-Saharan Africa prepared by the economist
Elliot Berg, which signified the conversion of the World Bank to neo-liberalism. This presented a frontal assault on state intervention in Africa, especially
in agriculture and in the rural economy, and laid out a strong argument in
support of the view that the key to the problems of African development lay
in 'getting the prices right'. At the same time came the publication of Robert
Bates's book on *Markets and States in Tropical Africa* (1981), offering an explanation for why it was that African political elites persisted with policies and
programmes such as the Integrated Rural Development Programmes which
manifestly failed to realize their stated objectives. Bates showed that failed
interventionist policies and programmes might still serve the political interests of ruling elites very well, and in opposition to the needs and interests of
those whom they ruled. It was a restatement, in some respects, of Lipton's
earlier argument about the power of 'urban bias' in development processes.
A little later came the most powerful and influential statement of the neo-
liberal position with the publication of Deepak Lal's tract on *The Poverty of
Development Economics* (1983). The whole case for a distinctive body of economic theory dealing with the specific problems of poor, developing countries was subjected to critique, and from about this time those who practised
development economics often began to be treated as the poor relations of
the economics profession. Through the decade, in response to the crisis of
the debt-led growth of the 1970s – the Mexican default came in 1982, marking the arrival of the Debt Crisis – stabilization and structural adjustment
programmes, designed after neo-liberal thinking, came in many countries
to replace the sorts of policies and projects that had been advocated, for example, in *Redistribution with Growth*. By 1990 the neo-liberal approach to
development was summed up neatly and influentially by John Williamson in
the idea of the 'Washington Consensus' (Williamson 1990).

In the sphere of development practice, meanwhile, the decade saw the
emergence on to the scene of a powerful new set of actors, the NGOs. It is
not that NGOs were, so to speak, 'invented' in the 1980s, but agencies such as
Oxfam or the Save the Children Fund, which had been in existence for a long

time already, became much more prominent, largely as a result of their very public engagement in action against famine in Ethiopia and Sudan. It was actually from someone with a strong academic background, but now working with NGOs – Michael Edwards – that an attack on the 'irrelevance' of academic development studies came, at the end of the decade (Edwards 1989). For Edwards the irrelevance of development studies was reflected in its failure with regard to practice in the field. For me the hubris of development studies in the early 1980s was the result of the failure adequately to recognize, much less analyse, fundamental trends of global political economy.

It is little wonder, under the impact of the kind of 'double whammy' wrought by Thatcherism and Reaganomics, within the university world and in that of development policy and practice, that development studies should have experienced what one writer described as an 'impasse', or that doubts about the whole post-war development project should have started to creep in from increasingly influential postmodernist writers (Jameson 1991). The idea of the 'impasse' was put forward by David Booth in an article published in 1985, which drew responses from several other scholars, and the debate among them was reviewed subsequently, and very fairly, by Booth himself in an essay that begins with the claim that:

> In the early 1980s there was a widely shared sense that social research and theorizing about development had reached some kind of an impasse. Interesting and valuable work was still being done but in many areas of inquiry there had been disappointingly little cumulative advance along the lines mapped out during the 1970s. Initially stimulating theoretical debates, most of them originating within or on the fringes of the Marxist tradition, had run into the sand, bequeathing few if any guidelines for a continuing research programme. *Crucial real world questions were not being addressed* [my emphasis] and the gulf between academic inquiry and the various spheres of development policy and practice had widened to the point where practitioners were raising fundamental doubts about the 'relevance' of academic development studies. (Booth 1994: 3)

I believe that David Booth's analysis contained much that was perceptive and well reasoned, notably the point that 'crucial real world questions were not being addressed'. But was a sense of there being an 'impasse' really very widely shared among scholars and researchers in development studies through the 1980s, outside a relatively small group of those critical scholars who had been most influenced by neo-Marxism in the 1970s, whom Booth was specifically addressing, and who were now exposed politically and intellectually by the surge of neo-liberalism? In spite of the hubris that had checked the ambitions of development studies of the 1960s and 1970s, for many the decade of the 1980s was a time of creative research and of the flourishing of new ideas; new shoots amid the debris. It was a time of major new intellectual developments, notably in the work of Amartya Sen on reconceptualizing development in terms of capabilities (Sen 1985; Dreze and Sen 1989; Sen 1999), and in the work of those scholars who identified the 'developmental state'. These were to come to provide the platforms for counter-attack against economic liberalism.

Green shoots amid the hubris of ambition The new intellectual developments included the work of Amartya Sen and others, on poverty and famines; new stimuli from the applications of feminist thinking to development problems, and the attacks on patriarchy and the systemic exclusion of women that followed from these; and the emergence of new concerns linking environment and development, reflected most influentially in the publication of the Brundtland Report on this theme in 1987. Some scholars recognized that a major shift was taking place in the whole regime of capital accumulation, and that a new 'global division of labour' was being established. But it was also a time of the revival of interest in the role of the state, especially through the study of the developmental states of East Asia, which began to counter neo-liberalism even as the latter gathered force.

The African famines of the earlier 1980s lent even greater influence to the work of Amartya Sen, which had begun with his paradigmatic analysis of the Bengal famine of 1943, published in the *Cambridge Journal of Economics* (1977). This article had first laid out the argument that food crises may occur not because of 'food availability decline' but because of a lack of effective demand resulting from a decline in the exchange entitlements of some actors. The argument was amplified with reference to other cases in *Poverty and Famines* (1981), work that was subsequently referred to, seventeen years later, in the citation for Sen's Nobel Prize in economics. Among a number of substantive studies of food crises and famines published around this time, perhaps the most outstanding was Mike Watts's *Silent Violence* (1983). But Sen's work also stimulated the efforts of NGOs, in particular, and of governments to establish famine early warning systems. It also started to influence understandings of poverty, which began to be seen in terms that were much broader than those of an income definition. A seminal study, in my view, was that of the Indian economist N. S. Jodha, who in 1984 wrote a paper based on field research in villages in his native region of western India which showed very clearly just how differently people themselves may regard their living conditions from the way they are captured in the economists' conventional definition of income poverty (Jodha 1989). Jodha's analysis was taken up by Robert Chambers in an essay on concepts of poverty which brought out the importance of distinguishing between 'subsistence', 'security' and 'self-respect' as criteria of poverty, and so emphasized its multi-dimensional character (Chambers 1988). These ideas also influenced Chambers' contribution to the Brundtland Report on Environment and Development in which he advocated the idea of 'sustainable livelihoods' that was to become an important focus for research and development practice in the 1990s. At the same time engagement with Jodha's work confirmed Chambers in his view that in order to understand the problems of development it is necessary to enter into dialogue with people, rather than presuming that both analysis and answers can be derived from theory or from Western science. Chambers (1983) marked the beginning of the trail that led to the extraordinary flourishing of participatory rural appraisal in the 1990s, and later to participatory poverty assessments. An important statement on similar lines but with particular regard to agricultural research and development came with Paul Richards' *Indigenous Agricultural Revolution* (1985). All this work entailed an implicit challenge to the ruling market orthodoxy and emphasized the need for non-market interventions, whether from the state, as in Sen's argument about famine relief, or communities, as in Chambers' work on participation in development.

Critical studies of agrarian change, meanwhile, far from being locked in an impasse, moved out of the kind of stalemate that had been created ten years or more earlier through the opposition of Leninist and Chayanovian views on the fate of the peasantry with the development of capitalism. Critical exchanges between Henry Bernstein and Peter Gibbon and Michael Neocosmos (1985; and see Bernstein 1990 for a brief and simple summary of the arguments) established the recognition that the development of capitalism involves the constant creation and destruction of places for petty commodity production. In agriculture petty commodity production may persist over long periods not because it is necessarily more efficient than large-scale agricultural production, in the terms either of neo-classical or of Chayanovian economics, but rather because of what the Indian economist Krishna Bharadwaj referred to as the 'compulsive involvement' of small producers in markets, to the benefit of owners of money capital (Bharadwaj 1974, 1985).[18] She and Amit Bhaduri (1983) showed how the ways in which real markets work are very far from the model of the market in mainstream economics, and how the conditions of what Bhaduri defined as 'forced commerce' are instrumental in the reproduction of poverty and may give rise in some circumstances to famine. Mike

Davis has recently shown this with extraordinary power in his *Late Victorian Holocausts* (2001), a book that has been described as 'The Black Book of Liberalism' because of the way in which it shows how the doctrinaire pursuit of liberal policies may result in the destruction of lives.

A new line of development in agrarian studies concerned the causes of environmental degradation and the beginning of the rise of what has come to be known as political ecology, stimulated significantly by the publication of Piers Blaikie's book *The Political Economy of Soil Erosion* (1985; and see also Blaikie and Brookfield 1987). Deploying a simple but effective framework that led outwards from local symptoms of land degradation, Blaikie showed how such degradation can be explained as an outcome of the ways in which particular agrarian economies work, and how these in turn are influenced by state and international structures of power. The re-emergence of environmentalism in development studies was charted in a book by Michael Redclift (1984), and the same author wrote critically about the idea of sustainable development at about the same time that the idea was given currency by the Brundtland Report (Redclift 1987; WCED 1987). An important theme within the literature on environment and development, and with a theoretical significance extending well beyond it, was that of the use of common property resources, whether of grazing land, water or forests. Research was encouraged by the National Science Council in the United States, and major studies were those of Robert Wade, on the local management of irrigation in southern India, in the book *Village Republics* (1988), and then by Elinor Ostrom, whose *Governing the Commons* (1990) remains the fundamental reference point on the subject. Another great advance of this period was the establishment of gender perspectives. Though the Swedish economist Esther Boserup had drawn attention to women's distinctive economic roles in a book first published as early as 1970, the publication of the collection *Of Marriage and the Market* (Young et al. 1981) was perhaps especially influential in bringing gender concerns into the mainstream of development studies and of development practice at this time, as was later work such as that of Diane Elson (1991).

The most significant ideas that entered into development studies in the 1980s were thrust upon us by events in the world little anticipated by development studies in the 1970s which had to do with what was described as 'the new international division of labour' (to which attention was, however, drawn by Frobel and others in the 1970s; see Frobel et al. 1980), the recognition of the NICs (the Newly Industrializing Countries) of East Asia, and what Nigel Harris memorably called 'the end of the Third World' (the title of his book first published in 1986). These were all indicative of what has come to be understood

35

as an epochal shift in the whole regime of capital accumulation and was influentially recognized as such by David Harvey in *The Condition of Postmodernity*, first published in 1989. In the same year Alice Amsden published her book on South Korea, *Asia's Next Industrial Giant*, anticipating by a year the publication of Robert Wade's *Governing the Market*. These studies gave substance to the generalization of Chalmers Johnson's idea of 'the development state', first proposed with regard to Japan, but elaborated more generally by Gordon White and others at IDS (1988). So they started to 'bring the state back in' (to use the title of an influential collection published in the United States in 1985 by Evans et al. which did not, however, specifically address the concerns of international development) even as neo-liberal thinking seemed to have become almost hegemonic. This work started to lay out a new agenda for development studies and to provide the basis for a fight back against neo-liberalism. What Amsden and, more pointedly, Wade showed was that the notion that the development experience of South Korea and of Taiwan exemplified the success of neo-liberal policies is simply wrong (see Wade 1996 for an account of the battles in the World Bank over this).

Reinvention in the 1990s and the challenge of Act V

If times were hard for academic development studies in Britain in the 1980s the final decade of the twentieth century saw something of a renaissance. Both the London School of Economics and the School of Oriental and African Studies, for instance, started new postgraduate programmes in development studies at the beginning of the 1990s, and both met with immediate success in terms of student demand. Teaching in development studies became widespread, generally, in higher education in Britain. Meanwhile, changes in the funding of development research by first the Overseas Development Administration and then the Department for International Development assisted the rise or the consolidation of other research centres in addition to the Institute of Development Studies. Core funding was gradually withdrawn from IDS and competition between centres for research funding was encouraged. It is a matter of intense debate as to whether the change in policy has generated more innovative or more effective research, though it is certainly the case that the emphasis on project funding, and the reliance of so many research centres and of university departments upon 'soft money', has discouraged independent scholarship. Committees, whether of development agencies like the Department for International Development or of funding bodies such as the Economic and Social Research Council, are not notably good at identifying research frontiers, and in so far as their new policies have discouraged independent scholarship they may have reduced creativity and originality.

From adjustment to governance, 'human development' and 'getting the social relations right' At the same time the world of development policy began to change. Recognition of the failures of stabilization and adjustment programmes, notably by the World Bank, started to draw attention back to the role of the state. Bank policies were subjected to critique by scholars from among those who had helped to create RwG twenty years earlier. Richard Jolly and Frances Stewart, with Giovanni Cornia, wrote *Adjustment with a Human Face* (Cornia et al. 1987), in part renewing many of the ideas of the 1970s, and these scholars and others came together to define the Human Development Index and to initiate the annual publication by the UNDP of its *Human Development Report*. The HDI was an attempt to operationalize Sen's conceptualization of development in terms of capability expansion, but the main purpose of its construction was a polemical one, to provide a means of critiquing liberal orthodoxy (Meghnad Desai, personal communication). By the time of the publication of the first *Human Development Report* in 1990, however, there were indications that the World Bank had already begun to move away from the positions of the 1980s. The *World Development Report* for 1990 saw the Bank return to a concern about poverty, and the strategy that it laid out included employment-intensive growth most effectively brought about in the view of the Bank, to be sure, through market policies, but also poverty-focused service provision and provision of a safety net. There were signs here, too, of a return to some of the ideas of RwG.

The new approach was further marked by the publication in 1992 of the World Bank paper on *Governance and Development*. That paper was introduced as follows:

> In this booklet, governance is defined as the manner in which power is exercised in the management of a country's economic and social resources for development. Good governance, for the World Bank, is synonymous with sound development management. *The Bank's experience has shown that the programs and projects it helps finance may be technically sound, but fail to deliver anticipated results for reasons connected to the quality of government action.* (World Bank 1992: 1; my emphasis)

The course was now set for the establishment of what came to be known as the Post Washington Consensus, which, with its recognition of the significance of 'governance' and, in this, of the importance of aspects of 'social relations', has given renewed impetus to multi-disciplinary development studies. 'Governance' was just one of the new words that entered into the development lexicon in the 1990s. Others were 'civil society', 'social capital' and 'participation', referring to important elements in what the Bank conceives of as 'good governance'. In this it is extremely important, in the words of one slogan that is reported as having currency in the World Bank, 'to get the social relations right' by encouraging the formation of social capital.[19] It is interesting that the draft research strategy paper produced by the Department for International Development at the time of writing of this essay should make hardly any mention at all, with regard to social science research, of research in economics, whereas it lays some emphasis on the importance of work in politics, and in general on cross-disciplinary research, including that where the 'crossing' is between social science disciplines and the natural sciences. The importance of such efforts has been very clearly demonstrated in research in the field of environment and development by Michael Thompson, Melissa Leach, James Fairhead and Robin Mearns, who were in part following the trail blazed earlier by Piers Blaikie (Thompson et al. 1986; Fairhead and Leach 1996; Leach and Mearns 1996). These scholars have shown not only how environmental problems but also science itself are socially constructed.

The 'governance' words are not the only new entries into the lexicon. Another is 'war', or 'conflict'. Of course, this is not in and of itself a new word, but it has entered into the discourse of development studies as it did not before. The irony in the fact that war was arguably the world's greatest growth industry in the period of neo-liberal ascendancy has not gone unremarked; and the rise of what are called 'new wars' (Kaldor 1999) has stimulated a great deal of research and teaching, some of it within development studies. Development scholars are now contributing as they did not before to debates on security issues (see Harriss 1995; Duffield 2001).

Conclusion: critical engagement with globalization

The most important of all the new words that have entered into use in the 1990s is that of 'globalization'. This did not appear, I think, in David Harvey's *The Condition of Postmodernity* (1989), though that book is about what comes a little later to be discussed under the title of 'globalization'. It did appear, however, in Anthony Giddens' *Consequences of Modernity*, first published a year later (Giddens 1990); and by the end of the 1990s it had both entered into popular language and become the vehicle for a whole new academic growth industry. The implications both of 'actual' globalization and of academic 'globalization studies' for development studies are ambivalent, and they partly help to account for the possibility of eclipse, as well as of resurgence, in the last act of the drama. This is because there is a strong sense in which what we may reasonably call 'the globalization project' (for the phenomena described under the rubric of globalization are driven by particular agents, and especially by American-based finance capital: see Wade 2000), and 'the development project' are in opposition to each other. But the challenge that is posed by globalization may also further stimulate the resurgence of development studies, if development scholars are able to redefine the 'development project' in the light of the understanding that they can bring to the analysis of the real histories of development in different parts of the world, in the way that was demonstrated a decade or so ago by Robert Wade and Alice Amsden. There has been a recognition even from within the World Bank itself of the inadequacy of development theory and of the failure of the long-standing attempts to improve that theory on the basis of econometric analysis of large cross-country data-sets, and of the need instead to understand circular and cumulative causation in the processes that drive economic growth, and hence an appreciation of the importance of history (see Kenny and Williams 2001). These more technical and methodological arguments coincide with the case being made by mainstream economists such as Rodrik and Stiglitz, as well as those from outside that tradition, by, for example, Ha-Joon Chang (Chang and Grabel 2004), against the prescriptions of the Washington Consensus or the Post Washington Consensus, that countries, and this means the states of those countries, have to find their own pathways to growth.[20] Whether they are able to do this or not will depend significantly on the trajectory of US imperialism, the recognition of which has latterly provided a focus for the resurgence and renewal of the radical current within development studies, and for renewed activism in the struggle against global capitalism.

The challenge for development studies now, therefore, lies not so much in resisting the critiques that derive from postmodernism, in 'post-development' theorizing exemplified by *The Development Dictionary* (Sachs 1992) and especially by Escobar's *Encountering Development* (1995),[21] as in renewing its relevance through improved historical understanding of development, and of the moral and practical requirements of global justice (see Little 2003; Pogge 2002). This calls for a *critical* engagement on the part of development scholars with development policy-making rather than placing development studies at the service of the fads, such as 'social capital' and 'participation', of the policy-makers.

Notes

1 As my frequent references to his comments show, I have benefited a great deal from stimulating remarks made on an earlier draft by Teddy Brett – to the point where I think I cannot entirely exonerate him from responsibility for what appears here. I am also grateful to Stuart Corbridge for encouragement and advice, and to Uma Kothari for sound editorial guidance.

2 Even this is a matter for debate, for Teddy Brett tells me that (Sir) Hans Singer considers that development studies first had distinct form in the 1940s, through the work of a UN committee, chaired by (Sir) Arthur Lewis, and of which he himself was secretary. The big 'foundation texts' of development studies are in works by Lewis, and by Paul Baran, published in the 1950s (Lewis 1954; Baran 1957).

3 It is not sufficiently recognized, for instance, how much the Indian economic nationalists, such as Dadabhai Naoroji and Romesh C. Dutt, contributed to the development of dependency theories.

4 See, for example: Bates 1981, 1989, 2001; Berry 1984, 1993; Evans 1979, 1995, 1996; Grindle 1985; Hart 1986, 2002; Scott 1976, 1985, 1998; Watts 1983.

5 See, for example, Almond and Coleman 1960; Geertz 1963; Huntington 1968; Rostow 1960.

6 Positivism, of course, has never gone away, and current claims about markets are no less justified on positivistic and technocratic grounds than were earlier arguments for planning. Colin Leys speaks of a particular 'positivist orthodoxy'.

7 Henry Bernstein noted in his introduction to his influential early Penguin Reader, *Underdevelopment and Development* (1973), that none other an authority than Seymour Martin Lipset (writing in 1969) had written that 'it is obvious that any effort to treat development in economy, politics and society as separate processes simply makes little sense' (cited by Bernstein 1973: 18).

8 Teddy Brett writes to me that 'The key issue was not a crisis of positivism [though I don't think Leys was saying this: JH], but of planning and economism. It was also a crisis of Import Substituting Industrialisation (which was not just about planning) and of the manifestly increasing poverty, leading to a focus on "the social" as you say, but also to the dramatic emergence of the dependency school. For me the "road to Damascus" moment was Richard Sklar's address to the East African Social Science Conference, in Kampala, in 1967.'

9 This is somewhat unfair to the teaching of Dick Grove and Ben Farmer at that time. Both took more nuanced and critical views of what they had observed in West Africa and Ceylon, respectively.

10 This claim is based on the fact that I was, I believe, the first research student to have been identified with the embryonic School of Development Studies that established the first teaching programme with this title.

11 See, for example, Martin Wolf's exchange with Robert Wade in *Prospect*, March 2002. Wade's main point is that the uncertainties surrounding the measurements make statements like Wolf's irresponsible. Latterly Wolf has published a kind of panegyric for economic liberalism in a book on *Why Globalisation Works* (2004).

12 V. M. Dandekar and Nilakanta Rath's 'Poverty in India – dimensions and trends', which launched a vast body of research in India, and had a seminal influence elsewhere, too, was first published in 1971.

13 One of them was Robin Murray, who I remember commenting at a conference on rural technology at IDS that what he had listened to seemed to him to be like sitting around talking about improved harrows in the midst of the Highland Clearances.

14 This perhaps understates the significance of the work of Eric Wolf, whose little book *Peasants* (1966), as well as *Peasant Wars of the Twentieth Century* (1971), remains outstanding.

15 See my reader *Rural Development: Theories of Peasant Economy and Agrarian Change* (Harriss 1982a).

16 But there were also some analytically substantial empirical studies done of development in particular countries that drew on a dependency perspective. The most notable of these was Peter Evans' work on Brazil (Evans 1979).

17 This is an argument about the relative weight of different specialisms within development studies. Of course, there were active scholars, such as my colleagues Chris Edwards and Rhys Jenkins, whose interests were emphatically in international political economy. I simply want to make the point that, with the advantage of hindsight, it appears to me that there was a disproportionate emphasis in teaching on 'local' questions.

18 This argument is the underpinning of my own, regarding capital accumulation in an agrarian region of southern India, in *Capitalism and Peasant Farming* (1982b).

19 For an intellectual history from within the Bank, see Bebbington et al. (2004); and for critical views, on the whole governance agenda, see Fine (2001) and Harriss (2001).

20 Teddy Brett argues that this line of thinking constitutes the 'second leg' of a pluralist strategy that has been emerging in response to the double impasse that is given by the crises of both statist and market fundamentalisms. The other leg is the inheritance of RwG, concerned with the need for social and political support for small and medium enterprises and for poverty-focused services. The 'developmental state leg' deals with macro-policy issues having to do with national macroeconomic management and global interventions.

21 This is a task that has already been taken up effectively, for example by Lehmann (1997) and by Corbridge (1998).

References

Alavi, H. (1965) 'Peasants and revolution', *Socialist Register*

Almond, G. and J. S. Coleman (eds) (1960) *The Politics of Developing Areas*, Princeton, NJ: Princeton University Press

Amsden, A. (1989) *Asia's Next Giant: South Korea and Late Industrialization*, New York: Oxford University Press

Baran, P. (1957) *The Political Economy of Growth*, New York: Monthly Review Press

Bates, R. (1981) *Markets and States in Tropical Africa: The Political Basis of Agricultural Policies*, Berkeley: University of California Press

— (1989) *Beyond the Miracle of the Market: The Political Economy of Agrarian Development in Kenya*, Cambridge and New York: Cambridge University Press

— (2001) *Prosperity and Violence: The Political Economy of Development*, New York: Norton

Bebbington, A., S. Guggenheim, E. Olson and M. Woolcock (2004) 'Exploring social capital debates at the World Bank', *Journal of Development Studies*, 40(5): 33–64

Bernstein, H. (ed.) (1973) [1976] *Underdevelopment and Development: The Third World Today*, Harmondsworth: Penguin

— (1990) 'Taking the part of peasants?', in H. Bernstein, B. Crow, M. Mackintosh and C. Martin (eds), *The Food Question: Profits versus People?*, London: Earthscan

Berry, S. (1984) *Fathers Work for Their Sons: Accumulation, Mobility and Class Formation*, Berkeley: University of California Press

— (1993) *No Condition Is Permanent: The Social Dynamics of Agrarian Relations in Sub-Saharan Africa*, Madison: University of Wisconsin Press

Beteille, A. (1965) *Caste Class and Power*, Berkeley: University of California Press

Bhaduri, A. (1983) *The Economic Structure of Backward Agriculture*, London: Academic Press

Bharadwaj, K. (1974) *Production Conditions in Indian Agriculture*, Cambridge: Cambridge University Press

— (1985) 'A view on commercialisation in Indian agriculture and the development of capitalism', *Journal of Peasant Studies*, 12: 7–25

Blaikie, P. (1985) *The Political Economy of Soil Erosion*, London: Longman

Blaikie, P. and H. Brookfield (1987) *Land Degradation and Society*, London and New York: Methuen

Blaikie, P., J. Cameron and D. Seddon (1980) *The Crisis of Nepal: Growth and Stagnation at the Periphery*, Oxford: Clarendon Press

Booth, D. (1975) 'Andre Gunder Frank: an introduction and appreciation', in I. Oxaal, T. Barnett and D. Booth (eds), *Beyond Dependency*, London: Routledge & Kegan Paul

— (1985) 'Marxism and development sociology: the impasse', *World Development*, 13(7): 761–87

— (1994) *Rethinking Social Development: Theory, Research and Practice*, Harlow: Longman

Boserup, E. (1970) *Woman's Role in Development*, London: Allen & Unwin.

Brenner, R. (1978) 'The origins of capitalist development: a critique of neo-Smithian Marxism', *New Left Review*, 104: 25–92

Brett, E. A. (1983) *International Money and Capitalist Crisis: The Anatomy of Global Disintegration*, London: Heinemann

— (1985) *The World Economy since the War: The Politics of Uneven Development*, London: Macmillan

Byres, T. J. (1972) 'The dialectic of India's green revolution', *South Asian Review*, 5: 99–116

— (1979) 'Of neo-populist pipe-dreams', *Journal of Peasant Studies*, 6: 210–44

Chambers, R. (1983) *Rural Development: Putting the Last First*, Harlow: Longman

— (1988) *Poverty in India: Concepts, Research and Reality*, Discussion Paper no. 241, Institute of Development Studies, University of Sussex

Chang, H.-J. (2002) *Kicking away the Ladder: Economic Development in Historical Perspective*, London: Anthem Press

Chang, H.-J. and I. Grabel (2004) *Reclaiming Development: An Alternative Economic Policy Manual*, London and New York: Zed Books

Chayanov, A. V. (1966) *On the Theory of Peasant Economy*, ed. D. Thorner, B. Kerblay and R. E. F. Smith, Homewood, IL: published for the American Economic Association by R. D. Irwin

Chenery, H. et al. (1974) *Redistribution with Growth*, Oxford: Oxford University Press

Cole, K., J. Cameron and C. Edwards (1983) *Why Economists Disagree: The Political Economy of Economics*, London: Longman

Corbridge, S. (1998) 'Beneath the pavement only soil: the poverty of post-develop-ment', *Journal of Development Studies*, 34: 138–48

Corbridge, S. and J. Harriss (2000) *Reinventing India: Liberalization, Hindu Nationalism and Popular Democracy*, Cambridge: Polity Press

Cornia, G., R. Jolly and F. Stewart (1987) *Adjustment with a Human Face* (2 vols), Oxford: Oxford University Press

Davis, M. (2001) *Late Victorian Holocausts: El Niño Famines in the Making of the Third World*, London and New York: Verso

Desai, M. (2001) *Marx's Revenge: The Resurgence of Capitalism and the Death of Statist Socialism*, London: Verso

Dreze, J. and A. Sen (1989) *Hunger and Public Action*, Oxford: Oxford University Press

Duffield, M. (2001) *Global Governance and the New Wars: The Merging of Development and Security*, London and New York: Zed Books

Edwards, M. (1989) 'The irrelevance of development studies', *Third World Quarterly*, 11(1)

Elson, D. (1991) *Male Bias in the Development Process*, Manchester: Manchester University Press

Escobar, A. (1995) *Encountering Development*, Princeton, NJ: Princeton University Press

Evans, P. (1979) *Dependent Development: The Alliance of Multinational, State and Local Capital in Brazil*, Princeton, NJ: Princeton University Press

— (1995) *Embedded Autonomy: States and Industrial Transformation*, Princeton, NJ: Princeton University Press

— (ed.) (1996) *State–Society Synergy: Government and Social Capital in Development*, University of California at Berkeley, International and Area Studies, Research Series no. 94 (reprinted from *World Development*, July 1996)

Evans, P., D. Rueschmeyer and T. Skocpol (1985) *Bringing the State Back In*, Cam-bridge: Cambridge University Press

Faber, M. and D. Seers (eds) (1972) *The Crisis in Planning* (2 vols), London: Chatto & Windus for Sussex University Press

Fairhead, J. and M. Leach (1996) *Misreading the African Landscape: Society and Ecology in the Forest–Savanna Mosaic*, Cambridge: Cambridge University Press

Farmer, B. H. (ed.) (1977) *Green Revolution? Technology and Change in Rice-growing Areas of Tamil Nadu and Sri Lanka*, London: Macmillan

Fine, B. (2001) *Social Capital versus Social Theory: Political Economy and Social Science at the Turn of the Century*, London: Routledge

Frank, A. G. (1966) 'The development of underdevelopment', *Monthly Review*, 18(4)

— (1967) *Capitalism and Underdevelopment in Latin America*, New York: Monthly Review Press

Frobel, F., J. Heinrichs and O. Kreye (1980) *The New International Division of Labour: Structural Unemployment in Industrialized Countries and Industrialization in Devel-oping Countries*, Cambridge: Cambridge University Press

Geertz, C. (1963) *Agricultural Involution: The Process of Ecological Change in Indonesia*, Berkeley: University of California Press

Gerry, C. (1978) 'Petty production and capitalist production in Dakar: the crisis of the self-employed', *World Development*, 6(9/10): 1147–60

Gibbon, P. and M. Neocosmos (1985) 'Some problems in the political economy of "African socialism"', in H. Bernstein and B. Campbell (eds), *Contradictions of*

Accumulation in Africa. Studies in Economy and State, Beverly Hills, CA: Sage Publications

Giddens, A. (1990) *The Consequences of Modernity*, Cambridge: Polity Press

Griffin, K. (1974) *The Political Economy of Agrarian Change*, London: Macmillan

Grindle, M. (1985) *State and Countryside: Development Policy and Agrarian Politics in Latin America*, Baltimore, MD, and London: Johns Hopkins University Press

Harris, N. (1986) *The End of the Third World: Newly Industrializing Countries and the Decline of an Ideology*, London: Tauris

Harriss, J. (ed.) (1982a) *Rural Development: Theories of Peasant Economy and Agrarian Change*, London: Hutchinson

— (1982b) *Capitalism and Peasant Farming: Agrarian Structure and Ideology in Northern Tamil Nadu*, Bombay: Oxford University Press

— (ed.) (1995) *The Politics of Humanitarian Intervention*, London: Pinter

— (1998) 'Development studies and the development of India: an awkward case?', *Oxford Development Studies*, 26(3): 287–310

— (2001) *Depoliticizing Development: The World Bank and Social Capital*, Delhi/London: LeftWord/Anthem Press

Hart, G. (1986) *Power Labor and Livelihood: Processes of Change in Rural Java*, Berkeley: University of California Press

— (2002) *Disabling Globalization: Places of Power in Post-apartheid South Africa*, Berkeley: University of California Press

Hart, K. (1973) 'Informal income opportunities and urban employment in Ghana', *Journal of Modern Africa Studies*, 11: 61–89

Harvey, D. (1989) *The Condition of Postmodernity*, Oxford: Blackwell

Huntington, S. (1968) *Political Order in a Changing World*, New Haven, CT: Yale University Press

ILO (International Labour Office) (1977) *The Basic Needs Approach to Development: Some Issues Regarding Concepts and Methodology* (by Dharam Ghai et al.), Geneva: International Labour Office

Jameson, F. (1991) *Post-modernism, or the Cultural Logic of Late Capitalism*, London and New York: Verso.

Jodha, N. (1989) Essay in P. Bardhan (ed.), *Conversations amongst Economists and Anthropologists*, Delhi: Oxford University Press

Johnson, C. (1982) *MITI and the Japanese Miracle: The Growth of Industrial Policy 1925–75*, Stanford, CA: Stanford University Press

Joy, L. and E. Everitt (1976) *The Kosi Symposium*, Sussex: Institute of Development Studies

Kaldor, M. (1999) *New and Old Wars: Organized Violence in a Global Era*, Cambridge: Polity Press

Kay, G. (1975) *Development and Underdevelopment: A Marxist Perspective*, London: Macmillan

Kenny, M. and D. Williams (2001) 'What do we know about economic growth? Or, why don't we know very much?', *World Development*, 29(1): 1–22

Kitching, G. (1982) *Development and Underdevelopment in Historical Perspective*, London: Methuen

Lal, D. (1983) *The Poverty of Development Economics*, London: Institute of Economic Affairs

Leach, M. and R. Mearns (1996) *The Lie of the Land: Challenging Received Wisdom on the African Environment*, Oxford: International African Institute with James Currey

Lehmann, D. (1997) 'An opportunity lost: Escobar's deconstruction of development', *Journal of Development Studies*, 33(4): 568–79

Lenin, V. I. (1899) *The Development of Capitalism in Russia* (various edns)

Lewis, A. (1954) 'Economic development with unlimited supplies of labour', republished (1963) in A. N. Agarwala and S. P. Singh (eds), *Economics of Underdevelopment*, New York: Oxford University Press

Leys, C. (1995) *The Rise and Fall of Development Theory*, Oxford: James Currey

Little, D. (2003) *The Paradox of Wealth and Poverty: Mapping the Ethical Dilemmas of Global Development*, Boulder, CO: Westview

Lipton, M. (1968) 'The theory of the optimising peasant', *Journal of Development Studies*, 4: 327–51

— (1970) 'Interdisciplinary studies in LDCs', *Journal of Development Studies*, 7: 5–18

— (1974) 'Towards a theory of land reform', in D. Lehmann (ed.), *Agrarian Reform and Agrarian Reformism*, London: Faber

— (1977) *Why Poor People Stay Poor: Urban Bias in World Development*, London: Temple Smith

Mellor, J. (1976) *The New Economics of Growth*, Ithaca, NJ: Cornell University Press

Mitrany, D. (1951) *Marx against the Peasant: A Study in Social Domination*, London: Weidenfeld & Nicolson

Moser, C. O. N. (1978) 'Informal sector or petty commodity production: Dualism or dependence in urban development?', *World Development*, 6(9/10): 1041–64

Myrdal, G. (1968) *Asian Drama: An Inquiry into the Poverty of Nations* (3 vols), Harmondsworth: Penguin

Ostrom, E. (1990) *Governing the Commons*, New York: Cambridge University Press

Owen, R. and R. Sutcliffe (eds) (1972) *Theories of Imperialism*, London: Longman

Pogge, T. (2002) *World Poverty and Human Rights*, Cambridge: Polity Press

Popkin, S. (1979) *Rational Peasant: The Political Economy of Rural Society in Vietnam*, Berkeley: University of California Press

Redclift, M. (1984) *Development and the Environmental Crisis: Red or Green Alternatives*, London: Methuen

— (1987) *Sustainable Development: Exploring the Contradictions*, London: Methuen

Richards, P. (1985) *Indigenous Agricultural Revolution: Ecology and Food Production in West Africa*, London: Hutchinson

Rostow, W. (1960) *The Stages of Economic Growth: A Non-communist Manifesto*, Oxford: Oxford University Press

Sachs, W. (ed.) (1992) *The Development Dictionary: A Guide to Knowledge as Power*, London: Zed Books

Schmitz, H. (1982) 'Growth constraints on small-scale manufacturing in developing countries: a critical review', *World Development*, 10(6)

Schumacher, E. F. (1973) *Small Is Beautiful: A Study of Economics as If People Mattered*, London: Blond and Briggs

Scott, J. (1976) *The Moral Economy of the Peasantry*, New Haven, CT: Yale University Press

— (1985) *Weapons of the Weak: Everyday Forms of Peasant Resistance*, New Haven, CT: Yale University Press

— (1998) *Seeing Like the State*, New Haven, CT: Yale University Press

Seers, D. and L. Joy (eds) (1971) *Development in a Divided World*, Harmondsworth: Penguin

Sen, A. (1981) *Poverty and Famines: An Essay on Entitlement and Deprivation*, Oxford: Oxford University Press

— (1985) *Commodities and Capabilities*, Amsterdam: North-Holland

— (1999) *Development as Freedom*, New York: Knopf

Sethuraman, S. V. (1981) *Urban Informal Sector in Developing Countries: Employment, Environment and Population*, Geneva: International Labour Office

Shanin, T. (ed.) (1971) *Peasants and Peasant Societies*, Harmondsworth: Penguin

Streeten, P. and M. Lipton (eds) (1968) *The Crisis of Indian Planning*, Oxford: Oxford University Press

Sutcliffe, R. (1971) *Industrialisation and Underdevelopment*, London: Addison-Wesley

Taylor, J. (1979) *From Modernisation to Modes of Production: A Critique of the Sociologies of Development and Underdevelopment*, London: Macmillan

Thompson, M. et al. (1986) *Uncertainty on a Himalayan Scale*, London: Milton Ash

Wade, R. (1988) *Village Republics: Economic Conditions for Collective Action in South India*, Cambridge: Cambridge University Press

— (1990) *Governing the Market: Economic Theory and the Role of Government in East Asian Industrialization*, Princeton, NJ: Princeton University Press

— (1996) 'Japan, the World Bank, the art of paradigm maintenance', *New Left Review*, 217: 3–36

— (2000) 'Wheels within wheels: rethinking the Asian crisis and the Asian model', *Annual Review of Political Science*

Wallerstein, I. (1974) *The Modern World System*, London: Academic Press

Warren, B. (1980) *Imperialism: Pioneer of Capitalism*, London: NLB and Verso

Watts, M. (1983) *Silent Violence*, Berkeley: University of California Press

WCED (World Commission on Environment and Development) (1987) *Our Common Future: The Brundtland Report*, Oxford: Oxford University Press

WCSDG (World Commission on the Social Dimension of Globalization) (2004) *A Fair Globalization: Creating Opportunities for All*, Geneva: International Labour Office

White, G. (ed.) (1988) *Development States in East Asia*, Basingstoke: Macmillan

Williamson, J. (1990) *Latin American Adjustment: How Much Has Happened?*, Washington, DC: Institute for International Economics

Wolf, E. (1966) *Peasants*, Englewood Cliffs, NJ: Prentice-Hall

— (1971) *Peasant Wars of the Twentieth Century*, London: Faber

Wolf, M. (2004) *Why Globalization Works*, New Haven, CT, and London: Yale University Press

Wolpe, H. (ed.) (1980) *The Articulation of Modes of Production*, London: Routledge & Kegan Paul

World Bank (1992) *Governance and Development*, Washington, DC: World Bank

Young, K. et al. (eds) (1981) *Of Marriage and the Market: Women's Subordination in International Perspective*, London: CSE

3 | From colonial administration to development studies: a post-colonial critique of the history of development studies[1]

UMA KOTHARI

In this chapter I foreground and explore a different history of development studies to that which is conventionally rehearsed. Here I examine the colonial genealogy of development studies through the lives and experiences of individuals whose careers stretch across different historical moments, encompassing the administration of colonies and the establishment and emergence of development studies in institutes of higher education in the UK. The post-colonial analysis of the history of development studies that is presented here challenges orthodox versions of its history and questions the conventional start date of 1945 as marking the beginning of development. The aim is to identify the traces of colonialism that pervade the workings of the post-independence international development aid industry and highlight the extent and form of the relationship between colonialism and contemporary development studies. Furthermore, through the narratives that are presented in this chapter, former colonial officers offer their own historical perspective and critique of development. This analysis of relationships and trajectories of ideas, institutions and people is important because it deepens our understanding of why and how development studies has evolved.

The following section, which analyses the recent and varied approaches to understanding the colonial legacy of development, is followed by discussions as to why development studies rarely acknowledges these colonial roots. I argue here that there is a perceived imperative for many of those within contemporary development studies to distance themselves from the negativity that surrounds this genealogy and instead present a rather truncated version of its history. The third section is based on research with former colonial officers who, following the formal independence of former colonies, subsequently worked in the field of development studies. Here, through their stories and recollections, I demonstrate the relationship between colonialism and development, focusing particularly on the experiences and skills that they took into development studies and how, if we are not to deny historical continuities, these have shaped the culture and direction of post-independence development. The chapter concludes by attempting to draw out what this particular historical reading highlights in terms of the continuities and divergences between colonialism and development.

Understanding the colonial legacy of development studies

Post-colonial analyses examine the historical effects of colonialism and the persistence of colonial forms of power and knowledge into the present. In exposing colonial discourses and practices, post-colonialists attempt to reveal how contemporary global inequalities between rich and poor countries have been, and continue to be, shaped by colonial power relations. Through problematizing, deconstructing and decentring the supposed universality of Western knowledge, post-colonial perspectives critically engage with and resist the variety of ways in which the West produces knowledge about other people in other places and interrogate hegemonic histories that often obscure the continuing effects of colonialism (see Kothari 2005a). Much of this type of interrogation, however, has taken place outside of development studies.

A discursive analysis of development began in the 1980s with the emergence, and increasing prominence, of so-called 'alternative' approaches to development, such as gender and development, environmental and sustainable development and participation and empowerment, as well as alternatives to development advocated by post-development theorists such as Escobar (1995). Investigations of the links between colonialism and contemporary international development have, however, emerged only recently (see Sylvester 1999). Influenced by the types of analyses that underpinned dependency and world systems theories in the 1970s, much critical literature from the 1980s that emerged out of post-colonial and post-development critiques focused on how the development project creates and perpetuates uneven and unequal development between First and Third World countries. These approaches centre on an analysis of development discourse and how it shapes and defines different realities. Post-development theorists attempt to deconstruct the idea of post-war development and some call for a total abandonment of the project. They argue that development discourse is ahistorical and obscures the political realities of the development industry. Further, they suggest that it is hegemonic in its construction and regulation of Third World identities and limits the adoption of alternative ways of organizing and achieving social progress. Some of these critics have argued that development is a 'neo-colonial' project that reproduces global inequalities and maintains the dominance of the South, through global capitalist expansion, by the North. In questioning the history, objectives and means of development, some of these critics have argued for the recognition that the current economic, social and political situation in developing countries, and the continuing interest of the West in the Third World, cannot be properly understood without an adequate understanding of their historical, and particularly colonial, background (Chandra 1992; Crush 1995; Cowen and Shenton 1996). Others have specifically traced the origins of the field of development studies in order to explore how development mediates, extends, entrenches or counters colonial legacies (Pieterse and Parekh 1995; Rahnema and Bawtree 1997).

There is ample evidence that colonialism survives the post-independence period in the form of economic and political relations and social and cultural representations. There are, however, a number of different perspectives and emphases that have emerged to account for these ongoing relationships and their contemporary articulations and consequences. Said (1989), for example, is clear that 'to have been colonised was a fate with lasting, indeed grotesquely unfair results' (207; see also Miege 1980). Goldsmith (1997) develops this idea when he claims that development reproduces a form of unequal trade that is reminiscent of colonial forms of economic control and exploitation. Others such as Mamdani (1996) have located continuities and divergences in institutional and administrative structures while Cooke (2003) provides evidence for the continuities between contemporary development management and colonial administration, arguing that these reveal colonialist power relations. The colonial legacy of other fields of contemporary development practice has also been explored through, for example, genealogies of participatory approaches (Cooke and Kothari 2001), gender and development (Radcliffe 1994; Parpart 1995; McEwan 2001), community development, and conservation and development (Adams and Mulligan 2003).

The historical continuum can also be understood in terms of how colonialism and international development articulate similar notions of modernity and progress. For example, Dirks (1992) suggests that colonialism can be seen as a cultural, not just an economic, project which created and maintained classifications and hierarchies between groups of people. Consequently, dichotomies of, for example, the 'modern' and the 'traditional' and the 'West' and the 'rest' are embedded within development discourse, and this reassertion of colonial classifications of difference is often invoked to justify development interventions. The representation of peoples in and of the 'Third World' as 'backward', 'traditional' and incapable of self-government further embeds global distinctions developed during the colonial period.

Despite this evidence of colonial continuities into the present day, it would be a mistake to suggest that present-day development discourse is simply a reworking of a (neo-)colonial one since development is not always and inevitably an extension of colonialism. Brigg (2002) has suggested that critiques of development need to take into account issues such as moral responsibility and humanitarianism and not focus solely on the perpetuation of colonial forms of authority and rule. While this is valid, it assumes that colonialism was not concerned with these issues but more problematically, by implication, that development necessarily is. An apt quote from Cecil Rhodes interestingly put these sorts of assumptions in perspective: 'imperialism was philanthropy plus a 5 per cent dividend on investment' (Rhodes, quoted in Lawlor 2000: 63). As I argue below, however, we need to be wary of histories of development that deny this colonial genealogy and attempt to create distinct and artificial boundaries between the exploitation of empire and the humanitarianism of development.

Obscuring a colonial genealogy

The discussion above highlights the recent recognition by some critical analysts of a historical trajectory that links colonialism to contemporary processes of globalization generally, and development more specifically. Attempting to understand and analyse this interconnectedness, however, is not a mainstream preoccupation within development studies. Indeed, much of the post-colonial debate has been located within, for example, sociology, anthropology, literary criticism and geography, and rarely in the development studies literature. Said, however, reminds us of the need to locate our field of study historically and contextually when he writes, ' ... there is no discipline, no structure of knowledge, no institution or epistemology that can or has ever stood free of the various socio-cultural, historical, and political formations that give epochs their peculiar individuality' (Said 1989: 211).

Moreover, an ahistorical approach to development studies, or one that presents an epochal historicization, obscures both the colonial genealogies of development and the historical continuities in the theory and practice of development. More generally, Chambers (1993) reminds us that with the accelerated rate of obsolescence of development ideas and the constant renewal of technical fashions in development practice, the need to revisit the past and be cognizant of the history of development appears increasingly important.

Although there are ongoing critiques of development, as shown above (see, for example, Escobar 1995; Slater 1995), much research and teaching in development studies still tends to embed 1945 as the key year in which development was initiated with the establishment of the Bretton Woods institutions. This limited historical analysis in much orthodox/mainstream development studies reveals the largely unreflexive nature of the discipline, partly engendered through the imperative to achieve development goals and targets. With a few notable exceptions (Crush 1995; Grillo and Stirrat 1997), most historical reviews of development rehearsed in development research and teaching have tended towards a compartmentalization of clearly bounded, successive periods characterized by specific theoretical hegemonies that begin with economic growth and modernization theories, moving through theories of underdevelopment and culminating in neo-liberalism and the Washington Consensus (see Hettne 1995; Preston 1996). An alternative version is one that is mapped on to particular events and processes; a political economy trajectory that traces by decade the history of development from the golden years of the 1950s through import substitution industrialization in the 1960s to the debt crisis in the 1970s, structural adjustment programmes in the 1980s and subsequently alternative development and the Millennium Development Goals in the 1990s and after.

Another critical factor that shapes the continuing rehearsal of this rather shortened version of history that dominates the discipline has been the perceived need to effectively distance development thought and practice from the contemporary negativity surrounding Britain's imperial history. This concealment of a colonial past thus becomes, perhaps unwittingly, part of a project that creates and maintains a dichotomy between a colonialism that is 'bad', exploitative, extractive and oppressive and a development that is 'good', moralistic, philanthropic and humanitarian. This separation from colonialism absolves those in development studies of the responsibility of addressing how our work is related to the various forms of rule, authority and inequality that characterized so much of the colonial period. And, as the narratives from former officers presented below demonstrate, the extent to which engagement with the colonial encounter may also question our homogenizing assumptions about those involved in colonial administration towards the end of empire. As one interviewee challenges, 'You know, someone who sort of brands me as a sort of colonial, imperial exploiter, I'd say – OK, I can see that in the bigger picture you can see me in that role but that isn't what I was actually doing.'

Overall, then, there has been a political imperative to distance the international aid industry from the colonial encounter so as to avoid tarnishing what is presented as a humanitarian project far removed from the supposed exploitation of the colonial era. This chapter suggests that not only is there a need to question the comparison made whereby development can only be 'good' as it is set against a colonialism that is wholly 'bad', but that in presenting a different history of development we can see how development works in and against its colonial past.

A further reason for the dearth of critical analysis and extended historical view is perhaps related to the policy and practice focus of much work within development studies. Many of those engaged with these aspects of development see themselves primarily as practitioners, and therefore presume to have little use for theory. This division between the relative importance of theory and practice is an ongoing debate within development studies.

The relatively few studies that have engaged with the continuities and divergences from colonialism to development have tended to focus on institutional histories, analyses of the origins of the 'doctrines' of development and the colonial genealogy of ideas and practices of development (see Cowen and Shenton 1996; Havinden and Meredith 1993; Munck and O'Hearn 1999). In this chapter I want to introduce an additional focus of analysis in the form of personal narratives that I argue can provide a further resource for understanding histories of development generally and interrogating comparisons between colonialism and development specifically. Below I show how the experiences and recollections of individuals involved in both colonial administration and subsequently in the field of development studies as teachers, researchers and expatriate consultants can inform our understanding of development studies and in so doing provide another history of the discipline, its discourse and practice. I begin in the next section with a note on memory and history, arguing that the process of collecting narratives, and not simply the content of the stories, provides us with evidence with which to interrogate alternative histories of development studies

Memory, narratives and history

Changes brought about by political independence in former colonies led many of those employed in the British Colonial Office to leave Africa and Asia and find employment back in the UK. Among those embarking on second careers were a group of individuals who found employment in the newly emerging and rapidly expanding international development industry in the UK, where they are (or were until retirement) involved in teaching development studies in institutes of higher education, devising policies to address issues of Third World development and carrying out research and consultancy work for multilateral, bilateral and non-governmental organizations. The research on which much of this chapter is based traced the genealogy of post-war international development through the personal testimonies of those individuals whose experiences and skills as expatriates in the colonial service were thought to be particularly suited to the work of international development. Between 2001 and 2002 I interviewed fifteen people who had previously worked for the

UK Colonial Office and subsequently became engaged in development studies. The interviewees, whose stories are reflected upon here, had been posted to sub-Saharan Africa during their time in the colonial service. Most have now formally retired although many continue to be active as development consultants, research associates in academic institutions, or in charitable foundations.

The taped interviews, only a greatly reduced version of which are presented here,[2] focused on their motives and aspirations for joining the colonial service and their subsequent decision to become involved in post-independence development work, and explored changes in their roles and responsibilities as they continued their careers in development studies. These life histories and narratives articulate continuities through the telling of events and experiences over time and highlight how subjective and collective understandings of past and present are imbricated. For example, individual stories about the period of Britain's colonial rule are unavoidably informed by an awareness of contemporary critiques of colonialism along with a more complex and varied Western attitude towards the outside world. Crucially, their accounts draw upon collective visions and themes, since life stories are inevitably located in the social contexts of meanings, languages and institutional and national cultures. As Jameson notes, the narrativization of an individual story and experience inevitably invokes the history of the collectivity itself (1986). Furthermore, as bearers of culture, the narrators are unavoidably influenced by historical and contemporary understandings of social relations, norms and customs that have become internalized. In this case, the negativity, or at least awkwardness, surrounding Britain's imperial history significantly shaped how stories were told, the language used and the form of self-criticism.

The lasting effects of colonialism are also manifest in the Overseas Pensioners Association, to which some of the interviewees belong. Colonial officers who felt abandoned by the UK government at the time of independence established the Association, whose main objective is to support those without adequate pensions. Interestingly, the Association also welcomes and supports activities that it feels will rescue the colonial project and its servants from the perceived negativity that surrounds that part of British history. There is a desire to 'set the record straight about the good work done under colonialism', to proffer a more nuanced testimony which foregrounds the positive impacts individuals could make in colonized spaces.

This contemporary context clearly informs their stories and the ways in which they recall and interpret the past and their role within it. The narratives provide evidence of how certain aspects of the past are invoked and others concealed in order to justify an individual's role and actions. Hobsbawm and

Ranger (1983) and Anderson (1991) have shown how the 'invention of tradition' and the construction of an imaginary past enable this legitimization. As Ranger writes, 'Some traditions in colonial Africa really were invented, by a single colonial officer for a single occasion. But customary law and ethnicity and religion and language were imagined, by many different people and over a long time' (Ranger 1993). The 'imagined community' of 'home' and 'away', invoked by the colonial officer, was also significant in shaping their experiences, the decisions they took and the framing of their recollections. While Gowan's (2002) study of imperial elites returning to Britain from India demonstrates the construction of imagined geographies of 'home', in the narratives of former colonial administrators, there is also an imagined geography of 'away'. For many, their lives were never as good as during the colonial period, partly because of the privileges of 'race' and gender but also because of what and whom they represented overseas. Therefore, as agents of colonialism they 'often display nostalgia for the colonized culture' (Rosaldo 1993: 69) evident in the romanticized vision they continue to hold of, for example, Nigeria, Tanzania or Kenya. These representations and imaginings of home and away, imperialist notions of dominance and the civilizing mission in much colonial discourse were transferred and translated into the sphere and context of post-independence development studies.

Importantly, through oral history, individuals can inscribe their experiences on the historical record and offer their own interpretations of the processes that connect their individual narratives with understandings of wider contexts and processes of change. Accordingly, these living memories can complement official and dominant sources and explanations of change, contest and challenge conventional discourses and interpretations, and attribute alternative versions of processes of change. Oral history not only allows evidence from a new direction but it also opens up new or under-researched areas of enquiry. In doing so, the diverse complexities of reality are illuminated while simultaneously this more nuanced understanding of different realities reveals common themes and trends. Thus personal testimonies of colonial officers can challenge established accounts, and provide significant justifications as well as critiques of colonial and development policy and practice. Furthermore, these personalized narratives can explain trajectories and processes that have led to more recent events and provide information that alludes to future aspirations and strategies (see Kothari and Hulme 2003). Finally, remembering is also about forgetting. Some former colonial officers feel that they have been forgotten in official versions of the history of colonialism and in contemporary understandings of colonialism, and that their testimonies correct this marginalization while at the same time there are also 'absent' memories in their own accounts.

These narratives demonstrate how colonial administrators and development professionals transfer ideas about other people and places over time and space but also rework these dominant discourses once 'in the field' since their experiences and approaches are inevitably subjective and contextual. I do not wish to suggest that the effects of colonialism were benign; however, while we can, at one level, generalize about colonialism and development, on another we must accept that there are multiple stories challenging the notion of a singular trajectory. Thus, historiographies of development studies may simultaneously reveal patterns and continuities but also identify what Crush (1995: 8) refers to as the 'conflicting intellectual currents flowing through the contemporary domain of development'.

I have argued above that the process of constructing a narrative and not only its content provides evidence of the continuing effects of colonialism. This was further reflected in how my own subjectivity as interviewer, grounded in a particular ethnicity, gender and familial history, inevitably influenced the interviewees and their responses in a variety of covert and overt ways, ranging from use of language to describe other people and other places to articulations of the benefits or otherwise of colonialism. Since individual recollections reflect collective and contemporary attitudes and perceptions, interpreting people's stories then became a process of analysing interpretations of the past and how memory is shaped by these influences, as much as about 'real' events and experiences. The individuals whose stories are reflected upon here, who worked in development studies and were in the past part of the colonial administrative service, reveal the embodiment of historical continuities and reflect particular historiographies.

From colonial administration to development studies

This section focuses on the relationship between colonial administration and development studies by identifying the sorts of skills and experiences that former colonial officers brought to post-independence development, their experiences of the transition from colonial administration to development studies, and their thoughts on what development has come to mean. The section argues that these personal and collective historiographies provide evidence for the institutionalized links between colonialism and development and how they became embodied in the individual. Furthermore, they have wider implications in terms of understanding the origins of contemporary development discourse and practice.

Said emphasizes historical continuities. He writes, 'Imperialism, the control of overseas territories and peoples, develops in a continuum with variously envisaged histories, current practices and policies, and with differently plotted cultural trajectories' (Said 1989: 219). Similarly, the era of colonialism, like the historical evolution of development and its ongoing formation, never embodied unchanging and homogeneous objectives and practices.

The practical implications for some colonial officers during the late colonial period were that their responsibilities were directed towards the preparation of colonies for indirect rule and self-government rather than the expansion of colonial territories. This no doubt created some ambivalence for those officers who were aware that their jobs were increasingly concerned with preparing nations for independence, an objective that could ironically result in the loss of their own employment and status. While the administrative workings of colonial rule appeared to be changing, so did the motives of many who joined the service in the late colonial era. Many felt that independence was imminent and therefore this was a very exciting period of global change (Kirk-Greene 2000), but at the same time feared for their future security of employment.

Although the narratives reflected upon here are those of a small number of former administrators and their accounts are inevitably subjective, interestingly they all saw themselves as development practitioners prior to the formal end of colonial rule. They did not view their activities in the context of the expansion or even of the maintenance of empire, but in latter-day colonialism they felt that they were already 'doing' development. Thus, they were not only colonial officers but were simultaneously development practitioners, and therefore are able to reflect on a very specific transitional moment.

A quote from one of the interviewees referring to the moment when he was required to leave the colonial service reveals the perceived link between the work carried out in the late colonial period and the work of post-war development.

> And I thought, right, if I can no longer do this job and work out here the next best thing is to be working for the development of Kenya in the development field – after all, it is the same thing. Yes, I was fed up in that it was clear that the winds of change meant you couldn't stay on for ever. But what's the point of chasing a dwindling colonial empire around – let's get back and get our teeth into something that will be important – helping Third World countries.

Clearly, then, towards the end of the colonial period there were some administrators who felt that their jobs in the colonial service were more closely related to development work. Indeed some of them had originally been posted to the colonies as teachers under the auspices of the Colonial Education Department, or as forestry and agricultural officers addressing issues of 'community development'.

At the time of independence those employed in the colonial service had to make decisions about their future, and although some stayed on after independence they realized that this was always going to be a short-term strategy as 'it was obvious the Africans were going to go for the administrative jobs and maybe also the top jobs in the police'. Others chased a dwindling empire around, but they were just delaying coming back to the UK and 'in the end even they were washed away by the tide of independence'.

Finding a job on their return to Britain was not always easy, partly because 'in this country there was this attitude that "Oh God, he's been in Africa for twelve years; he won't be much use to us!"' Some ex-colonial officers, however, did find jobs in the legal profession or as teachers in schools, while others joined the newly emerging and rapidly expanding international development industry. Those who were based in academic departments taught courses in public administration primarily to overseas students from newly independent states (see Clarke 1999; Minogue 1977) and periodically returned overseas as consultants on development projects (see Chambers, this volume; Cameron, this volume). Others worked for multilateral agencies such as the UN and the World Bank, bilateral institutions and international non-governmental organizations.

It is not the intention here to homogenize the institutions or the individuals operating within them, as clearly they do not have fixed and singular identities but are spatially and temporally varied. Decolonization, processes of globalization, the workings of the Bretton Woods institutions and the nature of international finance and trade have altered the environment within which development takes place. Moreover, within the development process, changing discourses of foreign aid and theories and policies of international development successively shaped practices, as did the evolving relations between Britain and its former colonies. Thus, while there are continuities, the workings of the Colonial Office and the role and mission of a colonial officer within it changed significantly from the early colonial period to the lead-up to independence. Similarly development organizations are distinguished in their objectives and global reach, which vary from place to place and over time, as the individuals within them are differentiated by their specific roles, responsibilities and location.

What this transition meant for former administrators is revealed in their narratives, which reflect on their induction into the development industry, focusing particularly on their subsequent critique of the development process and a perceived contrast between the forms of expertise and practice they mobilized in colonial and immediately post-colonial contexts and the very different skills and procedures of contemporary development professionals. They also assess apparent disjunctures and continuities between colonial and development praxis, further questioning the overwhelmingly negative perception of colonialism as a totality irrespective of specific and individual endeavours. These recollections deepen our understanding of how their experiences and skills came to shape the direction and form of post-independence development studies. That is, the experiences of former colonial administrators moving into development studies can tell us something about the ideologies and practices upon which post-independence development was formulated.

Some of the interviewees recalled that to work in development studies departments in UK institutes of higher education in the early days: 'The argument was that you must do development if you are going to teach it. So you must have done development in some way or another.' Many former colonials felt, however, that this was 'later watered down and we had people who were really only theorists'.

Thus, many of those who worked overseas as part of the aid mission were often not viewed by former colonial officers as 'experts'. As one interviewee notes: 'the conditions where lots of people could live for a decade or two in Africa and Asia are gone ... As the cynic would say, they don't want too much expertise on a single country.'

This reduction of in-depth knowledge of other places and people was expressed as a considerable problem within development studies: 'We want to be able to teach courses here where we can say this is going to be the best approach for this sector in Africa, but the point I'm trying to make is we should not continue to generalize about Africa. Each country is unique.' This was compounded by the antagonism between those in development who had a background in the colonial service and younger development 'experts' who did not.

Importantly, former colonial officers were unimpressed with the policies and strategies being devised in post-independent development: 'I shouldn't say this but I will. When I meet young chaps who now work as development advisers or listen to people talking about development aid, and they say "We're doing X, Y and Z", I think "Oh my God, we were doing that twenty years ago and we failed as well!" I am astonished sometimes that we go on inventing the wheel and the wheel goes round, and I don't think that this is just a silly old man talking.'

In order to contextualize these tensions between those who began their careers in development studies and those who had a background in the colonial service and whose working environments now overlapped it is necessary to understand their histories. Specifically, the practical skills, knowledge and accumulated experience that they felt they had acquired from living for long periods in former colonies they believed were subsequently being mistakenly devalued.

During the late colonial period, the skills required to become a colonial administrator included the practical skills and capabilities of living for extended periods in often geographically isolated areas, including speaking the local language (Kirk-Greene 2000). More often than not these administrators came through public and grammar schools, and many graduated from Oxford and Cambridge. All new recruits were required to attend a twelve-month course known as the Devonshire A course in which they were educated on, among other subjects, imperial history, language skills, the judiciary and ethnology (see ibid.). For colonial officers language skills were thought to be particularly important, alongside training in developing a disposition that encouraged a practical engagement and cultural and social immersion in the place of work. In development studies, on the contrary, language, while not unimportant, is often considered secondary to specific forms of theoretical or technical expertise. Indeed, these are conceived as far more relevant than regional experience and geographic specialism.

Some colonial officers felt that they had much greater geographic knowledge than younger development 'experts'. They were trained in the local language before being posted overseas, and although they were moved from one posting to another, the scale of movement was limited and most stayed within the same country. Thus, whereas specialisms of the colonial era tended to be based upon a knowledge of particular geographical areas, the Africanist or Asianist has largely been replaced by those with thematic and/or technical expertise in, for example, translocal foci such as gender analysis, rural development, impact assessment or participatory rural appraisal. They seemingly move unproblematically between and within countries, taking with them their particular expertise, but often with limited knowledge of the different historical, social and cultural contexts in which they are required to apply it. Thus, the interviewees feel that while they had experienced enduring and profound engagements with the places to which they were posted, the contemporary development 'expert' tends to move within a world of fleeting consultancies.

Academic background was not as significant a criterion in the recruitment process of colonial officers, although many did come through Oxford and

Cambridge. It was more the ethos and discipline nurtured in the culture of these establishments than the academic status which was valued. As one interviewee recalls, 'the Colonial Office didn't want people who are too clever, on the other hand they don't want people who are too thick'. Indeed, reliability, honesty and 'good character' were valued much more highly than academic knowledge and technical skills. This 'good character' and ability to deal fairly with people, albeit within the context of an unquestioned superiority, were valued in the colonial service, and one way of measuring these qualities was through an individual's extra-curricular activities, of which sport was the most significant. Sporting capabilities were seen to reflect qualities of leadership and fairness as well as fitness (see Furse 1962). The significance of sport goes beyond reflecting individual character, however; it was also something particularly British. This focus on character, personal qualities and sport also reveals the importance of class and it was the background in grammar and public schools followed by Oxford or Cambridge which generally ensured this. Although there were also those from more working-class backgrounds, they had often been awarded educational scholarships and hence had been educated in primarily middle- and upper-class institutions.

So the colonial officer was typically someone with a good second-class degree from Oxford or Cambridge, a sportsman with an ability to live and work in 'difficult' environments. When they moved into the field of development after independence, these qualities and behaviours were initially valued or at least accepted; as younger development professionals joined the industry, however, these mores were perceived to be not only less important but more crucially old-fashioned and unprofessional. Other criteria for recruitment were valorized which placed greater importance on technical skills and expertise than on personal character. The cultural capital and the specific relevance of class background in assigning an individual's status in the colonial hierarchy were being eroded and replaced by divisions based on other criteria. Indeed, in development the status ascribed to an individual consultant often relates to that of the institution they represent in terms of the extent of its financial resources, and political and global sphere of influence, whether they are from a multilateral agency such as the World Bank, a donor agency, an NGO or an academic institution.

The end of empire also brought with it a social distancing from colonialism. One British high commissioner said that he had to demonstrate that he was very different to previous colonial expatriates. Some former colonial servants feel, however, that this negativity towards all things colonial was misplaced since, given their extended stay overseas, they have greater knowledge and experience of other countries than those who rely on short-term overseas assignments.

In part, this discord reflects the changing boundaries of what development studies involved in the early days of the establishment of UK academic development institutes and what it later evolved into. At the time of the establishment of development studies institutes in Britain, former colonial officers' jobs in these centres included a range of activities that were less 'academic' and more related to the provision of professional training courses, with individuals associated with them being involved in short- and long-term consultancies overseas and secondments to bilateral and multilateral development agencies. Therefore, many people could be associated with a development studies institute but still spend long periods of time, sometimes two or three years, working overseas. Thus, many of the former colonial officers' comments about post-independence development refer to a period when it was more difficult to distinguish between development studies and the broader field of the development aid industry. Their references primarily draw out comparisons with post-independence professional 'experts' and technical assistance rather than relating more generally to the teaching and research carried out within what has become development studies. Indeed, the divisions between researchers and consultants, and policy-makers and academics, became more distinct as these institutes started to provide more academic training in the form of masters courses and PhD programmes. Importantly, the modifications necessary post-independence, and the profound resentment between the 'old' and 'new', were compounded by the adjustments former colonial officers inevitably had to make in terms of the loss of power and control, cultural capital and status that had been their privilege while overseas.

In this section I have presented colonial officers' personalized accounts of the implications of the end of empire and their perceptions about the changing nature of the relationship between Britain and overseas as articulated by what development studies, broadly understood, has become.

Continuities and divergences

That the experiences and attitudes of former colonial administrators who moved into development studies should not be carried over after formal independence denies historical continuities and the perpetuation of certain kinds of discourse over time and space. Certain regularities and consistencies, as well as distinct and contrasting practices, stand out from these interviews and other recent critical literature on colonialism and development.

At a fundamental level, both colonial administration and development studies involve an engagement with institutions and ideas that originate in the West and have a global reach. Most obviously, continuities are borne in the experiences of colonial officers and many of those involved in development studies through their travel to places outside Europe and so involve an encounter, at the level of the individual in the 'field', with other places and other people. Thus, colonialism and development articulate relationships between Britain and overseas, and the British and others. Even for those who do not travel, teaching development studies in UK institutes of higher education can invoke past relations, since a large proportion of students come from former colonies. These missions are inevitably embedded in relations of power, control and knowledge that intersect and are expressed and mobilized by the colonial administrator and the Western development 'expert' who become embodied sites of power, exercising forms of control and imparting knowledge in and among people from other parts of the world. In order to understand how this relationship is played out it is suggested here that the shift from colonialism to development represents a process involving a redistribution of ideas, institutions and people.

While there are continuities in terms of individuals, there are also divergences between the projects of colonialism and development in that the relationships between colonial officer and colonized, development practitioner and aid recipient and teacher and student are articulated variously and take different forms. The changing importance of particular types of experience, skill and expertise, particularly the shift from regional, geographic knowledge towards a valorization of technical or thematic specialisms, highlights significant divergences between colonialism and development. Furthermore, the decolonizing process heralded a more equitable and varied social mix, opening up possibilities that diverged from the conventional segregations of colonialism.

To say that development represents a continuation of colonialism is for some axiomatic and for others an unfair generalization. But what I have tried to suggest in this chapter is that through individual experiences we can see how the development industry works in and against its colonial past. Personal narratives simultaneously complement and critique official accounts not only of colonialism, but more importantly of mainstream and orthodox versions of the history of development. The characterization of colonialism as 'bad', however, or indeed the denial of a colonial genealogy, has allowed many of those in the aid industry to work unquestioningly and unproblematically in, and on, Third World countries. This ahistoricism is continually legitimized by the pervasive representation of development as Western philanthropy, as a humanitarian mission that bears no resemblance to the perceived inequalities and exploitations of empire. Thus, development can only be 'good' when set against a colonialism that was 'bad'. This dichotomy absolves those of us teaching, researching and advising in the field of development studies of the responsibility of examining the ways in which we may be perpetuating and entrenching notions of Western superiority, difference and inequality.

This dichotomy problematically ignores the experiences of those 'demonized' former colonials in at least two ways. First, it neglects to identify the perpetuation of inequities from the colonial era which entrenched notions of Western superiority and difference. A form of Eurocentrism continues to articulate First World–Third World relations in the post-independence period of development aid. It would, however, be disingenuous to construct development studies solely as a neo-colonial discipline. Clearly, individuals in development studies today are far more diverse in terms of gender, class and ethnicity than were the colonial officers, and this has necessarily meant an opening up of the field and the emergence of multiple strands of thought and practice. It is also evident that 'development professionals' are immersed in broader ideas and possibilities, reflected perhaps in the move from nation-state-led Eurocentrism to globalized values. Second, the separation between development and colonialism neglects to study those numerous examples of individual colonial practice which, although embedded within unequal relations, provided instances of processes grounded in local cultural context. Many former low-ranking colonial officers feel, therefore, that the broader knowledge acquired by development professionals has come at a cost: in contrast to the colonial specialist, deeply familiar, yet superior within, his geographic environment, the universalizing of thematic, theoretical and technical expertise within development studies is less able to be mobilized in the local cultural field. Additionally, theoretically and empirically separating the moment of colonialism from the time of development limits the extent to which contemporary processes of global change can be understood and evaluated, rooted as they are in (unequal) relations over time and space.

To produce a post-colonial development that critically re-evaluates development theory and practice and disconnects it from what has variously been termed its neo-colonial, re-colonial and imperial context and articulations requires, as a starting point, a historical analysis that identifies the particularities, and varied expressions, of the continuities between colonialism and development. It is hoped that this chapter has contributed to this analysis, to enable development studies to move beyond its complicity with Western knowledge and power, understand why it has evolved in the ways in which it has and, importantly, provide an alternative historical context with which to evaluate its future potential.

Notes

1 I am grateful to the former colonial administrators whose narratives are anonymously referred to here.

2 For a more detailed description and analysis of the narratives of former colonial officers, see 'From colonialism to development: reflections of former colonial officers' (forthcoming), *Journal of Commonwealth and Comparative Politics*, and 'Authority and expertise: the professionalization of international development and the ordering of dissent' (2005), *Antipode* 37(3): 425–46.

References

Adams, W. M. and M. Mulligan (eds) (2003) *Decolonizing Nature: Strategies for Conservation in a Post-colonial Era*, London: Earthscan

Anderson, B. (1991) *Imagined Communities: Reflections on the Origin and Spread of Nationalism*, London: Verso

Bell, M. (2002) 'Inquiring minds and post colonial devices: examining poverty at a distance', *Annals of the Association of American Geographers*, 92(3): 507–23

Brigg, M. (2002) 'Post-development, Foucault and the colonisation metaphor', *Third World Quarterly*, 3(3): 421–36

Chambers, R. (1993) *Challenging the Professions*, London: Intermediate Technology Publications

Chandra, R. (1992) *Industrialisation and Development in the Third World*, London: Routledge

Clarke, R. (1999) 'Institutions for training overseas administrators: the University of Manchester contribution', *Public Administration and Development*, 19: 521–33

Cooke, B. (2003) 'A new continuity with colonial administration: participation in development management', *Third World Quarterly*, 24(1): 47–61

Cooke, B. and U. Kothari (2001) *Participation: The New Tyranny?*, London: Zed Books

Cowen, M. P. and R. W. Shenton (1996) *Doctrines of Development*, London: Routledge

Crush, J. (1995) (ed.) *Power of Development*, London: Routledge

Dirks, N. B. (ed.) (1992) *Colonialism and Culture*, Ann Arbor: University of Michigan Press

Escobar, A. (1995) *Encountering Development: The Making and Unmaking of the Third World*, Princeton, NJ: Princeton University Press

Ferguson, J. (1994) *The Anti-politics Machine*, Minneapolis: University of Minnesota Press

Furse, R. (1962) *Aucuparius: Recollections of a Recruitment Officer*, London, Oxford University Press

Goldsmith, E. (1997) 'Development as colonialism', *The Ecologist*, March/April, 27(2): 69–77

Gowan, G. (2002) 'A passage from India: geographies and experiences of repatriation, 1858–1939', *Social and Cultural Geography*, 3(4): 303–23

Grillo, R. D. and R. L. Stirrat (eds) (1997) *Discourses of Development: Anthropological Perspectives*, Oxford: Berg

Havinden, M. and D. Meredith (1993) *Colonialism and Development: Britain and Its Tropical Colonies 1850–1960*, London: Routledge

Hettne, B. (1995) *Development Theory and the Three Worlds*, London: Longman

Hobsbawm, E. and T. Ranger (eds) (1983) *The Invention of Tradition*, Cambridge: Cambridge University Press

Jameson, F. (1986) 'Third World literature in the era of multinational capitalism', *Social Text*, 15: 65–88

Kirk-Greene, A. (2000) *Britain's Imperial Administrators, 1858–1966*, Basingstoke: Macmillan

Kothari, U. (2002) 'Feminist and postcolonial challenges to development', in U. Kothari and M. Minogue, *Development Theory and Practice: Critical Perspectives*, Basingstoke: Palgrave

— (2005a) 'Postcolonialism', in T. Forsyth (ed.), *Encyclopedia of International Development*, London and New York: Routledge

— (forthcoming 2005b) 'Authority and expertise: the professionalisation of international development and the ordering of dissent', *Antipode*

Kothari, U. and D. Hulme (2003) 'Narratives, stories and tales: understanding poverty dynamics through life histories', Global Poverty Research Group Working Paper

Lawlor, E. (2000) *Murder on the Verandah: Love and Betrayal in British Malaya*, London: Flamingo

McEwan, C. (2001) 'Postcolonialism, feminism and development: intersections and dilemmas', *Progress in Development Studies*, 1(2): 93–111

Mamdani, M. (1996) *Citizen and Subject: Contemporary Africa and the Legacy of Late Colonialism*, Princeton, NJ: Princeton University Press

Miege, J.-L. (1980) 'The colonial past in the present', in W. H. Morris-Jones and G. Fischer (eds), *Decolonisation and After: The British and French Experience*, London: Frank Cass

Minogue, M. (1977) 'Administrative training: doublethink and newspeak', *IDS Bulletin*, 8(4)

Mohanty, C. (1991) 'Under Western eyes: feminist scholarship and colonial discourses', in C. Mohanty, A. Russo and L. Torres, *Third World Women and the Politics of Feminism*, Bloomington: Indiana University Press

Munck, R. and D. O'Hearn (eds) (1999) *Critical Development Theory: Contributions to a New Paradigm*, London: Zed Books

Parpart, J. (1995) 'Post-modernism, gender and development', in J. Crush, *Power of Development*, London: Routledge

Pieterse, J. N. and B. Parekh (eds) (1995) *The Decolonization of Imagination*, London: Zed Books

Preston, P. W. (1996) *Development Theory*, Oxford: Blackwell

Radcliffe, S. (1994) '(Representing) post-colonial women: authority, difference and feminisms', *Area*, 26(1): 25–32

Rahnema, M. with Victoria Bawtree (eds) (1997) *The Post-development Reader*, London: Zed Books

Ranger, T. (1993) 'The invention of tradition revisited: the case of colonial Africa', in T. Ranger and O. Vaughan (eds), *Legitimacy and the State in Twentieth-century Africa*, Basingstoke: Macmillan

Rosaldo, R. (1993) *Culture and Truth: The Remaking of Social Analysis*, London: Routledge

Said, E. (1989) 'Representing the colonized: anthropology's interlocutors', *Critical Inquiry*, winter, 15: 205–25

Slater, D. (1995) 'Challenging Western visions of the global', *European Journal of Development Research*, 7(2): 366–88

Sylvester, C. (1999) 'Development and postcolonial studies: disparate tales of the "Third World"', *Third World Quarterly*, 20(4): 703–21

4 | Critical reflections of a development nomad[1]

ROBERT CHAMBERS

Nomad ... n 1 a member of a people or tribe who move from place to place to find pasture and food 2 a person who continually moves from place to place; wanderer (*Collins English Dictionary*, Millennium Edition)

The Egocentric Reminiscence Ratio (ERR) (the proportion of a person's speech devoted to their past – 'when I was ... ' and 'I remember when ... ' etc.) is supposedly higher among men than women, rises with age, on retirement leaps to a new high level, is higher in the evening than the morning, and rises sharply with the consumption of alcohol. Since in what follows my ERR is close to 100 per cent, let me assure readers that I am sober and that I rarely work after seven in the evening. I am writing this less because of the compulsions of age, gender and ego (though of course they are there) and more (or so I would like to flatter myself by believing) because I have been asked to. All the same, writing about your experience is an indulgence. The only justification is if it makes a difference – whether through others' pleasure, insight or action, or through your own personal change.

Most of my working life I have been based at the Institute for Development Studies (IDS), Sussex, but much of this time has been spent abroad. I have experienced and lived through the changes which others in this book describe, but not in any mainstream. As an undisciplined non-economist, I have been on the fringes. In consequence, my view of development studies is idiosyncratic. Writing this has helped me to understand myself a little better. Others will judge whether it is of interest or use to them.

What have reflections on personal experience to do with development studies, and what might be radical about this? Answers to these questions vary according to how broad development studies is taken to be, and what is taken to be radical.

The scope of development studies can be broad in two respects. First, empirically, it can refer to what people in centres, departments or institutes of, or for, development studies actually do and have done. In the UK, development studies has also to embrace whatever the Development Studies Association considers, names or explores. What people do or have done includes not just research and teaching, but consultancy, advisory work, dissemination, advocacy, convening,

67

networking and partnerships. Some in development studies have also spent time as volunteers, or in governments, aid agencies, NGOs and foundations.

Second, normatively, if development is defined as good change, development studies are again broad. Values have always been there in the discourses of development, even if often half hidden by pretences of objectivity. Introducing values expands the boundaries beyond, for example, what one may find in a book on development economics or social development, and includes ethics, individual choice and responsibility. What is *good* is then for individual and collective definition and debate, as is what sorts of change are significant.

The reader can judge whether it is radical or not to take these two broad meanings together and reflect critically on what someone in development studies does in a lifetime.[2] To help and warn, the least I can do in my case is describe the more significant predispositions (aka biases, prejudices and blind spots) of which I am aware.[3] I am an optimistic nomad. My spectacles are rose coloured. Pessimists may be justified in claiming more realism. For whatever reasons, cups to me are more often half full than half empty.[4] Life is more enjoyable this way, and I have a fond and possibly delusional belief that naive optimism has a wonderful way of being self-fulfilling. Enthusiasm is another weakness, bringing with it the dangers of selective perception, and of doing harm when combined with power.

As for being a nomad, it would be flattering to explain this in terms of a drive to *explore*; and when writing I like to use that word. But I have been running away more than running to. I have run away from whatever was dull, difficult or conflictual. This has meant avoiding the challenges in the heartland of any discipline or profession and instead seeking life and livelihood in other, emptier spaces. Being nomadic and marginal like this has been exhilarating, fulfilling and fun, a mix of solitary wandering and collegial solidarity with others in a small tribe. But when the tribe grows, it is time to move on.

Two themes – reflexivity and choosing what to do – thread through this account. They are hidden in Section 2, 'Nomad and journey', which the reader may wish to skip, come into the open in Section 3, 'Reflections', and finally inform Section 4, 'A radical agenda for future development studies'. This last draws on the preceding critical reflection to ask what are some of the things we – development professionals with one or more feet in development studies – should try to do in the future.

Nomad and journey

The five phases that follow are separated for purposes of description but were experienced as a flow.

Uprooting and running away I was born and brought up in a small English provincial town (Cirencester). My parents were middle class, both thwarted in their education. My mother had fought for more years in school, but still got fewer than her brothers. My father's schooling was downgraded and short-ened when his father lost his cattle and farm to foot-and-mouth. I think they passed their frustrations on to me. I do not regret it. I was sent to prep school and to boarding public school. These were followed by National Service and university. My script was to come top in school, to be a good little boy basking in approval, and go on and on to become Prime Minister or Director-General of the BBC. In the jargon of an earlier social science, I had a high N-ach or need for achievement.

From early on, though, I wandered, pulling up roots and moving on. After School Certificate (O-levels) I did a year of mathematics, then switched to botany, chemistry and zoology for A-levels, then to history at university, and then public administration, becoming, as I have happily remained, undisci-plined. Ever since university I have been running, and running away, never staying for long in one place or with one subject. I ran away from a safe family firm of estate agents in provincial England. I went on a scientific expedition with friends to Gough Island in the south Atlantic (Holdgate 1958). Then there was a year in the USA on an English Speaking Union scholarship studying for an aborted PhD on changes in the American ideal of success. I ran on then to my first regular job, in Kenya as a district officer in what was known by then (1958) as Her Majesty's Overseas Civil Service. I made it clear that I was only interested if I could be spared another year at Cambridge on what was known as a Devonshire Course. This was a sort of proto-development studies for those going into colonial administration, including history, social anthropology and other subjects considered relevant.

And that was how I got into 'development'.

Decolonizing It is difficult to convey to others the exhilaration of the decolon-izing experience in Kenya. As a district officer I would have been seen by some as a wicked colonialist. I am not here defending or glossing any of the outrages of colonialism. But the task then was to prepare for independence and one could not have wished for a better job.

Whether for my supposed left-wing political views or because of my love of mountains,[5] I shall never know, but I was posted for two and a half years to the 'remote' Samburu district in northern Kenya where I was told there was 'no politics'. There was work as a third-class magistrate, administering the Tribal Police, and a great deal of walking and riding horses. The most constructive part was finding dam sites, building dams and managing grazing control to save the Samburu pastoralists from destroying their environment. Or so I believed. This was followed by North Tetu Division in Nyeri district, where people were exploding with energy, and work included negotiating sites for new primary schools when existing ones exceeded their size limit, encouraging coffee planting, and getting tree seedlings to people who insatiably seized them to plant on their land.

There were then two big challenges in Kenya: training for the takeover of government with independence; and settlement of Africans on the former White Highlands. I wanted to get involved in one or the other. Because I was a mountaineer, and had accompanied a training course on Mount Kenya, the door opened to be a trainer. I was recruited to the new Kenya Institute of Administration (KIA) and was responsible for three back-to-back six-month courses for Kenyan administrators who were taking over. This was an extraordinarily intense experience, innovating and improvising on the run, and beginning to learn how to avoid having to lecture: this was anyway essential as I did not know enough about anything to be able to talk about it for any length of time. The last course of twenty-four graduates straight from university, mainly Makerere in Uganda, challenged ('Why do we need to climb Kilimanjaro in order to be able to run our country?') but did not subvert the somewhat muscular approach of the training, which stressed character and self-confidence. The subjects covered included law, accounting, government procedures, natural resources, making district plans in real districts, and aspects of public administration covering all major ministries and departments (see Fuller 2002: 240–43). We put together practical case studies using real government files with the names unchanged. Through these, trainees dealt with real problems and could compare their solutions and the memos they wrote with those of known senior colonial officers (Chambers 1964). Another exercise was dealing with an overloaded in-tray which we trainers had much fun composing. One of my subjects was politics, for which I concentrated on European pathologies as sources of lessons.[6] For better or worse these were probably the most influential six months of my life (several on the courses were permanent secretaries in under two years). Then suddenly there was no one left to train. De-Europeanization had been so fast that Kenyans could no longer be spared for training. Kenya was independent and I was put in charge of the KIA library. It was time to move on.

Retreading and research After rejecting the idea of a career in politics in the UK (the Liberal Party, which I supported, was in deep, possibly terminal, decline), I opted, as did a few others, to retread as an academic, registered for a part-time PhD at Manchester under W. J. M. (Bill) Mackenzie, and joined Guy Hunter, who was launching the East African Staff College.[7] We ran three-week courses in Nairobi, Kampala and Dar es Salaam in rotation, for senior civil servants and business managers. We began asking participants to make population projections to 1980, and debated disbelief at the dramatic rise in rural as well as urban populations. Government and business case studies played a part, as did talks and discussions with political leaders. My 'research' narrowed to the administration of settlement schemes, and especially the well-documented and much-visited Mwea Irrigation Settlement north of Nairobi, a honey pot which attracted other researcher bees, or flies, besides myself.[8] Mwea, with its strong disciplinary management, and its agricultural and economic success, was regarded as a model for development and much visited and referred to in policy discussions. The seminal, much-cited and misquoted research of Jane Hanger and Jon Moris (1973), however, showed that women were much worse off on the scheme. Settlement schemes were a great subject at the time: they had high political priority, they were much researched, there was a burgeoning grey literature, and comparative analysis and practical lessons were in demand.

Camouflaged by a PhD, I then became a 'lecturer' in the Department of Politics and Sociology in Glasgow for three years. Development studies was not yet a subject at Glasgow. My mentor, Bill Mackenzie, was a wonderfully humane polymath, deeply committed to development in Africa, and gave me freedom to continue research and to write. I never had to give a lecture and did little teaching. I met and married Jenny, who did lecture, in psychology. I got into writing and editing, and then moved in 1969 to an honorary fellowship at IDS, Sussex, then three years old, and an appointment to IDS Nairobi to coordinate evaluation for the Kenya government's Special Rural Development Programme (SRDP). After that and a spell in Botswana, while still based at (a very tolerant) IDS, I had two years mainly in Sri Lanka and Tamil Nadu with Barbara and John Harriss and Indian and Sri Lankan colleagues, as assistant director to Benny Farmer, doing fieldwork on agrarian change and the lack of a green revolution in rice (Farmer 1977).

UNHCR and the Ford Foundation Much of the time when I was physically at IDS is a blur. The periods abroad from IDS stand out more, two in particular. For a year and a half (1975–76), I was the first evaluation officer with UNHCR, based in Geneva. This was an organization largely staffed and dominated by lawyers recruited to deal with refugees from eastern Europe. Their professional training and inclinations were to deal with legal issues. In terms of the breadth of concerns in development, and so also in development studies, UNHCR was a sort of coelacanth, a survivor from an earlier, less evolved age. It had no in-house competence in health, education, resettlement or agriculture. At the same time there were millions of rural refugees in Africa. I concentrated on them and tried to bring them to light as people not just statistics, and to counteract convenient myths that they could be taken care of by African hospitality. Colleagues could not believe that I would leave UNHCR after only eighteen months, but by then I had fulfilled the main task. And someone had warned me that I was beginning to become like a UN civil servant, which I took as a health warning, since many were such political animals.[9]

Later (1981–84), based in Delhi, I was the last Ford Foundation staff member to be a project specialist (meaning someone who works substantively on a subject). As a programme officer I was responsible for making and managing grants for irrigation management and social forestry. In this I was singularly unsuccessful, but had tremendous access and opportunities for learning and taking part in professional discussions and debates. These led on to thinking and writing about irrigation management, livelihoods, trees, common property resources, rights and access.

Methodology and participation From the early 1970s methodology became more and more central to what I found myself doing. Questionnaire surveys had proved ponderous, slow and inefficient, even when as well carried out as they were with the SRDP in Kenya and the rice-related research in South Asia. RRA (rapid rural appraisal) was evolved by practitioners in many places who were seeking more cost-effective alternatives. In the late 1970s there was a workshop and then an international conference on RRA at IDS. In 1985 the international conference on RRA at Khon Kaen in Thailand (KKU 1987) was a landmark. RRA training and field visits in Ethiopia, Kenya and West Bengal pointed to the potential of group-visual methods. I was then privileged to have two years (1989–91) based in Hyderabad with the Administrative Staff College of India at the time when Indian innovators were evolving PRA (participatory rural appraisal) approaches and methods, and the PRA explosion began. 'Bliss was it in that dawn to be alive', or so it seemed. It is difficult to express the amazement and exhilaration of those days when we discovered that 'they can do it', that poor people, without education, women, children and men, had capacities to map, diagram and analyse of which we had not dreamt. After that I spent most of the 1990s back in IDS, collaborating with the International

Institute for Environment and Development (IIED), networking and trying to support the spread of PRA and of good practices, latterly with colleagues in the Participation Group at IDS, who were working across a wider range of subjects, including participation in governance, human rights, citizenship, poverty and policy.

Reflections

Reflections on these experiences relate to what we do and how we do it in development studies. We all have different endowments, opportunities and trajectories. As other chapters describe, development studies themselves, radical or not, undergo radical changes. They are, and should be, in constant flux and evolution. They are, and should be, influenced by and influencing the ever changing external environment of development policy, power, relationships and practice. But development studies are not an external given. They are also populated, animated, influenced and evolved by us individuals who are engaged in them. Our pathways and life experiences are both moulded by and mould development experience and development studies. We are many sorts of people. Some readers will identify themselves also as actual or would-be development nomads. There are still a number of us but we may be an endangered species.

Reflecting on my wanderings, and rationalizing after the fact, I can see four aspects that illuminate and in part explain what happened, and which may point to more general insights and lessons for those of us in development studies: comparative advantage and luck; making mistakes; reversals – standing on one's head (or, more prosaically, seeing things differently); and issues of development nomadism and ecosystem change. This last concludes that most of us in development studies options are more constrained by funders than we were.

Comparative advantage and luck Before drawing lessons, we have to recognize luck. I have been lucky, and luck and coincidence have provided a sort of personal comparative advantage which few others will have. Here is some of my luck, in roughly chronological sequence.

The first example was studying the Italian Risorgimento (the unification of Italy) at university. This entailed critical analysis of primary documents, with all their contradictions and even forgeries. It embedded a scepticism about evidence which has lasted well, and about sources and methods in research, and how knowledge is, as we now say, constructed, and fallible and always open to questioning and doubt.

73

Then I was fortunate in patrons and colleagues. A sequence of patrons were inspiring and enabling, giving me confidence and opportunities, and launching me out. These include Bill Mackenzie at Manchester and Glasgow, Guy Hunter at the East African Staff College, and Benny Farmer at the Centre for South Asian Studies, Cambridge. I can think of no other contemporary who was so privileged. The same goes for my colleagues in fieldwork in Kenya, Sri Lanka and India, who were friends then and have become friends for life. Throughout, my colleagues at IDS blessed me with a benign tolerance. And there were others in other institutions such as the IIED, the Overseas Development Institute (ODI) and Wye College, who were congenial co-conspirators with the solidarity of heretics who are a minority.

Another debt is to those who taught me that I did not know how to write. At school I was told, 'Chambers, your sentences are too angular.' Charles Chenevix Trench, my first district commissioner in Kenya, passed on to me his love of strange and funny events, of whimsical anecdote and of stories told against oneself, which he constantly wrote up for the entertainment of others (e.g. Chenevix Trench 1964). A big learning here was to relish unusual experience, to enjoy writing about it, and above all to laugh at oneself and not to take oneself too seriously. Charles wrote in my final confidential report, 'He is incurably verbose on paper.' Alan Simmance, at the KIA, went through one of my texts crossing out about one word in five. Harry Hanson, who examined my thesis, hammered me for a pretentious quotation from Talcott Parsons. After over a year with UNHCR in Geneva I was told, 'You are beginning to write like a UN civil servant.' I vividly remember these shocks. They startled me into trying to write more clearly and enjoying playing with words and their patterns.

A less obvious piece of luck was not having to lecture. To lecture, you have to read and remember what others have written, reinforcing it then through public repetition. I did not know enough of any relevant subject to be able to give a formal lecture during my three years at Glasgow, and am amazed to realize that I have only ever given one lecture in thirty-five years at the University of Sussex. Instead I have taken the easier option of participatory workshops, trying, but not always succeeding, to do something new each time. Optimal unpreparedness and trying to facilitate more open-ended participatory learning in place of more closed didactic teaching have helped. But lack of time and energy, laziness and having found exercises and sequences that seem to 'work' have lured me into repetition. In consequence I have deceived myself, constructing through speech and public performance false beliefs, progressively discarding caveats and fitting what I say to the needs of the occasion. I do not think many lecturers realize that giving a lecture again and again is, like a catechism, disabling and conservative because each time we say something we embed it, remember it better and believe it more, diminishing our doubts, finding it easier to repeat, and to a degree closing our minds.

Yet another comparative advantage came from an interstitial existence between disciplines. This meant that I did not need to master or meddle in dominant development studies debates. Once I asked John Harriss whether I should make the effort to understand the mode of production controversies which were raging not least in the pages of the *Economic and Political Weekly*. I have since applied his advice, that it would not be worth my while, to other transient turbulences in the academic mainstream, complacently assuring myself that I was adhering to the principle of optimal ignorance. There was, after all, plenty else to do that was more exciting and less demanding.

The most significant and decisive lessons have come from failure and humiliation. When it became clear with the SRDP evaluation in Kenya that I was a hopeless manager, I ran away to consultancies, research and writing, and remained free from having to manage anything substantial for the rest of my life.[10] Later, being turned down for a chair by the IDS appointments board was a brilliant reinforcement and confirmation: it liberated me from posing as an academic, and the humiliation and hurt became a driving force of anger and energy.

The most important condition of all was security and freedom: a fellowship at the IDS provided a stable base and an organization and colleagues who tolerated and even encouraged my physical and intellectual nomadism. In development studies, the like of this no longer exists. The IDS was a good place to be at and go away from, and then to return to. It was more than just a dry-season reserve pasture. It had a reputation, convening power and, through its core funding, flexibility. Much of this was in the days when reappointment was reasonably safe if you wrote a book every five years or so and contributed something to courses when you were around. It was a busy and challenging place, and work was hard. But I was free to go on secondment to other jobs, and also to explore. There was a precious, glorious freedom to spend time in other countries, and to move from topic to topic (see also below).

So it was that much of my comparative advantage came from not having to lecture, not having administrative responsibility, not being promoted, not having research projects to manage, and not having to invest time as many do now in the often demoralizing business of preparing competitive bids.

On being wrong I have often been wrong and have made many mistakes. Four

75

stand out and are common enough to deserve description, as warnings and learning for myself and perhaps for others.

COMBINING COMMITMENT, ENTHUSIASM, EDUCATED IGNORANCE AND POWER These compounded each other with grazing schemes in Samburu district in Kenya. It was arrogant and wrong to try to induce the Samburu pastoralists to accept an alien system. The water introduced probably did more harm than good by allowing heavy grazing of areas earlier protected by lack of water. Like other missionaries blinded by their belief in themselves, I was wrong to think that meaning well was enough. Subsequently, I have come to understand how as a district officer I was doubly disabled: by 'education' and by power. The education – a 'good' degree in history at a 'good' university – led me to think I knew when I did not know; power as an administrator (executive and judiciary in the same person) reinforced this disability by reducing the need to compromise or adapt to others. I am astonished by the arbitrary decisiveness of some of the things I did. The collapse of grazing schemes in Samburu was a salutary slap in the face. It symbolized the failure of a mindset, behaviours and attitudes and demanded critical examination both of the system (which was transforming anyway with independence) and of myself. There are questions here for those development professionals with power in aid agencies, governments, NGOs, university departments, research institutes and consultancy agencies.

ACCEPTING CONVENTIONAL METHODOLOGY AS A GIVEN I was slow to question questionnaires. In Kenya I passionately advocated repeating a survey with a control area to identify the impacts of the Zaina Gravity Reticulated Water Scheme. But any results would have been useless. In the South Asia work I was slow to realize how much better we would have done if we had used local categories, for example of soil types, instead of composing a questionnaire in Cambridge. It took me too long to see the need to challenge methodology and to have the courage to do so. The lesson (see below) is to strive for self-critical epistemological awareness and to seek new ways of doing things.

IMPOSING A MANAGERIAL MINDSET This manifested itself in studying Mwea and writing it up. Jon Moris pointed out to me that on every point of contention between the management and the settlers – and there were many – I took the management's point of view. It took me years to recognize and offset this hangover from my days as an administrator and decolonize my mind. Even when later studying canal irrigation management in South Asia, this same top-down orientation still predisposed me to managerial solutions to bad distribution of water in canal systems: discipline was to be tightened among the staff who controlled and distributed water. Mick Moore disagreed. Subsequent experience showed that the solution was not the top-down discipline that I advocated but bottom-up participation with the empowerment of groups of irrigators. The lesson is introspection to understand and offset the way life experiences predispose us to interpretations, conclusions and recommendations.

BEING OUT OF DATE After my time with the Ford Foundation in India (1981–83) I sat down to write about canal irrigation management. The material and mindset that I had were mainly from the 1970s. But irrigation was moving on. In the mid-1980s, while I was writing the book (published only in 1988!), two new topics were coming to the top of the agenda: financing irrigation, previously heavily subsidized; and farmer participation. But the book was already too long, I was no longer able to update it in the field, and I badly wanted to get it out of the way and move on. This was a cost of nomadism. It is also a warning of the costs of long gestation for books based on empirical data – the danger of being out of touch, late and out of date by the time they are published. The lesson is to strive to write, publish and share with little delay, fortunately now with the Web much easier than it was; and to be ruthless with oneself in rewriting and updating rapidly before publication.[11]

In sum, the lessons are personal: to be critically self-reflective, alert and aware, and ever willing to question and to change.

Reversals: standing on one's head 'Reversals' was the word that summed up changes that were taking place in the 1980s and 1990s both in development orientations and in my own life. Polarizations and dichotomies, paired lists of contrasts, comparing normal professionalism and a new professionalism that expressed the reversals, coming to see the contrasts as between a paradigm of things and a paradigm of people – unsubtle and stark though these oppositions were, they served to summarize the paradigmatic contrasts and tensions that many were perceiving and experiencing. As the verses celebrating Hans Singer's seventy-fifth birthday had it (the first is from *Alice in Wonderland*):

> 'You are old, Father William,' the young man said,
> 'And your hair has become very white;
> And yet you incessantly stand on your head –
> Do you think, at your age, it is right?'

and

> Normal professionals face the core

And turn their backs upon the poor
New ones by standing on their head
Face the periphery instead.

(Clay and Shaw 1987: 229, 253)

As more and more development professionals 'stood on their heads', things came to be seen differently. In many fields, reversals and professional transformations began or continued and gathered momentum and even respectability.

Transforming reversals occurred, for example, in agricultural science and knowledge. Robert Rhoades' *The Art of the Informal Agricultural Survey* (1982) stressed changes in behaviour of researchers with farmers, and Paul Richards' *Indigenous Agricultural Revolution* (1985) demonstrated in detail the value and validities of indigenous technical knowledge. Both were landmarks, widely influential and revolutionary in their implications. Not just the knowledge but the experimental abilities of farmers were increasingly recognized. Jacqui Ashby's International Centre for Tropical Agriculture (CIAT) video *The IPRA Method*, and Michel Pimbert and P. V. Satheesh's International Crops Research Institute for the Semi-arid Tropics (ICRISAT, 1991) video *Participatory Research with Women Farmers*, had a huge impact in the 1990s. In the mid-2000s we have moved so far that in the International Agricultural Research Institutes it is now common for farmers to be involved not just in evaluating varieties, but in the whole breeding processes, including selecting the original crosses, a degree of participation unthinkable in the 1980s. Beyond this, in the 2000s there is a new critical awareness of research process and relationships with the emergence in the Consultative Group for International Agricultural Research (CGIAR) system of the theme of Institutional Learning and Change (Watts et al. 2003),[12] reflecting back critically on the system itself.

Reversals of behaviours and relationships, and transformations of mindsets, went together. With much that changed, practice came first, and theory later. One part of this was the explosion of innovation with PRA (originally participatory rural appraisal, now sometimes participation, reflection and action, or simply PRA), with outsiders changing their behaviour and becoming facilitators and local people the analysts, expressing their own realities. The epicentres of innovation were in countries of the South, especially in South Asia and sub-Saharan Africa. In the 1990s many university faculty members in the South and North were left standing, while students asked to be taught and to use the new visual and group approaches and methods, and the behaviours and attitudes that they demanded. Development studies courses and university departments lagged behind field practice, and when they did begin to adopt the new approaches and methods their understanding and teaching were often flawed, suffering from the inexperience of university faculty. Practitioners from the South were at times appalled by the ignorance of teachers in the North. Abuses have now diminished and practice has improved as the significance of behaviour, attitudes and relationships has gradually sunk in. More generally, more participatory approaches to teaching and learning in development courses have also been evolved[13] and are spreading (Taylor and Fransman 2003).

Nomadism and ecosystem change To be geographically, institutionally and intellectually nomadic seems to require two conditions: emerging gaps or patches to graze or cultivate; and funding and freedom.

It was good fortune that gaps were there to be found and explored: methods for rapid appraisal, canal irrigation management, tropical seasonality, trees as savings, water and poor people, micro-environments unobserved, farmer-first approaches in agricultural research and extension, vulnerability as a dimension of deprivation, sustainable livelihoods, and so on. Today, change in many dimensions seems to be accelerating, which should mean that new issues and gaps, and the opportunities and needs they present, will continue to open up for us all.

But funding and freedom are more the problem now. Organizations need funds to create posts and people need security and opportunities to move around. The IDS was privileged, and the envy of others, with its core funding in the 1970s and 1980s. It allowed freedom not only for longer-term work but also for rapid opportunism and leaping on serendipitous leads. Here is an example. In the late 1970s someone remarked in a seminar that they had found births peaking during the monsoon in Bangladesh. Richard Longhurst, just back from fieldwork, said he had found the same during the rains in northern Nigeria. So we asked – why? And at once we were into the rich and wonderfully complex subject of seasonality. Richard and I wrote a two-page note and were allocated £10,000 from the IDS budget for a conference on tropical seasonality and poverty, a subject as enthralling as it was neglected and important, and a book resulted. Today, we are so projectized and log framed that we would lack the flexibility to open up a subject like that. It does not fit in any box. We would face negotiation, hassle, delay, uncertainty and worry, wondering how we were going to earn our way while we took the risks of making a proposal that had not been asked for. Seasonality remains a Cinderella in development, vital, pervasive, enormously significant for many poor people, cross-cutting

79

disciplines, and still systemically under-perceived by professionals at huge cost in stress, suffering and impoverishment to hundreds of millions of poor people.[14] Yet it is hard to imagine funding now to support work on tropical seasonality as a general subject.

Research agendas in the 2000s appear to be determined more by funders than they were. Core funds are scarcer and scarcer. There is less trust, more targets, less flexibility, more 'accountability' upwards to where the money comes from. I am vulnerable to the fantasy of a past golden age. Yet even allowing for that, it seems to me that development studies now suffers from too much centralized decision-making linked to funding, with a loss of nimble opportunism. Do we not need more nomadism and more nomads? And if so, what are the implications for those who fund development studies?

A radical agenda for future development studies: qualifications, caveats and context

In some circles, to be radical, or to label oneself as radical, is approved and politically correct. There can then be a danger of posturing as radical for radicalism's sake. In development studies, I believe there is a case for persisting with and continuing to evolve many of the good things that are already being done, some of them bequeathed by yesterday's radicalism, no longer very new, but with far still to go: concerns, for example, with gender relations, participation and sustainability. There is a case, too, for continuity of in-depth research. What is radical can also rotate; some cutting edges move in circles. This can mean, for example, reviving and reinforcing the orientations and concerns with redistribution and equity from the 1970s.

It is also important to recognize that over the past two decades, in the UK at least, much has changed for the better. First, dissemination used to be a blind spot: on ESCOR in the 1970s it was again and again necessary to argue to *raise* the budgets of research projects to include provision for workshops, publications and other forms of dissemination. That has now been corrected. Second, international collaboration and South–South and South–North links are more common, and relationships more collegial. Long past are the days when the South came to the North mainly to be trained: learning now is reciprocal, and flows of innovation and learning are increasingly from South to North. Third, in the UK priority subjects are more systematically opened up jointly with institutions in the South through the Development Research Centres, for example Chronic Poverty at Manchester and Citizenship, Participation and Accountability at IDS. Finally, the agenda does move, and quite rapidly. Recent examples on the social side alone are human rights, violence, conflict, disability, chronic poverty, poor people's concepts of ill-being and well-being, and dimensions of power and relationships (e.g. Groves and Hinton 2004). And each discipline and sector has its own evolving agenda.

A case can also be made for a historical view and learning from the past. Rediscovering wheels has its value in learning for oneself. Unfortunately, though, much learning is expensive and unnecessary because old lessons have been lost. Community-driven development driven by the World Bank and participatory natural resource management driven by national bureaucracies are relearning the costly but forgotten lessons of community development in the 1950s and 1960s. Here as elsewhere one can ask whether the experience of the past has been studied enough and the lessons presented to those who make policy today.

All that said, immobility, inertia and conservatism give grounds for concern. I sense that there is less inclination and opportunity for development professionals to change types of jobs and organizations and that fewer people do it. I have no supporting statistics, and I hope I am wrong. To be sure, there are still people who move in and out of NGOs, aid agencies and research and academic institutions, but they appear a minority. In the UK in the 1960s and 1970s, development studies was a growth industry: new institutes and centres were being founded. But now in the 2000s the security of an expanding job market has passed, and I think more people hang on in their posts rather than risk a transition. In IDS in the 1970s and into the 1980s, fellows were *expected* on average to spend a third of their time on spells abroad, funded from other sources. So it was that I could work on evaluation in the IDS Nairobi, on rice-related field research in South Asia, on rural refugees with UNHCR in Geneva and Africa, on irrigation and social forestry with the Ford Foundation in Delhi, and on PRA with the Administrative Staff College of India. Today there seems less latitude for such spells abroad, which for me were so challenging, energizing and formative; and that is a loss.

There is, of course, a case for specialization, by subject, by country or by region. There is a case for spending time in one organization or place. But specialization and isolation have been responsible for many of the worst errors in development policy and practice. To offset these requires that development studies be polymath, grounded in and continually keeping up to date with micro and macro realities, and theoretically informed but open to an eclectic pluralism. Loss of mobility, with careers limited to one organization and one place, whatever their benefits, has costs in the range of experiences and learning forgone.

Conclusion: a radical reconfiguration?

There will be many views about what might be a radical agenda for future development studies. The reader may wish to make a personal list before reading mine. What follows draws on current ideas and insights from colleagues, and is where my journey as a nomad has brought me. There is much, much else besides what follows here.

Radicalism often refers to analysis, advocacy and action for major social change. What follows in no way negates such activities. But there is a complementary critical radicalism which introduces and explores new dimensions and activities that cross-cut subjects and contexts. These dimensions and activities are little recognized, attract few funds and are not represented by any one discipline or profession – or if they are, not by one that is prominent in development studies. These dimensions and activities overlap and interact. Those I shall outline are: methodologies, critical reflexivity, agency and the personal, power and relationships, and pedagogy for the powerful, all combining to become a critical reconfiguration.

Methodology refers to the ways we do things and their patterns. Methodology is implicit in every development studies activity – research, teaching, learning, convening, networking, writing, conferences and so on. There is also a meta subject of how methodologies can be developed. This is even more neglected. In participatory research, however, experience has been that each topic and context needs invention, piloting and refining of its own tailor-made methodology.[15] Despite this experience, though, methodology is still a relatively neglected subject in development studies. Habits persist: in fieldwork, bad questionnaire surveys survive. There are brilliant examples of RRA and PRA, but quality and ethics are often problematic. Significant innovations are overlooked; for example, little interest in the mainstream has been shown in participatory approaches and methods for generating statistics. How things are done and can or could be done is an issue across subjects and topics, not just those well established in disciplinary mainstreams, but also in others such as bureaucratic procedures, participatory poverty assessments, accountabilities upwards and downwards, natural resource management, advocacy, training for new concerns such as human rights, work on HIV/Aids, chronic poverty, and many more. One methodology we need is to know better how to analyse the links between our choices, and acts of commission and omission, and those who are meant to benefit, and so to learn to make better decisions about what to do.

Critical reflexivity refers to reflecting critically on oneself. The academic debates of development studies have been weak on transparent reflexivity.

Willingness to examine and present personal predispositions seems inversely related to the conviction, passion and rigidity with which views are held and taught. This is independent of right or left, and largely independent of discipline. It was there as much with some of the old-style Marxists of the 1960s and 1970s as with some of the neo-liberal marketeers of the 1990s and 2000s. It is a matter not just of the inherent validity of an ideology or world view but also of personality and personal orientation. This is not at all to say that the Marxists or the neo-liberals were or are all wrong. It is, rather, to say that it would be easier for all of us to get closer to useful understanding and good ideas about what can and should be done, and for others to form sound judgements about their views, if they could examine and be transparent about their life experiences and conditioning and the predispositions to which these have given rise.

Development studies especially needs self-critical *epistemological* awareness – that is, being critically aware of how knowledge is formed by the interplay of what is outside, and what inside, ourselves. Outside ourselves, this concerns being aware not just of methodology but also of the external processes of observation and interaction which inform us; and inside ourselves, this concerns trying to be aware of our own predispositions to select, interpret and frame. This makes doubt a virtue, and being able to say 'I don't know' and 'I was wrong'. And it can lead to modifying how we seek to learn, changing the approaches and methodologies we use, trying to understand and offset our mindsets and orientations, and to be more sensitive to, and aware of, the realities of others.

Agency and the personal dimension follow on. This is so self-evident that it is embarrassing even to make the point. But what happens in development results largely from human action, from the choices and actions of actors. For many actors in development studies, making a difference is a major, if not the major, motivation. Yet, and again strangely, there is little systematic analysis of the causal links between our work – that book, that conference, that idea – and the poor, deprived, vulnerable and excluded people whom we seek to serve. There is little analysis of career trajectories and life experiences, or of the best balance between specialization and nomadism, between working in one sort of organization and in several. Unsurprisingly, I would argue we need more semi-nomadic, perhaps transhumant, professionals who move around and gain experience in different contexts, countries and organizations. In North and South alike, this would mean more people who had spent different parts of their lives in other countries, in aid bureaucracies, NGOs and research institutes, who had done grassroots fieldwork, and who could bring to their

83

work, in whatever context, a kaleidoscope of experience. To do this is harder than it was but it needs to be encouraged and made easier.

Power and relationships have only recently become a major focus of attention in development studies. Although power in political science has a long genealogy, power in relationships between development actors has received little attention. In their edited book *Inclusive Aid: Power and Relationships in International Development* (2004) Leslie Groves and Rachel Hinton have placed it firmly on the agenda, with the challenge to change behaviour, attitudes and mindsets, and procedures, principles and conditionalities, to make real the rhetoric of partnership, empowerment, ownership, participation, accountability and transparency.

Methodology, reflexivity, agency and making a difference, and power and relationships, converge and overlap, and together with parts of my life experience point to the need for a pedagogy for the powerful or (with apologies to Paulo Freire, though I hope he would have approved) for the oppressors, or more tactfully, the non-oppressed. My power, ignorance and ignorance of my ignorance as a district officer led me to do harm when I meant to do good and thought I was doing good. In the history of development there are many good things, but the avoidable errors are appalling. Tens, perhaps hundreds, of millions of poor people were deprived, suffered and often died as a result of policies of structural adjustment alone. We need better ways, procedures, methodologies and experiences to enable those who make and influence policy, and ourselves in development studies, to be more aware, to get it right and to do better. The big priority now is realism, to bridge and close the chasm that has opened even wider between the incestuous love-hate relationships of lenders, donors and policy-makers in their capital-city and five-star-hotel meetings and workshops, and the poor people for whose benefit our development industry is said to exist. Recognizing their power in development studies, we can ask too whether we need a pedagogy for funders.

There is no magic wand, no one solution. But one process shows promise of practicality and impact. It is the practice of immersion.[16] In this, outsiders – policy-makers, powerful people, development professionals of all sorts including academics – have the opportunity to spend a few days hosted by a poor family or community, sharing some of their life, helping them in their daily tasks, learning their life histories, and seeing things from their, peripheral, perspective. Pioneered by Karl Osner in the 1980s, used by the World Bank for senior managers and others since the mid-1990s and now spreading to other agencies and organizations, immersions have shown a potential to make a radical difference to those who can make a radical difference. When

I reflect on my own past in development and development studies, and my errors and failures of understanding, I can speculate on how differently (and better) I would have acted had I had the experience of participatory research and regular immersions.

A radical reconfiguration of development studies would then include more individual reflexivity, especially self-critical epistemological awareness, and deliberate efforts, through practices such as immersions, to gain the experiential learning of reversals. It would pay more attention to methodology. It would entail more conscious actions to support some nomadism, and to avoid the traps of isolation, insulation and complacency to which we are so vulnerable, especially, but not only, those of us in and from the North. Above all, it would recognize the importance of policy-makers, the wealthy and others with power, and make it a priority to learn about how they, as well as ourselves, can change and act more for the better. For they are the biggest blind spot in development studies. If we are serious about poverty, we have to be serious about powerful people as people.

Notes

1 I am grateful to Uma Kothari for constructive critical reflections on drafts of this chapter.

2 There are markers of ageing. One is the first time you are, if thin, described as 'sprightly'. Another, which I recently passed, is when you are introduced as having '... spent a lifetime ... '.

3 This is not the place for detail on subjects such as relationships with parents, childhood traumas, early toilet training and the like, although we know these have a profound effect on us. To recount these would not, I think, significantly illuminate what follows.

4 Another form of optimist, perhaps more common in our credit-for-consumption Northern world than before, drains the half-full glass and asks for more.

5 I suspect that there was a security file on me dating back to wild days during National Service and carrying the motion 'This House welcomes the advent of communism in China'. This was at the time of the Korean War. In my interview for HMOCS I was probed for my reasons, perhaps political or ideological, for wanting to go to Kenya, a 'difficult' colony with minority problems. It ended happily enough with 'Oh, my dear chap, if you want to go to Kenya for the *mountains* ... ' and I was through.

6 As teaching material I requested the British Council to send us two books: Isaiah Berlin on Karl Marx, and *Mein Kampf.* The response was that these could not be supplied because of their political nature. Perhaps someone feared a parliamentary question: 'Is the minister aware that the British Council in Kenya is supplying ... ?' We asked for Lord Lugard's diaries instead. These were deemed acceptable.

7 The East African Staff College had headquarters in Nairobi in what are now the income tax offices. It subsequently grew in size and scope, and has become ESAMI (the Eastern and Southern Africa Management Institute) with a multi-storey building in Arusha, Tanzania.

8 So many researchers descended on Mwea that Jon Moris and I were able to edit a book on the scheme, *Mwea: An Irrigated Rice Settlement in Kenya*, Weltforumverlag, Munich, 1973.

9 Before I joined it UNHCR was described to me as a *'panier de crabes'* (a basket of crabs).

10 I have to qualify this. In the 1990s at IDS I found myself managing a substantial budget but was immensely fortunate that before it got completely out of hand John Gaventa came and took over.

11 I smile at my hypocrisy in writing this. I have a book that has been with the publisher for nearly three months during which much has happened. Instead of up-dating it urgently, I am trying to complete this chapter to meet its third deadline. The kindest gloss I can give this is that there are always trade-offs.

12 This paper symbolizes the scope for reversals and the vicissitudes of develop-ment: the authors' names are in reverse alphabetical order; and within months the International Service for National Agricultural Research, which published the paper, had ceased to exist.

13 For example, an innovative MA in Participation, Social Change and Develop-ment was launched by IDS and the University of Sussex this year (2004).

14 A recent manifestation of the neglect of the multiple interlocking dimensions of seasonal deprivation for poor people is an artefact of the top-down, insulated, centre-outwards analysis which is informing efforts to achieve the Millennium Development Goals. Perhaps this is only to be expected from season-proofed, mainly Northern professionals.

15 See Cornwell et al. (2001) and Barahona and Levy (2003) for examples from Malawi. Many professionals persist in thinking that they can take participatory meth-odologies off the shelf, as though they were like questionnaires.

16 For an overview and sources see Eyben (2004); for fuller analysis and distil-lations of experience, Irvine et al. (2004); for an example and outcomes, Chen et al. (2004); for practical guidelines, Osner (2004); and for a participatory research variant, Jupp (2004).

References

Barahona, C. and S. Levy (2003) 'How to generate statistics and influence policy using participatory methods in research: reflections on work in Malawi 1999–2002', IDS Working Paper 212, Sussex: IDS, November

Chambers, R. (1964) 'The use of case studies in public administration training in Kenya', *Journal of Local Administration Overseas*, 3(3): 69–174, July

Chambers, R. and J. Moris (eds) (1973) *Mwea: An Irrigated Rice Settlement in Kenya*, Munich: Weltforum Verlag

Chen, M., R. Jhabvala, R. Kanbur, N. Mirani and K. Osner (eds) (2004) *Reality and Anal-ysis: Personal and Technical Reflections on the Working Lives of Six Women*, Working Paper WP 2004-06, Department of Applied Economic and Management, Cornell University, Ithaca, New York, April, <http://aem.cornell.edu/research/researchpdf/wp0406.pdf>

Chenevix Trench, C. (1964) *The Desert's Dusty Face*, Edinburgh and London: Black-wood

Clay, E. and J. Shaw (eds) (1987) *Poverty, Development and Food: Essays in Honour of H. W. Singer on His 75th Birthday*, Basingstoke and London: Macmillan

Cornwell, E., P. Kambewa, R. Mwanza and R. Chirwa with the KWERA Development Centre (2001) *Impact Assessment Using Participatory Approaches: 'Starter Pack' and Sustainable Agriculture in Malawi*, Network Paper no. 112, Agricultural Research and Extension Network, London: Overseas Development Institute, January

Eyben, R. (2004) *Immersions for Policy and Personal Change*, IDS Policy Briefing, Issue 22, Sussex: IDS, July

Farmer, B. H. (ed.) (1977) *Green Revolution? Technology and Change in Rice-growing Areas of Tamil Nadu and Sri Lanka*, London and Basingstoke: Macmillan

Fuller, C. (2002) 'Training the new administration', in J. Johnson (ed.), *Colony to Nation*, pp. 239–43

Groves, L. and R. Hinton (eds) (2004) *Inclusive Aid: Power and Relationships in International Development*, London and Sterling, VA: Earthscan

Hanger, J. and J. Moris (1973) 'Women and the household economy', in R. Chambers and J. Moris (eds), *Mwea*, pp. 209–44

Holdgate, M. (1958) *Mountains in the Sea: The Story of the Gough Island Expedition*, London and New York: Macmillan

Irvine, R., R. Chambers and R. Eyben (2004) 'Learning from poor people's experience: immersions', *Lessons for Change in Policy and Organizations*, 13, Sussex: IDS

Johnson, J. (ed.) (2002) *Colony to Nation: British Administrators in Kenya 1940–1963*, Banham: Erskine Press

Jupp, D. (2004) *Views of the Poor: Some Thoughts on How to Involve Your Own Staff to Conduct Quick, Low Cost but Insightful Research into Poor People's Perspectives*, available on request from <djupp@tiscali.co.uk>

KKU (1987) *Proceedings of the 1985 International Conference on Rapid Rural Appraisal*, Rural Systems Research and Farming Systems Research Projects, University of Khon Kaen, Thailand

Osner, K. (2004) 'Using exposure methodology for dialogue on key issues', in M. Chen et al., *Reality and Analysis*, pp. 84–94

Rhoades, R. (1982) *The Art of the Informal Agricultural Survey*, Lima: International Potato Centre

Richards, P. (1985) *Indigenous Agricultural Revolution*, London/Boulder, CO: Hutchinson/Westview Press

Taylor, P. and J. Fransman (2003) 'Learning to participate: the role of higher learning institutions as development agents', IDS Policy Briefing 20, November

Watts, J., R. Mackay, D. Horton, A. Hall, B. Douthwaite, R. Chambers and A. Acosta (2003) *Institutional Learning and Change: An Introduction*, Discussion Paper 03-10, The Hague: International Service for National Agricultural Research, October

5 | Secret diplomacy uncovered: research on the World Bank in the 1960s and 1980s

TERESA HAYTER

My first period of research and writing on the World Bank[1] was from 1967 to 1970 at the Overseas Development Institute (ODI) in London. The Overseas Development Institute had published the first report I wrote for them on French Aid (1966). But my report on the World Bank in Latin America was censored by the ODI and the World Bank. It was eventually published in 1971 as *Aid as Imperialism*. I then worked as a research assistant to Professor Ian Little at Nuffield College in Oxford and in Kenya, and later wrote a short book on imperialism entitled *The Creation of World Poverty* (1981). From 1981 to 1984 I returned to research on the World Bank with a grant from the Social Science Research Council (SSRC) and wrote *Aid: Rhetoric and Reality* (1985).

When I initially carried out research and wrote about foreign aid in the 1960s I believed that its real, and not just stated, purpose was to improve the situation of poor people in developing countries. At the time, there was virtually no published material arguing anything else, and my illusions were widely shared. As I learnt more, and in particular when I began to do research on the World Bank and the International Monetary Fund, I came to believe that the purpose of aid is, and cannot be other than, to serve the economic interests of the major capitalist powers, especially the USA, and of their big corporations and banks. It became clear that these two international institutions are not even enlightened defenders of the capitalist system as a whole, but instead give priority to the interests of their major funders. Their claims to political neutrality have no foundation in reality. The result is that the effect of foreign aid, including the 'aid' provided by the two major international institutions, on the poor of the Third World is, on balance, negative. This chapter explores these issues through experiences of working on the World Bank over a period of about twenty years from the 1960s to the 1980s, and my subsequent disillusionment about the real purposes of 'aid'.

The purposes of aid: early illusions at the Overseas Development Institute

At the ODI in the 1960s, we believed that our task was to lobby for more aid, and to make it 'more effective'. By this we meant that aid should be reformed or improved so that it made a bigger contribution to promoting 'development' in what were euphemistically called developing countries. There was little attempt, however, to define development. Instead, there was an unquestioned assumption among the staff that 'development', whatever it was, would lead to improvement in the situation of poor people. The ODI prided itself on the fact that it was not funded by government, and its studies could be quite critical of the failures of government aid policies to promote the purposes for which we believed it was intended. The ODI was, on the other hand, funded by Barclays Bank, Unilever and others with banking and commercial interests in developing countries. This began to sow some seeds of doubt in my mind as it became clear that we could not, for example, produce research that questioned the contribution of foreign private investment and lending to 'development'. Any attempts at staff meetings to raise questions about this issue were not popular. My first book written for the ODI, *French Aid* (1966), however, complied with the necessary ideological framework and met with approval. Numerous interviews with French aid officials had convinced me of their good will and I was generally impressed, for example, with their claims that their intentions, when they intervened in the policies of governments mainly in former French colonies in West and North Africa, were to increase their independence and self-sufficiency in the medium term.

In 1966 the ODI organized a conference on 'Effective Aid', at which there were representatives of the World Bank and the bilateral aid agencies of France, Germany, the United Kingdom and the United States. Also present were the chairmen of Barclays Bank UK, and of the International Nickel Company USA. Naively, members of ODI staff assumed that 'effective' here meant in terms of the alleviation of poverty. In the report of the conference's proceedings, and in a section on 'Motives and objectives of aid' in a book entitled *Effective Aid* (1967), I dismissed the argument that aid could be justified on the grounds that it was in the economic or political self-interest of the countries providing it, and asserted that 'a sense of solidarity' which had made progress within states was now being extended to the world as a whole. The most debated topic at the conference was the legitimacy, effectiveness or otherwise of an activity called 'leverage'. This meant making aid conditional on the adoption, by receiving governments, of policies of a general nature, unrelated to the specific projects financed by aid. The participants divided roughly along national lines, with the United States Agency for International Development (USAID) representative, the French and also the World Bank favouring the idea, and the British and Germans against it. Michael Hoffman of the World Bank contributed a paper on the coordination of aid (1967) which hinted at the need for donors to examine the performance of recipients and coordinate their responses:

To put it a bit crudely, the potential donors are interested in getting the most for their development dollars and are, therefore, likely to approach the exercise [of aid coordination] with a critical eye on the economic performance of the claimant country and the reasonableness of its claim for external assistance ... The Bank ... is almost equally concerned about both increasing the general flow of development finance to worthy countries and encouraging maximum mobilisation of domestic resources in recipient countries and steadily improved general economic performance. (Hoffman 1967)

The USAID paper was a good deal more explicit, stating that:

AID has increasingly recognised that economic aid can promote development not simply by supplementing the host country's limited capital and technical resources but also by exerting influence on host country policies and programmes. As we have become more aware of aid's potential leverage role, we have experimented with techniques for exercising such leverage more effectively ... Existing government policies, priorities and administrative capacity should not be taken as immutable, but rather regarded as policy variables. (USAID 1966)

During the discussion, the British participants raised objections on the basis that donors did not always know best, and that, for example, an aid agreement with Chile incorporated a wages policy agreement that went to the heart of the question of income distribution. Similarly, efforts to persuade countries to control their population could have large effects on the age and sex profile of the population. They suggested that these issues needed to be addressed with caution, as trying to intervene in these choices could be dangerous. Both the British and the German participants were worried by the prospect of 'intervention of one state in the internal affairs of another'. The US response was that they did it anyway, and they might as well make sure that the intervention was beneficial. An aid official was quoted in the proceedings as follows:

I think you intervene just as much by not doing anything but providing $100m to some existing government. Essentially you are supporting whatever that government wants to do, you are making the opposition of that government unhappy because you have supported that government. You cannot say that you are not intervening; you are intervening. (USAID 1966)

The representative of the World Bank, apparently, concurred, supporting the principle that:

The World Bank had been trying to obtain greater commitment to policies favourable to development in recipient countries for some time. Its efforts were increasingly accepted. Complaints of 'infringement of sovereignty' had in the past been heard much earlier in the process ... Finance ministers sometimes incorporated agreements with the bank on policy measures in their budget speeches. (ibid.)

The word 'dialogue', subsequently much used by the World Bank as an innocuous-sounding description of its attempts to persuade governments to change their policies, was introduced. A British participant told 'the story of the man who was asked whether he had persuaded another man. The answer was: "Yes, we sat up all night, I persuaded him, and in the morning his hair was as white as the snow."' There was much agreement that attempts to exercise influence were more likely to be successful if they were made through a multilateral organization, and that 'multilateral agencies could stick much more objectively to technical and economic considerations'. For example, 'a Frenchman with experience of trying to achieve the same policy changes in Africa through bilateral and through multilateral channels had found that the latter could be more effective'.

Research on the World Bank: an encounter with reality

Following the conference, the World Bank offered to fund research on its activities and policies by the ODI. I was subsequently invited to research the activities and policies of the World Bank in Latin America. I suggested to the ODI that I should examine the issues raised at the conference around the subject of 'leverage' (which was the original title given to the book I wrote in 1968, which, on publication, was amended to *Aid as Imperialism*). The World Bank accepted our proposal, which was couched in cautious language, but stated that the study would concentrate on 'activities which involve a fairly close relationship between the international agencies and Latin-American countries' and 'an examination of the potential role of international institutions and of economic aid as catalysts in development, assuming that more is involved than a simple transfer of resources or the setting up of isolated projects'. At the time I was fairly open-minded on the topic. The Bank later accused me of having a thesis to which I bent the facts; in fact the opposite was the case. Like the British and German participants at the conference, I had some doubts about excessive interference by foreigners in the policies of recipient countries. I assumed, however, partly because of the reformist rhetoric of the US-led Alliance for Progress in Latin America, which called for reforms such as increases in taxation to fund public services so as to avert the danger of more

Cubas, that the exercise of influence could be in directions that I considered progressive. In 1967 I set off for Washington and then, for three months, to Brazil, Colombia, Peru and Chile.[2]

In my three weeks in Washington, World Bank officials briefed me and were quite forthcoming with introductions and advice. But the Bank generally did not publish even the most final and sanitized of its country economic reports from which one might have gleaned what its policies were, and I was not given access to any of its unpublished materials and reports. I obtained from other sources some of its unpublished materials, and the disclosure of the existence of Operational Memorandum no. 204 (see below). There was at the time very little written material that analysed or questioned the role of the World Bank or aid, although I had read, and disbelieved, a paper published in Pakistan which argued that aid served the purposes of imperialism. I dredged through all the material I could find, and included it in long quotations and footnotes in my report. But the report was essentially based on numerous interviews with government officials, politicians and aid officials and some academics and journalists in Washington and in the four countries I visited. Of the aid officials, by far the most open were from USAID.[3] Most World Bank and IMF officials, apart from one or two mavericks, were on the whole extremely reticent and cautious. It became clear that they were, mostly, a tough lot, with a harsh right-wing ideology. Unlike the French officials whom I had earlier interviewed, they were unsubtle in their attitudes towards the countries and governments they dealt with.

My interviews with senior officials in the central bank and finance ministry in Rio de Janeiro began the process of opening my eyes. At the time there was a right-wing military dictatorship in Brazil; a more populist one had been ousted, with CIA assistance, in a coup in 1964. Yet a very senior central banker complained to me that World Bank officials knew nothing of the reality of Brazil. They merely, he said, travelled by car from their hotel to the finance ministry with their eyes closed, and refused to accept the evidence provided by the fact that the unemployed were sleeping in the street. It slowly emerged that the three aid agencies I was studying, the World Bank, the International Monetary Fund (IMF) and USAID, were thoroughly in favour of the policies of the dictatorship, and in fact considered them a model of 'monetarist' austerity. A few minor reservations were expressed by AID officials, one of whom said that the Brazilian economics minister Roberto Campos was 'more royalist than the king' and should, for example, have used some of Brazil's reserves to import food and consumer goods at a time when shortages were forcing up prices. But in general, as another AID official put it, the three agencies were 'all in it together'. Such pressures as they did exert were in the direction of cutting, not raising, levels of social expenditure, keeping wages below the rate of inflation and paying off debts.

Next was Colombia. In Colombia the three agencies were engaged in a battle with the government to get it to devalue its currency. In November 1966 President Lleras had announced on television that he would not devalue the peso because foreigners told him to, that he was breaking off relations with the IMF, and that he was reintroducing controls that his government had agreed to give up under an IMF programme of import liberalization. This agreement had in addition specified that if the IMF's measures did not result in Colombia meeting certain balance of payments targets, the IMF would stop lending. Colombia failed the balance of payments test even though it had complied with the IMF's conditions. The IMF and World Bank missions met USAID officials at the US embassy in Colombia and decided that devaluation was required. An IMF representative advised the Colombian government that the IMF would not renew its stand-by loan unless Colombia devalued, and apparently specified by what amount. The other two agencies, according to varying accounts, either initiated the demands for devaluation or even demanded more toughness, merely using the IMF as spokesperson, or alternatively fell in behind the IMF, supporting it with actions of their own. The World Bank, for example, apparently 'told' the New York banks to stop lending to Colombia.

In Peru the engagement of the international aid agencies in general economic policies was less evident, although there was some pressure to raise taxation in order to deal with problems of financial instability, and at the same time some pressure to cut public expenditure for social purposes and for a wage freeze. The main issues raised by Peruvian officials and politicians concerned projects, their objections to direct US pressures in the interests of US private investors in Peru, and the World Bank's refusal to take social and political considerations into account when determining project location, saying, for example, that 'people could be moved'. I subsequently discovered the existence of an internal Bank document called Operational Memorandum no. 204, adopted by its governors some time after the Bank was set up, which states that it may not lend to countries that default on debt repayment or servicing, which nationalize foreign-owned assets or which fail to honour agreements with foreign private investors. This memorandum was invoked in 1967 in Peru over the issue of long-disputed assets of the US International Petroleum Company, as well as in numerous other places and times.

In Chile the issues emerged with yet more clarity. The orthodox 'monetarist' or neo-liberal policies of the aid agencies were confronted by the modernizing, somewhat progressive but not anti-capitalist Christian Democrat government of Eduardo Frei. Frei's government initially intended to follow a middle way between the monetarists and the revolutionary left. It adopted some of the ideas of the Latin American structuralist school, attempting to achieve the hat-trick of less inflation, more growth and some income redistribution, including land reform. The aid agencies thought these aims were impossible to achieve and, as some Chilean government officials and politicians complained, had no sympathy with their ideas and made no attempt to understand them. What they wanted was financial stabilization, which for them meant cuts in government expenditure, lower wages and less land reform than even the Christian Democrat government intended. By the end of the Christian Democrats' term, they had largely caved in and abandoned their attempts at reform. When Allende's socialist coalition was elected, the IMF and the World Bank stopped lending, but with the overthrow of Allende's government, they got what they wanted – that is, uncritical support for their economic policies under Pinochet's brutal dictatorship, with their devastating effect on the Chilean poor.

It was becoming clearer to me whose interests the aid agencies represented. The IMF and the World Bank share a large building in the centre of Washington, their voting systems are weighted according to the size of member countries' financial contributions, and the USA with a few other major powers has a veto on decisions. Even that does not always provide the USA with the power it wants, since the US delegate requires the support of other delegates to exercise a veto, and the USA therefore intervenes at times to ensure that decisions do not reach the executive directors. Even more important, the World Bank raises the bulk of its funds from the major capital markets, especially Wall Street, and therefore depends on their approval; it also has a more immediate interest in the repayment and servicing of debts, its own and those of the private banks, than the IMF. While in theory financial stability is the business of the IMF and the World Bank is supposedly interested in investment and growth, in practice there is no clear indication that the IMF presses harder for austerity than the World Bank; it was sometimes the other way round. The aid agencies also pushed for the liberalization of imports and capital movements, policies in which the major industrialized powers have a clear interest.

All the presidents of the World Bank have been citizens of the USA. The IMF's managing directors have been Europeans; their deputies, and the heads of its Western Hemisphere Department, have been US citizens. The institutions have much autonomy even from the supervision of their boards and executive directors, and they are hierarchical and authoritarian. Most of the staff are from the USA, some are from Britain and other European countries, few are from the Third World; of the latter, the overwhelming majority have postgraduate degrees from major North American and European universities. Some of the Bank's senior staff, and all its presidents except McNamara, come from private US banks, and some return to them. The staff are normally located in Washington, and usually make only short trips to the countries they are dealing with, to avoid, I was told, the danger that they might 'go native'. The pay and perks are so good that there is also much incentive for staff to stay in line. In my various encounters with World Bank staff, I perhaps got most information from Indians at junior levels whom I met unofficially. Some of them knew exactly what was going on, knew it was not in the interests of the poor in the Third World, and were prepared to tell me so, and perhaps to add that they needed to save up enough money for themselves and their families to buy a house and eventually retire in India.

Reality is not for publication: the World Bank's attempts to 'bury' the ODI report

On returning to Washington it became clear that the senior World Bank officials had now understood, belatedly, what I was interested in. They told me that their objections lay not with my conclusions, which were not only still unclear even to me and which I had not conveyed to them, but with the subject matter of my research. I was summoned to an interview with two Bank officials and told that I should abandon my research and write about something else. My hair did not go white, but I had to retreat to recover from the Bank's onslaught. As I wrote later in the Appendix to *Aid as Imperialism*, 'I came out of this interview battered, but eventually realised that I was in a position not to be bullied out of my research; I had a lot of material on the Bank's activities, and merely wanted to hear from them their version.' Although all the officials I asked to interview, apart from the official most concerned with Colombia, agreed to see me, however, they were often hostile or suspicious and few were informative. The interview with Gerry Alter, director of the Western Hemisphere Department of the Bank, as I wrote in the Appendix to *Aid as Imperialism*, 'was devoted almost exclusively to unsolicited explanations of why the Bank preferred the public not to know about leverage, and also to an attempt to discover what my conclusions would be if, in spite of everything, I persisted in my desire to write about leverage'. He told me that he believed the Bank could operate less effectively if it was publicly known to be engaged in the business of leverage, and drew an analogy with 'secret diplomacy'. The IMF was even less helpful. I saw only one of the IMF officials whom I asked to see in Washington, although after they had received the draft of my book, they offered to 'arrange for an oral discussion between you and interested members of our staff' if I were to return to Washington.

On returning to London, I wrote the first draft of the findings of the research (1967–68). My ideas had radically changed, partly because of meeting people on the left, especially in Chile, but mainly because of my observations of the behaviour of aid agencies. I had become convinced that not only were they not, as they claimed, politically neutral (it was inconceivable that they could support socialism), but that they were not even interested in reforms which, according to some theories, might avert socialism. They supported a right-wing, monetarist orthodoxy whose main concern was the never-never land of financial stability that was to be achieved by cuts in government spending, wages and sometimes employment. They were interested in implementing policies that favoured foreign interests, such as debt servicing and import liberalization, supporting private enterprise, especially foreign private enterprise, and the so-called free market. They were barely interested even in economic growth, which they saw as following after, and as a more or less automatic consequence of, stabilization. I had also become convinced that there was little possibility that any real improvements in the situation of the rural and urban poor in Latin America could be achieved through reforms, and without a socialist transformation of society. This would of course entail expropriation of the interests of both local and foreign capital, and would therefore be unacceptable to the international aid agencies. The latter could not be reformed, given their sources of funding; the World Bank has a particularly close relationship with, and dependence on, the major financial markets of the rich countries, especially Wall Street, from which it raises most of its funds.

My employers at the ODI said that I should continue to write what I believed, provided I tried to put the agencies' case 'fairly'. They were not enthusiastic about the first draft produced in June 1968, saying among other things that it read a bit like Sunday-paper journalism. I made some changes in response to their criticisms, but it was some time before they agreed to send the second draft to the World Bank, IMF and others for comments. There followed a year of claims, counter-claims, many and voluminous criticisms and comments from the Bank, and some tedious redrafting by me. A Bank official said he hoped ODI would 'give very careful thought to publishing such a document. My main concern is whether it gives the impression that what the agencies do is wrong.' Another hoped the study 'could be quietly buried'. I was assured by ODI that the objections were primarily technical and that it was a matter of merely correcting 'factual errors'. Consequently, I produced a further draft, incorporating a few corrections of 'fact' that the Bank had pointed out, and, as requested, changing the order of the text to improve its presentation. At the beginning of 1969, I incorporated a short section on Cuba following a visit to the country and in response to the ODI's comments that I had failed to show what the alternative might be to the aid agencies' policies. The ODI's director and director of studies pronounced themselves satisfied, and said the study was 'now well on the way to publication by the ODI'. Three months later they wrote to me again, to say that 'Alas we are not home and dry yet, as the IBRD/IMF have written to us recently and raised the whole issue of the use of confidential information.' I was given a copy of their voluminous comments, including one from William Clark, former director of the ODI and then information director at the World Bank, which was at variance with my recollection of what had happened. He said:

> First thing on my return I have had the Hayter story in full storm on my desk ... It would be very unpleasant to exert any sort of a veto on publication, but I can see the extreme awkwardness of publishing what Bank people consider very confidential material. Lars Lind did go out of his way to ensure that Teresa saw all the top brass, and that they treated her as a colleague. They not unnaturally expect that their confidence would be respected. (quoted in Hayter 1971)

He went on to write, 'I should add that the opinions of the people who have read the revised draft remain very adverse on the grounds that it remains unbalanced and hence unscholarly' (quoted in ibid.). Gerry Alter, director of the Western Hemisphere Department of the Bank, wrote a long memo which included the statement that:

> I must say that, like the IMF, I had been assuming that ... steps were being taken to ensure that the paper would not be published in anything like its present form ... Our objections cannot be met by minor changes in drafting. The real trouble is that the author has tried to bend the facts to suit her thesis, and in the process she has not only got a lot of things wrong, but she has also made quite indiscreet use of information given her in confidence by people with whom she talked in the Bank and the Fund. (quoted in ibid.)

Most of the information to which Alter objected was of course not given to me by Bank officials, but generally by discontented officials of the governments on which the Bank was putting pressure. Alter then gave 'a few examples amongst many passages in the paper which, whether true or false (and most are false), could seriously embarrass the Bank in its relations with its member countries'. They included references to the discussions between the three aid agencies in the US embassy in Colombia, the failure of the Bank to inform even its board about its activities, the fact that the Bank's agreements looked like carbon copies of IMF agreements, the Bank's claims of success in persuading India to devalue, the Bank 'telling' the New York banks to stop lending to Colombia, its hostility towards land reform, the negative effects of stabilization programmes on growth, the pressure on Argentina to sack railway workers who 'could always go back to rural areas' (whence virtually none of them had come, unless perhaps the Bank official meant rural areas in Europe).

The IMF also responded, saying that:

> publication of this study would be most undesirable from the Fund and Bank's point of view, although it may be argued that it would do more harm to the ODI than the international agencies. Moreover, we feel, as we did on the first round, that the paper is so tendentious and so distorted throughout that it does not lend itself to amendment by specific comments. We intend so to inform Miss Hayter again, though more succinctly and probably more firmly than on the previous occasion.

They never did inform me again, but they added that the current director of the ODI had assured them, on an earlier visit to London, 'that the paper would not be published'. Had I been wasting my time in redrafting it?

I was told about, but failed to see, the Bank's next communication. Apparently it said, again, that the study was unscholarly, tendentious and inaccurate; that it made use of confidential material supplied by the Bank (without, apparently, specifying which material); and that if the ODI published the study, or allowed it to be published elsewhere, this would be a breach of confidence and the Bank would have to draw its own conclusions. ODI took this to mean that it would withdraw its financial support, a loss to the ODI of around £15,000. There followed a proposal from a member of ODI's staff that he should redraft the study to make it acceptable to the Bank, which of course meant mainly changing its ideological line, removing the reference to Operational Memorandum no. 204, removing any reference to alternative possibilities, and removing the section on Cuba. I turned down the proposal. The decision whether or not to publish was then taken to the executive committee of the ODI, which in October 1969 unanimously decided against publication. Writing to inform me of this decision, the director of the ODI said, among other things, the following:

> The Committee was of course aware of the views of the World Bank, and of its opposition to publication. But I can assure you that this influenced the decision only to the extent that it was felt that in such circumstances ODI had to be

completely confident about the craftsmanship of any study that was published – since it would obscure subsequent debate if fundamental hostility to the conclusions of the study could be presented as valid criticisms of its technical competence. This confidence was, I am afraid, lacking ... (letter to Teresa Hayter from the director of the ODI)

ODI did not, however, make any attempt to stop me publishing the study elsewhere, saying it did not 'have any right, legally or otherwise' to do so, and that this was fortunate, since otherwise they would be in 'an awkward situation', given that the Bank felt strongly the study should not be published by ODI or anybody else. I took the draft to Penguin, who published it virtually without changes, but with the addition of an appendix that contained the above quotes and a bit more. The book was on the Penguin 'bestseller' list for non-fiction publications, and sold around fifteen times the number of copies it would have if ODI had published it.

The World Bank revisited

In 1980 I applied through the Oxford Polytechnic for a Social Sciences Research Committee grant to revisit the conclusions of *Aid as Imperialism*. The grant was for three years and included travel expenses for me to go to India, Algeria, Peru and Washington. At the end of the three years I published, with Catherine Watson (a disaffected former 'token' environmentalist in the World Bank), a book called *Aid: Rhetoric and Reality* (1985). The offer of the grant was made conditional on my having a 'review panel' to 'provide balance', but the people who agreed to support my application in this way kindly made no attempt to influence the conclusions. The SSRC's other main concern was that I would not get access to Bank officials, which of course was potentially a bar to any critical research on the Bank. Although the Bank now claimed to believe that a policy of greater openness was desirable, when I asked for interviews the Bank's information department informed me that the Bank 'had been burnt once and did not see why it should be burnt again'. They gave me permission to request interviews on an individual basis. I gathered that a memorandum had been circulated instructing officials to talk to me only in general terms. I was able to see only one of the senior officials in the Latin American and Caribbean department of the Bank, whom I knew personally; he specified that the interview was on a personal basis and did not allow me to take notes. Elsewhere in the Bank some officials did talk to me quite openly. I believed, and believe, that their case for more openness should not have been weakened by their experiences with me; 'On the contrary,' I wrote in my preface to *Aid: Rhetoric and Reality*, 'the continued hostility of their colleagues provided further proof that the Bank had not significantly changed.' Some of the officials who refused to meet me had genuine excuses, or were perhaps nervous that they might divulge information they should not. 'Mostly,' I wrote in this preface, 'they were just the inveterate reactionaries who know quite well that they have nothing to gain by talking to me.' This meant that, as before, the bulk of my information came from the officials, politicians and economists whom I interviewed in the countries I went to. Cathy Watson wrote a detailed appendix to the book on 'working at the Bank' which contained a description of the nature of the staff at the World Bank, who, as she put it, 'treated us like scourges. As far as they were concerned, we were trouble ... '. She found that it was easier to respect the ex-colonials, mainly British and Australian, who held mainly technical positions in the Bank, in agriculture, for example, than the 'young professionals' straight out of graduate school who knew a good deal about neo-liberal economics but knew and cared very little about the real world.

This research followed the period, from 1968 to 1981, when McNamara was president of the World Bank. Many people believed that his tenure resulted in a substantial change in the Bank's policies and practice. Certainly its rhetoric changed. McNamara had been secretary of state for defence during the US war in Vietnam, and was held responsible for some of its more devastating acts. He appeared to have had a change of heart, believing that a better way to combat subversion was to promote development, and that the West needed to find a successful capitalist alternative to China. In 1966 McNamara asserted that 'order' and 'stability' were not possible without 'internal development of at least a minimal degree'. This at least was a more progressive position than, for example, Kissinger's, who is said to have believed that starving people do not make revolutions. McNamara recruited some relatively progressive economists, who talked and wrote about 'redistribution with growth' and 'basic needs'. Among observers of the Bank, affected no doubt by this rhetoric, there continued to be startling illusions about what the Bank was doing, or could do. For example, in 1982 the British Labour Party, then in opposition, published a report entitled *Development Co-operation*. It contained some strongly worded criticisms of the IMF's lack of political neutrality and its bias in favour of the market mechanism and the private sector. But it advocated increasing funding of the World Bank, as follows:

> Ten years ago, Teresa Hayter produced a damning report ... which suggested that [the Bank's] contribution to the Third World was 'negative'. There was a good deal of evidence to support this claim – the Bank strongly encouraged

'free enterprise' and especially the use of private foreign capital ... Since then, however, the Bank has produced a much more radical approach to the problem of the poorest countries, and is now concerned to improve the position of the most disadvantaged section of the population through a policy of 'redistribution with growth' ...We should therefore ... use our influence on its board of directors to support the progressive policies which it has been developing, and also encourage it to support forms of *socialist organisation* where these can make a visible economic contribution to Third-World development. (Emphasis added)

Apart from the rhetoric, the biggest difference from Bank policies in my earlier period of research was that the Bank was now willing, in fact quite eager, for it to be known that it was engaged in the business of persuading governments to adopt 'reforms', through what it called 'dialogue'. In 1980 it introduced 'Structural Adjustment Lending' (SAL) to supplement its project lending. Project lending was, and remains, the Bank's main form of lending. But it has clear disadvantages from the point of view of putting immediate pressure on governments to change their general policies. Structural Adjustment Lending has clear similarities with the IMF's long-standing tradition of stand-by loans, as both have a set of general economic conditions attached to them. Bank publications did not advertise what these conditions were; in theory they could have had something to do with adopting measures to alleviate poverty and redistribute income. In practice it became clear that they did not. When I asked what effect the Bank's new 'poverty orientation' was having on the policies it promoted through its SALs, its 'dialogue' and so on, it turned out that the effects, such as they were, were confined to *projects.* For example, as I wrote in *Aid: Rhetoric and Reality*:

> Thus an official close to McNamara, asked to give examples of pressure being put on governments to pay more attention to poverty and income distribution, cited the case of Brazil. Pressure was indeed put on Brazil: the government was told it had to begin negotiations on a rural development *project* before the Bank would negotiate on other projects. There was no fundamental reappraisal of development strategy and certainly no reassessment of the orthodox IMF/World Bank methods of achieving 'stabilisation'.

The proportion of the Bank's lending for 'social' or 'poverty-oriented' projects was, moreover, small. In the early 1980s projects financed by the Bank amounted to less than 2 per cent of total investment in the Third World. Of these, between a third and a half had what the Bank called a poverty orientation.

But nearly all of these (between 24 and 31 per cent of total projects) were in agriculture, which, as I wrote in *Aid: Rhetoric and Reality*, 'does not necessarily mean that income is redistributed to the poor, and may mean the opposite'. In general, the effects even of the other 'poverty-oriented' projects were doubtful. The Bank, true to its neo-classical doctrines, strove to achieve 'full cost recovery' on its projects. Projects had to pay for themselves. People would find their free, though unsatisfactory and polluted, supplies of water replaced by cleaner water which they had to pay for. Similarly with housing and education. Thus, as I wrote in *Aid: Rhetoric and Reality*, Bank officials accepted that:

> governments' methods of eliminating slums frequently involve merely bull-
> dozing them, and, where relocation does occur, people are moved to distant
> suburbs. As McNamara eloquently put it, 'there is one thing worse than living
> in a slum or squatter settlement – and this is having one's slum or settlement
> bulldozed away by the government which has no shelter of any sort to offer in
> its place'. So, in the Philippines, the Bank set out not to destroy slums, but to
> upgrade them. But, because of the principle of full-cost recovery, and in theory
> also so that the projects would be 'replicable', it wanted the inhabitants to pay
> for the improvements.

The Bank's claims that its projects in agriculture were of interest to the poor related almost entirely to the fact that they were located in rural areas with high concentrations of poverty. In reality their benefits went overwhelmingly to medium or large landowners.

On land reform, the Bank's attitude was unchanged. Its main stated concerns were whether land reform would create instability, and whether it would lead to disruption of production; a less often stated, but undoubtedly present, concern was its effect on the big landowners who supported the governments of which the Bank approved. A Bank official, who met me surreptitiously in a bar, told me that he had written a report demonstrating that, without expropriating large landowners who made little use of their land, there was no chance of improving productivity, let alone alleviating poverty, in the Brazilian north-east; the report, he said, was suppressed at higher levels in the Bank. A sample of the Bank's attitudes is contained in a 1980 confidential report entitled *Poverty, Basic Needs and Employment*, quoted in *The Development Debacle* (1982) by Walden Bello and others, which advocated retreat from partial land reform measures introduced by the Marcos government in the Philippines, partly on the grounds that:

> Some former tenants, and other potential tenants, were not really ready for a

shift in tenure status; they need and prefer the protection of the landlord, who is also their creditor, particularly for insurance against bad harvests. Indeed, [the Bank] complained that agrarian reform contributed, 'in many areas [to] disruption of healthy landlord/tenant relations'.

Bank reports welcomed the termination of land reform programmes. As I wrote in *Aid: Rhetoric and Reality*:

For example [the Bank's] laudatory presentation to the consultative group for Peru says with evident approval that 'the Agricultural Promotion Law ... ends the agrarian reform expropriation process – an important measure to instil investor confidence'. Another report on Peru describes the failures and 'negative effects' of land reform under previous reformist military governments and a report on the Peruvian agricultural sector states that: 'This entire period (1970–80) from its start has been characterised by ill-conceived and mal-administered sweeping land reform and economic control measures.' The sector report tells, at length, the sad story of an expropriated coffee grower, 'a highly respected professional living in Lima' ...

On the other hand, both in Peru and in Algeria, two of the countries I went to, the Bank did advocate 'land reform'. By this it meant the return of state farms to the private sector, or breaking up large-scale land reform cooperatives into small privately owned units.

The Bank was also, unsurprisingly, interested in a problem long experienced by the colonizers and others who embarked on Third World ventures: how to persuade small farmers to produce a surplus for export (so that the foreign currency earnings could, for example, enable their governments to service foreign debt, as well as giving urban elites access to the luxury imports to which they had become accustomed). Cheryl Payer, in her book *The World Bank*, published in 1982, quoted a Bank country economic report on Papua New Guinea as follows:

A characteristic of PNG's subsistence agriculture is its relative richness: over much of the country nature's bounty produces enough to eat with relatively little expenditure of effort. The root crops that dominate subsistence farming are 'plant and wait' crops, requiring little disciplined cultivation ... Until enough subsistence farmers have their traditional life styles changed by the growth of new consumption wants, this labour constraint may make it difficult to introduce new crops.

As for the general economic policies the Bank did promote in its 'policy dialogue' with governments, it turned out that there was little or no change.

Secret diplomacy uncovered

McNamara's recruits were largely confined to the research department of the Bank, and their influence on its central activities was limited. There were suggestions from these officials that the Bank might now view more favourably the policies of the Frei government. But this suggestion was counteracted, for example, by the fact that, although McNamara had appeared impressed by Sri Lanka's relative success in improving 'social variables', in practice the Bank joined the IMF in pushing, eventually with success, for the reimposition of orthodox economic policies and the ending of the rice subsidy. In the Bank's economic reports on countries, there was usually a section on poverty, but these were often tacked on at the end, and were extremely short. As before, attention to the problems of poverty was considered to be something that could come later, after the more pressing problems of debt, deficits and inflation had been dealt with. Although, as a Bank official informed me, there were 'some' countries in which poverty was the central issue, the Bank was often more insistent than the IMF on stabilization measures, cuts in public spending and the like. One IMF official commented that he had been summoned to a meeting at the Bank to discuss the demands being made on a particular government. He had expected the Bank to complain that the IMF had been too insistent on cuts. Instead, the Bank officials complained that the IMF was being too lax, and was 'pulling the rug from under our feet'.

The Bank, in insisting on neo-liberal austerity measures and reliance on market mechanisms, was clearly adopting a particular ideological position. The adherents of this ideological position claimed that it served the interests both of capitalism as a whole and of the peoples of the Third World. Both these claims are dubious. The Bank's policies frequently appeared to be biased in favour of the economic self-interest of the governments and corporations that provide the bulk of its funding. There were three fields in which this was particularly clear. These were the Bank's support for foreign private investment, its demands for import liberalization, and its reaction to the 1982 debt crisis. In the first of these the Bank has been unfailingly faithful to its original statutes, which enjoin it to promote an inflow of foreign private capital. The injunction to promote and facilitate this inflow is repeated ad nauseam in virtually all the Bank's publications and reports. As a senior Indian government official told me, the Bank's general remedy was to increase the role of the private sector, 'especially the foreign private sector': 'the more we moved to a market-oriented system the better off we would be'; it was 'something like a gospel', propounded 'every morning'. In India, Algeria and elsewhere, this meant bitter struggles against the Bank's demands for privatization of public sector enterprises and for new investments to be made in the private sector, which in practice meant the foreign private sector. An Indian official in the Ministry of Steel and Mines told me that the high-pressure salesmanship of foreign companies, and their tactics of bribing (which he said the World Bank cannot do, or does not do), were 100 per cent worse than the World Bank's insistence on imports. He nevertheless added that 'the stultifying of local manufacturing capacity is the greatest disservice done to us by the foreign aid agencies. If IDA stops, that will be the greatest service they can do to us.' In its project financing the Bank normally insists on international competitive bidding for contracts. Although it is rarely accused of corrupt practices, it has been known to manipulate the process so as to favour 'competition' from foreign suppliers. For example, in India the Bank insisted that a road project should be put out to tender not in the usual small sections suitable for local contractors, but as a lump, suitable for foreign bidding. The Bank does not just support the capitalist system in general; it supports the capitalists of the major powers that fund it in particular.

Free trade was another, related, Bank tenet. Its enthusiasm for the benefits of free trade at least equals the institutionalized enthusiasm of the IMF. Together with the IMF, it insists on overall limitations in demand and on devaluation rather than import controls or selective tariff barriers. It is systematically enthusiastic about programmes of import liberalization, supporting them when its friends and ideological soulmates in governments adopt them, as they did in Peru, and urging them elsewhere. Free trade clearly favours established, foreign producers and import liberalization can have devastating effects on local producers and employment, while leading to large increases in imports of luxury products. The Bank in the early 1980s was also strongly advocating the promotion of labour-intensive manufacturing for export. Its arguments in favour of export-led, rather than import-substituting, industrialization would have been more convincing if it were not for recession and increasing protectionism in the already industrialized countries, over which, of course, the Bank had no control. In addition, its favoured export-oriented production, unlike import-substituting manufacturing, relies heavily on very low wages and poor working conditions, achieved through government repression, about which the Bank showed little sign of concern.

Even more stark has been the behaviour of the Bank over foreign debt. The Bank was a leading and enthusiastic member of the lenders' cartel which was formed to ensure that debtors did not default on their debts to the private banks after the 1982 crisis. This was hardly surprising, given the Bank's close relationship with Wall Street, but it was shocking. In the nineteenth century Latin American governments regularly defaulted on their debts. In the late twentieth century the major reason why they did not do so was the powerful support the bankers received from their governments, and especially from the World Bank and the IMF. The banks had vaunted the recycling of petrodollars into the 'sinkhole' provided by Third World countries as a triumph of private enterprise. But when the capitalist crisis of the 1970s caused interest rates to be raised to unaffordable levels and threatened defaults and a crash in the banking system, the banks ran to their governments. These governments, with the assistance of the World Bank and the IMF in their 'dialogues' with debtors, succeeded in transferring the burden of the debt crisis not to the private banks, which according to the ideology were supposed to take risks, not to taxpayers in the countries where the banks were based, nor even to the governing elites of the Third World, but to the poor, who were the ones to suffer most from the cuts, wage freezes, redundancies and privatization of public services imposed by SALs and stand-bys to raise money to service debts.

With the advent of Clausen as president of the World Bank in 1981, its rhetoric changed again. Clausen said he wanted the Bank's image to be closer to the Bank's reality, and set out to prove to the bankers that the Bank had always defended their interests, and that the Bank's wilder critics in Congress, who had accused it of supporting socialism, were wide of the mark. Any lingering doubts that this was so ought to be dispelled by the Bank's continuing efforts to extract debt servicing from countries throughout the world, including countries in Africa where standards of living have been declining since the 1980s. One final piece of evidence is the Bank's systematic hostility to any government attempting to introduce socialist policies, to nationalize or renationalize their industries and resources, or even to engage in redistributive reforms. The Bank had stopped lending in such circumstances to a long list of countries, including Chile, Vietnam, Nicaragua, Grenada, Algeria, Peru, Brazil, Egypt and Jamaica, to name a few. Others, including the Soviet Union, eastern European countries, China, Cuba, Angola and Mozambique, have not joined the Bank/IMF, have only recently joined, or have withdrawn. The Bank says that it does lend to countries with left-wing governments, but in every case this is either short-lived, or it is because the Bank hopes to be able to shift their governments towards privatization and free market policies. The Bank and the IMF have of course played this role in eastern Europe, with sometimes devastating consequences. In the early 1980s in Algeria, officials claimed that the Bank's pressures for privatization were less severe than elsewhere because of their determination to resist; but pressures there were, and the direction is always predictable.

The World Bank is finally exposed

The show goes on. As the *Financial Times* of 25 September 2003 reported from the IMF/World Bank annual meetings in Dubai:

> The US-installed Iraqi administrators chose the meetings to announce an experiment in free-market economics so sweeping it suggested a bust of Milton Friedman might be erected in Baghdad to fill the plinth where the statue of Saddam Hussein once stood. Accordingly, the Iraqi ministers were busy with back-to-back meetings, with banks, investment advisers and debt restructuring specialists all lining up for a piece of the post-Saddam action.

I did no more research on the World Bank after 1984. But it remains clear that, whatever the latest changes in the rhetoric of the World Bank and the IMF may be, the institutions cannot be reformed. They should be abolished. Large numbers of people, moreover, and not only in the Third World, now know on which side of the barricades the World Bank stands. It has become thoroughly part of a rogues' gallery, linked with the IMF, the WTO and the G8, in campaigns against the exploitation and impoverishment of the peoples of the Third World. The World Bank's stabilization programmes are widely cited throughout the world as major causes of impoverishment and suffering. The World Bank/IMF annual meetings have been so disrupted by protests and demonstrations that, after Berlin and Washington, they have few places left to meet. Rightly so. People's eyes are, I hope, opened.

Notes

1 The International Bank for Reconstruction (IBRD) and the International Development Agency (IDA) are commonly known as the World Bank.

2 Flying economy class rather than, as had been expected of me, first class, in order to save the World Bank money, but staying in the best hotel on Copacabana beach in Rio de Janeiro because that was where a World Bank delegation was staying.

3 Perhaps this was because of the Freedom of Information Act, and the fact that some of them were academics on short assignments.

References

Bello, W., D. Kinley and E. Elson (1982) *The Development Debacle: The World Bank in the Philippines*, San Francisco, CA: Institute for Food and Development Policy

Hayter, T. (1966) *French Aid*, London: Overseas Development Institute

— (1967) *Effective Aid*, London: Overseas Development Institute

— (1971) *Aid as Imperialism*, London: Penguin

— (1981) *The Creation of World Poverty*, London: Pluto Press

— (2000) *Open Borders: The Case against Immigration Controls*, London: Pluto Press

— with C. Watson (1985) *Aid: Rhetoric and Reality,* London: Pluto Press

Hoffman, M. (1967) 'Effective aid', in Overseas Development Institute, *Effective Aid*, London: Overseas Development Institute

Overseas Development Institute (1967) *Effective Aid*, London: Overseas Development Institute

Payer, C. (1982) *The World Bank*. New York: Monthly Review Press

USAID (1966) 'Effective Aid', paper presented at Effective Aid conference, London: Overseas Development Institute

TWO | **Ideas and ideologies**

6 | Development studies and the Marxists[1]

HENRY BERNSTEIN

In British universities in the 1960s and 1970s, the institutionalization of development studies as a distinct field of teaching and research coincided with the rapid growth of Marxist ideas in the social sciences. This chapter considers aspects of development studies and Marxist work over the last forty years or so, including some intrinsic tensions that each brings to their encounters. I try to identify conditions and issues of intellectual production and its practical applications that may be useful to constructing and pursuing the project of a historical, and critical, sociology of knowledge of development studies, which this collection seeks to stimulate.

This essay employs a restrictive or institutional definition of development studies as the kinds of teaching and research done in development studies departments, centres, institutes, and so on, in British universities, as sites of an academic specialism of recent provenance. What justifies it as a specialism in its own right is the presumption that it is dedicated *and* equipped to generate *applied* knowledge of practical benefit in the formulation and implementation of development policies and interventions. This is what motivates students to enrol in university development studies programmes (typically with the hope of making careers in development work), and government and other development agencies to fund applied research on development by academics. As 'policy science', development studies is centred on two sets of issues: those of economic growth and how to promote it, and those of poverty and how to overcome it, principally in what is now known as the (global) South. Virtually all intellectual production in the name of development studies, and the claims made for it, can be assimilated to one or other of these over-arching goals, or seeks to link them.

This restrictive sense corresponds roughly to what Cowen and Shenton (1996) identify as the 'intent' to develop – constitutive of development discourses or what they call 'doctrines of development' – by contrast with 'immanent' development. Development studies in the restrictive or institutional sense, founded on such 'intent', eludes definition by any coherent object of study or intellectual paradigm, a problem highlighted by the porousness of its borders: intellectually with the social science disciplines (and the various approaches they contain), in applied work with governments, aid agencies

111

and other development organizations. There is much crossing of both types of borders and in both directions, with more and less happy experiences and outcomes for those who make such journeys. In mapping some of the contexts, contours and issues of the career of development studies I use a broad and schematic periodization that posits a founding moment comprising the conjuncture from the end of the Second World War to the institutionalization of development studies in British universities in the 1960s and 1970s, followed by that of the gathering neo-liberal ascendancy since the 1980s.

The questions I seek to pose, if hardly to answer in any comprehensive or definitive sense, include the following: if development studies in British universities continues to prosper institutionally during this current period of the neo-liberal ascendancy, does it also prosper intellectually when its agenda seems to be set – directly and indirectly – by bilateral and multilateral aid agencies, by state and quasi-state bodies, to a greater extent than in the past?

Development studies I. The founding moment: big issues and big ideas

As a recognized field of teaching and research in British universities, and those in other countries, development studies was a product of the decolonization of most of Asia and Africa from the late 1940s to the early 1960s, and the reorganizations of foreign policy, both political and economic, it generated in the North. Its institutional origins were thus closely linked to the formation and trajectories of agencies, policies and practices of development aid.[2] The colonial factor may partly explain the relative absence of the rubric 'development studies' in American universities; the USA had few colonial possessions but substantial historical experience of policy-making and intervention in 'informal empire', notably in Latin America.[3]

The centrality of development to the discourses and practices of governments in the conjuncture of decolonization, both North (in foreign policy) and South (in domestic policy), as well as of the major multilateral bodies established at the end of the Second World War (the United Nations, the World Bank), was shaped by the bipolar post-war world of the two superpowers. Their pursuit of influence (or control) in the newly independent states of Asia and Africa incorporated claims of the superiority of their own socio-economic systems, and their paths of development, as models to emulate. Irrespective of the rubric of development studies, for example, American universities produced some of the definitive texts of explicitly cold war development theory, of which Rostow's 'non-communist manifesto' (1960) was emblematic.[4] Rostow, like other contemporaries across the political spectrum, had a sharp sense of the historical moment he inhabited, of what was at stake when the victorious war against fascism had enhanced the political and military strength of the USA (as well as its economic dominance in the capitalist world) and of the USSR (now joined, for the time being, by revolutionary China), thereby contributing to the end of (most of) European colonial empire in Asia and Africa, which both superpowers, for different reasons, wanted to see dismantled.

In effect, the founding moment of development studies was one of world-historical drama, as appreciated by those who shaped the contemporary intellectual frameworks of the meanings and means of development, and engaged in their contestations. This was a moment, then, of asking big questions and pursuing big ideas, with an expansive intellectual agenda that sought to identify and explain key processes of change in the formation of the modern world and their effects. Among such effects in particular was the striking unevenness of forms and rates of economic growth in different regions and countries at different times, together with social, political and cultural forces associated with them and which may contribute to their explanation. That unevenness, of course, was – as it still is – manifested in the brute facts of massive social inequality within and between regions and countries. Key themes of this expansive notion of the study of development, which it often aspires to connect, include: transformations of agrarian societies, patterns of accumulation and industrialization; the formation and functioning of international markets and divisions of labour, and other aspects of a world economy (flows of people, capital, commodities, technologies and ideas, images and practices); the formation and functioning of modern states and of an international state system; the differentiated social agents who, individually and collectively, participate in and struggle over such processes and shape their outcomes.[5]

Much of this expansive agenda – especially concerning the conditions, mechanisms, nature and effects of development as the transformation of individual countries/societies – has a rich and diverse intellectual lineage that includes the great founding figures of social science, hence long pre-dates the notion of any distinctive field of development studies.[6] Moreover, for intellectual pioneers such as Adam Smith, Karl Marx and Max Weber, the transformations of their time(s) were being wrought by the development of *capitalism* and, for Marx, above all *industrial* capitalism. Marx also had a very strong sense of the *global* character and consequences of capitalism, albeit one that was relatively little specified or explored in his work. Certainly by the founding moment of development studies, issues of the development of individual poor ('underdeveloped') countries (the first set of themes outlined) were increasingly integrated with consideration of international economic and political conditions of development (the second and third sets of themes), which anti-colonial movements did much to impress on the agenda, as did the superpower rivalry of the USA and USSR (providing different examples of the fourth set of themes).[7]

Another vital ingredient in the powerful cocktail of this world-historical moment was the complex and compound legacies of European colonialism, and of 'Orientalism' more generally, for the constitution of 'development' as discourse and object of policy in both North and South. This is too large and important a topic to address here, where I note only that in the case of Britain (as of some other European countries, notably France and the Netherlands) the experience of colonial administration and of the 'developmental' phase of late colonialism contributed ideas and practices, and also personnel, to the emerging professionalization of development expertise in both national and international organizations (see the chapter by Uma Kothari in this collection).[8]

In the founding moment of development studies there was an assumption that the state in newly independent (and other poor) countries had a central role in planning and managing economic and social development. Indeed, this assumption held across a very wide range of the political and ideological spectrum, with a particularly marked influence in Britain (as in other countries of northern Europe) of social democratic ideas, associated with structuralist economics (or political economy) and a kind of international Keynesianism applied to issues of aid and trade.[9] Consequently both champions and critics of the newly established field of development studies shared an understanding that its rationale was to find ways of assisting state-led development.

While that understanding was a key route across the border with governments and aid agencies, the expansive framework and agenda of the study of development, embracing a plethora of objects of study, research and reflection, overflows the borders with all the social science disciplines, including history, law and the relative newcomer of international relations, hence are not unique to development studies, that even newer kid on the block. Indeed, it may be that in practice the latter is today less well placed to investigate, and produce knowledge of, processes of development in the intellectually expansive sense suggested, for reasons considered later. There are programmes of study and research on development in disciplinary social science departments in British universities, for example in anthropology, economics and politics, hence outside that particular space in the academic division of labour designated as development studies. There is also much research relevant to the study of development by social scientists with particular expertise, including linguistic and other cultural skills, in Asia, Africa and Latin America. They may thus be considered 'area studies' specialists in the term used in the American academy, are found mostly in anthropology and history, followed by politics and sociology, among the major social science disciplines, and some of them reject any identification of their work with development studies, for various reasons.

Development studies II. The age of neo-liberalism: how less becomes more, and more less

When the gathering ascendancy of neo-liberalism in development policy from the 1980s – the Washington Consensus – repudiated any significant interventionist role of states in the South in bringing about economic development, the question therefore arose as to whether development studies retained any purpose.[10] The question made sense. Development studies has not only survived the current period of neo-liberal ascendancy, however, but has prospered in British universities in terms of continued institutional growth.[11] An important, very general, part of the explanation for this is that neo-liberalism cannot write the state out of the script of contemporary capitalism, nor does it wish to do so (despite the usual excesses of political rhetoric), and certainly not in the realm of foreign, including aid, policy. In the North, the political course of neo-liberalism as a programme of state reform by various means of squeezing and splitting the state, in the terms used by Mackintosh (1992), combines redefinition of what states should and can do (less welfare, more 'security', for example) with attempts to re-engineer the ways in which they do it, rather than any diminution of the overall scope of state activity and the resources it commands. In the South the drive to 'roll back the state' was devised and is pursued by Northern governments through their bilateral aid programmes and collectively through multilateral agencies, above all the World Bank, which has established a unique ideological and intellectual hegemony in development policy discourse in the last twenty years or so.

The paradox is that less intervention in theory has meant more intervention in practice. The major shifts of development theory, policy discourse and design, and modalities of intervention in the period of neo-liberal ascendancy, spearheaded by the World Bank, require a great deal of work to replace what preceded them in the period of state-led development.[12] And the intellectual and political labour of deconstruction requires a greater practical labour of reconstruction, from the demands of legitimization by intellectual and technical expertise – including, not least, presenting claims to better results of neo-liberal policies – to the nuts and bolts of reforming particular institutions and practices.

After a brief initial moment of market triumphalism in the early 1980s (get the prices right and all else will follow: growth, prosperity and stability), it became evident that a few decisive strokes of policy to roll back states and liberate markets were not enough to achieve accelerated economic growth *and* reduce poverty. Matters were not as straightforward as they might have seemed, and here the first paradox meets another, whereby apparently less becomes substantially more. Freeing the market to carry out the tasks of economic growth for which it is deemed uniquely suited rapidly escalated into an extra-ordinarily ambitious, or grandiose, project of social engineering that amounts to establishing bourgeois civilization on a global scale. Comprehensive market reform confronted similarly comprehensive state reform (rather than simply contraction) as a condition of the former; in turn, the pursuit of 'good govern-ance' quickly extended to, and embraced, notions of 'civil society' and social institutions more generally. In short, the terrain of development discourse and the range of aid-funded interventions have become ever more inclusive to encompass the reshaping, or transformation, of political and social (and, by implication, cultural) as well as economic institutions and practices.

Bourgeois civilization comes as a complete package,[13] and completing it requires filling many gaps left by displacement of the framework of earlier state-led development, in which public investment and a state economic sec-tor were central to economic growth, and employment generation, strong provision of public goods and redistributionist measures were central to con-necting economic growth and the elimination of poverty (Seers 1969). In con-ceptual terms, the gap left by public investment in economic infrastructure and enterprise was to be filled by the structures of incentives and competitive pressures to efficiency provided by properly functioning markets and their price signals. In practical terms – and until such time as markets are able to provide – political considerations recommended trying to fill two of the major welfare gaps left by 'squeezing' and 'splitting' the state, namely losses in 'for-mal' employment and deteriorating provision of such strategic public goods as healthcare and education. These areas (and especially the latter), along with others bearing on livelihoods and basic needs, have been increasingly allocated to alternative provision through 'civil society', in practice NGOs (non-government organizations). As amply documented, and widely debated, recent decades have witnessed an explosive proliferation of development NGOs. They constitute an extensive international network – or hierarchy – through which a significant proportion of aid funding is disbursed, most of it in the first place through large international (Northern) NGOs acting as subcontractors to aid agencies.

Finally, two other aspects of the ever expanding agenda of development studies can be noted briefly. The first is the absorption and impact, however uneven and incomplete, of over-arching areas of concern of different kinds generated by wider intellectual and political currents, of which issues of gender (from the 1960s) and of the natural environment (from the 1970s) provide the most potent examples (see the chapters by Ruth Pearson and Admos Chimhowu and Philip Woodhouse in this collection). The second is that the demise of the USSR opened up a potentially vast new frontier to development studies from the early 1990s. Those with credentials in the many areas of applied research embraced by the pursuit of structural adjustment in Asia, Africa and Latin America were now able to stake claims to assist the course of market liberalization, state reform and good governance across the former Soviet bloc from the Baltic to the expanses of Central Asia.

The scope of development studies has thus expanded greatly, and it has done so, as implied by the above observations, principally by agglomeration. To what may be considered its constant topics – for example, in international economics (trade, investment and today – above all? – capital markets), macro-economics (exchange, interest, inflation and savings rates, employment, productivity) and social policy (health, education) – are added state reform, the (re)design and management of public institutions, democratization, civil society and the sources of social capital, new social movements, small-scale credit, NGO management, (environmentally) sustainable development, women/gender and development, children and development, refugees and development, humanitarian emergencies and interventions, and post-conflict resolution (among other examples). What has been largely abandoned from the earlier agenda of the founding moment of development studies is that central attention to issues of economic planning, public investment and accumulation, together with the expansive conceptions of public goods with which they were then associated.[14]

If development studies in British universities prospers institutionally, does it also prosper intellectually during this period of the neo-liberal ascendancy when its agenda is set – directly and indirectly – by bilateral and multilateral aid agencies, by state and quasi-state bodies, to a greater extent than in the past? An adequate answer to this question would be long and complex, exceeding the limits of space available (and the competence of the author, given the ever expanding terrain of development studies and its proliferating specialized subdivisions). Here, as throughout this chapter, I suggest only some elements of an answer, broadly sketched.

One must recognize, to begin, that there is always a tension between scholarship in social science and its appropriations by and for policy. How policy works in practice is shaped much more by political forces and processes than by the intrinsic merits of different intellectual paradigms and positions and their contestations (a rationalist fallacy to which intellectuals are prone). One of the constant intellectual tensions of development studies, then, is between its institutional identity and practical mission on one hand, and the expansive sense of the study of development as one of the definitive themes established by the classic origins of modern social science on the other hand. And, as noted, important contributions to the latter continue to be made outside the rubric of development studies, sometimes in intellectual and/or ideological opposition to the latter qua 'policy science'.

Tensions between scholarship, with its exacting disciplines (including the time it takes), and knowledge required, and packaged, for the practical pur-poses of policy design and implementation, do not amount to an unbridgeable divide between the two endeavours. Such tensions can produce more or less creative effects, depending on broader political and ideological conditions of intellectual production and the specific political complexions and purposes of those who commission or otherwise promote particular kinds of applied knowledge. In an ideal world, the rich intellectual resources for the study of development (in the expansive sense) would be available to the mission of development studies (in the restrictive sense), and systematically assimilated and assessed by the latter to inform its work of devising effective development policy and practice. It seems to me that this kind of tension was more crea-tive in the founding moment of development studies than it is today, when the stretching of the agenda of development discourse to near-omniverous proportions is driven by pressure to bridge the yawning gaps between now conventionalized formulae for market-led economic growth and evidence of growing social inequality and poverty in the South.

For example, one of the constitutive elements of the intellectual agenda of the study of development in its expansive sense is the (variant) relationships between different economic structures and patterns of growth in different places and times in the formation of a modern world economy and the reduc-tion or reproduction of poverty, as an aspect of social inequality intrinsic to *and* produced by capitalist development. This concern was also more evident in the founding moment of development studies, characterized by a more diverse and dynamic intellectual and ideological conjuncture, not least due to the influence and impact of Marxist ideas (see below). The key questions of development strategy were framed within serious attempts, from different viewpoints and yielding different interpretations, to understand the massive upheavals that created the contemporary world and continued to shape it.[15] This is now displaced by such notions as 'pro-poor growth', which expresses nicely the commitment of contemporary development discourse and doctrine to 'win-win' solutions *and* its faith that an inclusive – and globalizing – market economy (or more broadly bourgeois civilization) contains no intrinsic obstacles to a better life for all. There is so much to gain with relatively little pain; the only losers will be rent-seekers and others who fail to play by the rules of the game.[16]

The commitment to 'win-win' policy solutions to continuing problems of economic growth and poverty imposes one kind of constraint on the intellectual spaces of development studies. It is the credo of what Ferguson (1990) memorably termed an 'anti-politics machine' that 'depoliticizes' development doctrine (see also Harriss 2001), and marginalizes or displaces investigation and understanding of the sources, dynamics and effects of typically savage social inequality in the South, and of no less savage relations of power and inequality in the international economic and political system. It elides consideration of the often violent social upheavals and struggles that characterize the processes *and* outcomes of the development of capitalism.

Another type of constraint on intellectual work in development studies stems from the hegemonism of neo-classical economics, which has spiralled during the neo-liberal ascendancy, including the latest manifestations of its ambition to subsume much of sociological and political enquiry within its own paradigm (Fine 1997, 2001). This is as good an example as any of a theoretical model achieving supremacy as a world view, *and* global programme, owing to political and ideological conditions rather than intrinsic intellectual superiority. And neo-classical economics provides intellectual support, with more or less plausibility, to the good intentions of the 'win-win' discourse of development policy.

There may be positive aspects of the agglomeration of topics assimilated to the rubric of development studies, if not of the loss of some of the classic issues of development strategy of the previous period. What has also been lost to a considerable degree is the wider intellectual, and political, understanding of development as a process of struggle and conflict, and use of the diverse intellectual resources available to advance such understanding.[17] The expansion of topic range (and policy objects) is not the same as intellectual vitality and depth, or indeed pluralism, all of which, I suggest, have diminished for the reasons indicated. Such observations about the narrowing intellectual horizons, and more shallow intellectual base, of development studies – how more becomes less – will not meet with general agreement, of course, and require testing by more detailed, and empirical, investigation of its 'output', as well as by the normal course of debate.

The same applies to observations about connections between intellectual practices, and their shifting conditions, and the intellectual skills, experiences and career paths of those who work in development studies – an occupational sociology of the field, as it were. This bears on the key political (and existential) issue of the 'room for manoeuvre' – that is, of the positioning and practices, collective and individual, of those critical of the dominant ideological tendencies of development doctrine and of the powerful forces that promote them. This is a matter of the spaces available, or which can be 'captured' or created, *within* the discursive and practical fields of dominant development agencies (and not least their funding practices) to articulate, and implement, alternative ideas and courses of action. In turn, questions of such 'room for manoeuvre' connect with how notions of the tasks of intellectual and applied work are constituted, the capacities they are deemed to require, and of how to combine them.[18]

'Practitioners' have been present in development studies from its inception, across a spectrum from the former colonial administrators noted earlier (whose intellectual contribution was so limited) to architects of national development strategies and plans. The demand for practitioners has increased, however, along with the expanded range of development studies, and the political and institutional pressures that contribute to this agglomeration. Here are several examples. The first is neo-classical economists who are mathematically well endowed but somewhat challenged in terms of broader intellectual culture, both qualities that commend them for applied work in the 'hard' areas of macro- and microeconomic modelling and policy design. A second example is practitioners of public administration, required to deal with the many nuts-and-bolts aspects of comprehensive state reform, civil service restructuring and (re)training, decentralization, and other re-engineering of public institutions in the name of 'good governance'. A third is those recruited for, and aimed at, the 'soft' areas of welfare, community-level and other self-help interventions where NGO activity concentrates and the jargon of 'participation', 'empowerment', 'stakeholders' and the like is most pervasive.[19] Of these examples, only the first requires an academic formation of any intellectual presumption and rigour (within its very narrow culture), primarily the acquisition of a well-established analytical 'tool kit'.

The point of these examples is not to (pre-)judge the ethics, intentions or professional competence of such categories of practitioners which, one might reasonably expect, follow a (notionally) normal distribution across development studies as in any other comparable field of 'policy science'. Rather, it is to pose the question of the effects for the intellectual terrain of development studies of the neo-liberal hegemony of development discourse, and of its practical manifestation in the demand of aid agencies for expert advice across the spectrum of their policy concerns (from 'hard' to 'soft'), and by their willingness to contract some of that expertise from universities.[20] Part of the answer, I suggest – and one which also calls for more systematic empirical research – is that, in the circumstances sketched, efforts to identify and exploit 'room for manoeuvre', and the outcomes of such efforts, are more a matter of professional skill than intellectual position or substance, and especially skill in the institutional politics of aid agencies, which includes, of course, talking the(ir) talk. 'Practitioners' have to be seen, above all, as competent technicians, in the 'soft' as well as 'hard' areas of development policy and practice. And for this, their training, capacities and interests in development in the intellectually expansive sense proposed above are generally irrelevant and in some (many?) instances are no doubt best concealed in order for them to pass as competent technicians.

And the Marxists? I. Political struggle and intellectual dynamism

The history of Marxist ideas is as complex as those of the other great lineages of social theory that contribute to the study and understanding of development in its intellectually expansive sense, and perhaps more so. The reason is that it comprises at least three strands, each stamped with their own tensions and contradictions, as are the various ways in which they intertwine, namely those of Marxist intellectual work (and its specific social and political conditions in different times and places); of political parties and movements that contest the social order of capitalism and imperialism and seek to replace it with a Marxian version of socialism (and eventually communism); and of states that attempted to construct and pursue a project of socialist construction as a mode of development alternative, and superior, to capitalism – or claimed to do so.

All these strands, and their various effects for each other, were evident with particular dynamism and intensity in the 1960s and 1970s, which saw a massive increase of interest in, and influence of, Marxist ideas in British universities, as elsewhere, as part of the formation of a 'New Left'. In terms of intellectual resources, both reflecting and stimulating this interest were the first English translations of important texts, including some by Marx, especially the first full translation of the *Grundrisse*; notable editions of Gramsci's writings; texts by leading protagonists of the Bolshevik debates of the 1920s, for example Preobrazhensky and Bukharin; and, in addition to the official *Selected*

Works, writings of Mao Zedong then appeared in new editions of translation and commentary. The efflorescence of Marxist intellectual work and debate added university-based journals such as *Antipode, Capital and Class, Critique of Anthropology, History Workshop, Journal of Contemporary Asia, Journal of Peasant Studies, Race and Class, Radical Sociology, Review of African Political Economy* and *Review of Radical Political Economy* to existing independent Marxist journals such as *Monthly Review* and *Science and Society* in the USA and *New Left Review* in Britain. In the 1960s *New Left Review* soon made explicit its mission to translate and explore contemporary, as well as earlier, Marxist texts and debates – notably from France, Germany and Italy – to provide Marxist intellectual work with theoretical foundations lacking in the inheritance of British (and more generally anglophone) 'empiricism'.

This intellectual ferment was, of course, intimately tied to the political events of its time and the concerns they generated. One preoccupation was the effort to understand better the problems and prospects of economic and social development of poorer countries, only recently independent of colonial rule in most of Asia and Africa, with particular attention to (i) how their processes of accumulation were shaped by their internal social structures and associated forms of state, (ii) their locations in the social divisions of labour of a capitalist world economy – an 'imperialism (now) without colonies' – and (iii) how international and domestic class forces interacted. This expansive intellectual agenda included a commitment to exploring and testing the possible contributions to such understanding of knowledge of pre-capitalist social formations in different parts of the world; of paths of capitalist transition in the now developed countries of the North; and of Latin American, Asian and African experiences of colonialism and their legacies for subsequent processes of development/underdevelopment. All these became major themes in Marxist (and *Marxisant*) theoretical and historical work, with the first and third also central to the remarkable flowering of Marxist work in anthropology, and the second and third to an intellectually expansive, and historically minded, political economy of development.

If much of the focus noted was on the development of capitalism and its prospects in the South, this was also intimately linked to the Marxist left's concerns with anti-imperialism and transitions to *socialism*. Two of the defining global moments of the 1960s and early 1970s were the Vietnamese war of national liberation against US imperialism[21] and the 'Great Proletarian Cultural Revolution' (GPCR) and its aftermath in China. While international progressive support for the former was unanimous, comprehending the baffling course of the latter, and analysing its effects, generated (or further provoked) a range of sharp and symptomatic disagreements among Marxists about the conditions, strategies and prospects of socialist development in poor countries. Of course, casting its long shadow over those disagreements was the first and fateful experience of social revolution and draft industrialization in a mostly agrarian society, that of Russia/the USSR.

In this context marked by anti-imperialist struggles, by the increasingly evident difficulties of capitalist development in poor countries, and by scepticism about the USSR and communist parties across the world that were aligned with it (a distinguishing feature of the New Left),[22] it was probably above all the claims of Maoism – as political philosophy and model of development alternative to both capitalism and Soviet state socialism – which influenced Marxist intellectuals by both acclaim and rejection. Whether those claims amounted to filling gaps in 'classic' Marxism or to its fundamental (and fatal) revision – in the direction of 'Third Worldism', the absorption of anti-imperialism by nationalism, peasants (and lumpenproletarians) rather than the organized working class as the revolutionary force of the current epoch, and so on[23] – demanded attention and response across a wide terrain of analytical, empirical and political issues.[24] The moment of Maoism, as that of 'Third Worldism' more generally, certainly had the merit of forcing attention on two of the most problematic ideological currents that had long haunted Marxism in the real worlds of politics it has grappled with, not least by infiltrating the programmes and practices of Marxist parties and movements, namely nationalism and populism.

Two texts from the large corpus of (British) Marxist writing of this conjuncture illustrate its extreme diversity of approaches to and arguments about development. The better known is Bill Warren's highly contentious *Imperialism: Pioneer of Capitalism* (1980), published posthumously from drafts edited by Warren's former student John Sender. This may be regarded as a restatement of a classic Marxist view that the (full) development of capitalism across the globe is a necessary precondition of any project of socialist construction. By this token capitalism is a progressive force, the seeds of which were first planted in the South by colonial imperialism. While Warren's empirical argument sought to document the actuality of capitalist development, and its benefits, his book was more notorious for its polemical fire. This was directed against positions (sometimes claiming the heritage of Lenin's *Imperialism*) that denied the possibility of capitalist development (accumulation, industrialization, development of the productive forces) in the South, notably the 'development of underdevelopment' and dependency theories influential at the time, *and* against those nationalist and populist – and self-styled 'socialist' – currents in development policy in the South that blocked the contributions of international capital.

By way of contrast, *Social Construction and Marxist Theory: Bolshevism and Its Critique* by Philip Corrigan, Harvey Ramsay and Derek Sayer (1978) presented a serious and sustained intellectual argument for Maoism.[25] Its subtitle indicates its purpose, which was to liberate socialist theory (and practice) from what its authors regarded as that aspect of classic Marxism which privileged the development of the productive forces above mass politics, and was incorporated in Bolshevism: an index of its incomplete break with bourgeois ideas and of the troubled path of Soviet state socialism. In turn, mass politics and its forms of inclusive and dynamic participation, as theorized by Mao Zedong and epitomized by the GPCR in China, generated forms of development centred on satisfying basic needs through creative collective practices.

While, as ever, they bear the hallmarks of their specific moment of production, the contrast between these two works echoes long-standing tensions in the Marxist tradition. One such tension centres on interpretations of the relationship between, and relative emphasis on, the productive forces (the means of producing wealth) and their unique development in capitalism, and the social relations of production or class relations (the basis of politics). Another tension is inherent in Marx's famous observation (1976: 91) that 'The country that is more developed industrially only shows to the less developed the image of its own future' – if this is taken to mean that the latter are destined to advance to the same kind (or stage) of capitalist economic development through incorporation in a global capitalist economy shaped (and dominated) by the former. This view was embraced by Warren (above) and rejected by many other Marxists, as well as by many nationalists and populists in the South together with their Northern sympathizers. A somewhat different tension, on an existential as well as intellectual plane, concerns the conditions, purposes and effects of Marxist intellectual work in relation to contemporary political dynamics and struggles with all their contradictory impulses and the sheer messiness of what I term real-world politics, a matter to which I return. And, connecting in different ways with all these, is that pervasive tension at the core of any socialist or communist project between realism and utopianism, between the claims of Marxism as a science of social reality and a programme of human emancipation.

While these kinds of tensions (and many others) permeated Marxist intellectual debate on the general terrain of arguments about capitalism and socialism, and imperialism and development, as well as informing widely divergent political positions on contemporary events, how – and how much – did they connect with the concerns of development studies in its founding moment, described earlier? Here are several, once more preliminary or provisional, observations. First, the seemingly inexhaustible firepower of Marxist criticism was turned on other theories of, and prescriptions for, development, from the explicit anti-communism of the mostly American modernization school to the paradigms of mainstream social science to such closer ideological neighbours (and competitors?) as the varieties of dependency theory and social democratic (and nationalist) versions of structuralist economics – all this, of course, in addition to the usual internecine intensity of debates between Marxists. There was also a great deal of creative analytical *and* empirical Marxist work, however, ranging from, say, the investigation of intricate structures and processes of class formation in villages and rural localities to analysis of the functioning of international divisions of labour. Much of this work was published in the kinds of journals listed above, which were read widely by those on the left with intellectual interests and political concerns that extended far beyond development studies in its restrictive sense even when they were employed within it.[26]

Marxist academics employed in development studies, however, were not necessarily detached from its more applied work, even as they engaged in and contributed to wider debates within Marxism and across the social sciences. First, there was considerably more space for the expression of Marxist ideas in development studies in its founding moment, with its relatively more expansive horizons and recognition of the intellectual importance and power of Marxism, not least in large regions of the South, by (some) non-Marxists. Second, Marxists and many on the non-Marxist left, including more progressive social democrats, often shared political sympathies on particular issues, for example concerning the Cuban and Vietnamese revolutions, and a predisposition towards helping more progressive regimes and governments in the South to formulate and implement their development strategies. This is a lineage that can be traced from the 1950s in Nehru's India[27] through Nkrumah's Ghana and Sekou Toure's Guinea, and revolutionary Cuba, to Allende's Chile in the early 1970s and on to liberated Mozambique and Nicaragua of the Sandinistas.[28] Third, in the conjuncture described there were, as indicated, many apparently progressive regimes in the South to work with *and* an ideologically more conducive set of governments and aid agencies to support such work, especially in (social democratic) northern Europe (and Canada) and in some parts of the UN system.

The question remains: what, if anything, was specifically Marxist about the methods and techniques, as distinct from the commitments and motivations, *applied* by Marxist 'practitioners' in their employment by, or cooperation with, the efforts of progressive regimes in the South to promote economic and social development? Or, to put it somewhat differently: what distinguished the practical policy designs of Marxists from the prescriptive framework and planning methodology of structuralist economics more broadly (with which Marxism shares a common lineage of classical political economy)? My hunch is that the answer is probably 'very little'. On one hand, Marxists, like structuralist economists more generally, developed and debated the case for development strategies based in public investment, planning and coordination, and did so through arguments about methods of resource allocation and their efficiency/effectiveness which drew on elements of other paradigms in economics.[29] On the other hand, as W. Brus (1991: 339), one of the principal eastern European theorists of 'market socialism', observed in relation to possible affinities between planning in socialist regimes and under social democratic governments in the capitalist North: 'any analogy must be very tentative both because of the starting position and because of the profoundly different conditions of struggle for achieving the desired aim'.

It may well be that the questions just posed are not the right ones, and that Brus's reference to different starting points and conditions of struggle points towards more apposite questions for assessing the distinctive intellectual contributions, actual and potential, of Marxism to understanding – and facilitating – processes of development, to which I return below.

And the Marxists? II. Political defeats and beyond

If the founding moment of modern development studies seems part of an already distant past, the contrast between the conditions of Marxist intellectual work then (the 1960s and 1970s) and now (since the 1980s) appears as an almost epochal rupture. And, of course, it is a rupture marked not only by the demise (albeit by very different routes) of the 'actually existing socialisms' of the Soviet bloc and China but also by the retreat and disarray of social democratic politics, as well as the disappearance or mostly accelerated decline of historic communist parties in the European democracies. In short, the current moment is one of massive defeat of the left, both Marxist and non-Marxist, throughout the North, if not so comprehensively across the South.[30] This necessarily has a profound effect for the conditions, preoccupations and styles of Marxist intellectual work in universities in both North and South, and the ways in which it links with the wider political environment and its contradictions – or fails to do so.

Many formerly Marxist academics, whose formation was in the 1960s and 1970s, have abandoned Marxism; there is much less Marxism available to today's university students as part of their general education in the social sciences. The connections between Marxist intellectual work and the pro-grammes and practices of progressive political formations, both parties and regimes, have eroded with the demise or decline of the latter (and however vicarious such connections, or claims for them, sometimes were). To the ex-tent that one or another variant of Marxism exemplified a (fashionably) radical stance in the social sciences only a few decades back, this has been largely dis-placed by the various currents of post-structuralism, postmodernism and the like (loosely defined), the 'radical' ambitions of which rest on their subversions of the claims of existing forms of knowledge to objectivity and of any political aspirations to a project of universal emancipation. In relation to development studies, the effect of the postmodern(ist) 'turn' is to deny the validity of any conception of development other than as for an imperializing (Northern) dis-course imposed on the South. In short, in the conditions of political defeat outlined, the space for Marxist intellectual work – as for most intellectually expansive, and scholarly, endeavour? – within development studies has been reduced drastically by the ascendancy of a neo-liberal common sense of the epoch on one hand, and, on the other hand, by the self-regarding ambition of postmodernism to monopolize the modes of critique.[31]

More broadly, Marxist intellectual work today has lost two of its virtually definitive points of reference, and contestation, of most of the twentieth cen-tury, namely the existence and influence of regimes claiming the credentials of 'actually existing socialism' and a Leninist model of the party as the in-dispensable organizational vanguard, leader and shaper, of socialist politics. Those who retain a commitment to Marxist ideas confront a massive challenge with the loss of these intellectual-cum-political preoccupations, so long at the centre of intra-Marxist debate. Key questions of that challenge include: What explains the (global) victory of capitalism? What are the prospects and oppor-tunities of (what kinds of) capitalist development in different regions, and for different classes, in the South? And what remains politically with the demise of any evident socialist (development) alternative?

Most fundamentally, in the light of historical experience to date it may prove impossible to rethink notions of any feasible socialism(s), and of socialist de-velopment, that can be projected into a foreseeable future. The best that can be said, with no guarantee of success, is that paradoxically – or dialectically – that process of rethinking socialism should, and can, be informed by analyses of a now untrammelled, and ever more globalizing, capitalism, the contradictions that drive it and the social and political struggles it generates. Three aspects of this can be indicated which link with some of the themes already indicated in this essay.

The first is the critique of neo-liberalism in all its aspects from theoretical doctrine to the practices of development (and Northern foreign policy) interventions. There is no lack of such critique today and, as might be expected, it embraces a wide range of ideological currents – including various strands and combinations of nationalist, populist and deconstructionist elements – on various sites of contestation, and with different degrees of intellectual coherence and depth. In an important sense, then, the vitality of critique is assured, but this is no ground for intellectual complacency that assumes, in Manichaean fashion, its virtue and innocence by contrast with neo-liberal vice and guilt. Not only is such critique so diverse and so often confused, but the strength of its fervour can manifest an underlying sense of impotence in the face of an apparently rampant global capitalism. For Marxist intellectuals the *utility* of critique has to be informed and assessed by its contributions to developing a better understanding of changes in the world(s) they inhabit.

This leads to the second aspect: analytical and empirical work on the ways in which capitalism is changing today and its effects for economic growth and poverty/inequality in the South. In my view, this is the area in which university-based Marxist intellectuals, in the conditions of wider political constraint sketched, can make their most significant contributions. The work of critique, in Marx's sense, is addressed both to existing social relations and realities and to the ideas/ideologies that, in claiming to explain them, justify them. And such critique, as Marx was also clear about, can only be carried forward by generating analytically superior results. This, then, is a research agenda for Marxists concerned with development: to investigate, understand and grasp what is 'changing before our very eyes' in the world of contemporary capitalism (Bernstein 2004), and thereby to subject Marxist analysis to the necessary test of whether it can generate new knowledges and by what distinctive means available to historical materialism, both inherited *and* that can be created within its intellectual framework. This is the test of the reproduction of Marxist ideas in any dynamic, rather than antiquarian, sense.

Whether these new knowledges also disclose possibilities – 'imaginaries', in the jargon of the day – of different social relations and realities, and how plausibly and effectively they do so, in turn links to a third aspect: that of identifying and understanding, and supporting as appropriate, those forces that contest the capitalist social order in ways that, with all their inevitable contradictions, point to alternative, more progressive futures. Here the major challenges to the dynamic reproduction, hence relevance, of Marxist ideas – and the challenges that generate the most intense disagreements between Marxists of different stripes – centre on the analysis and assessment of the political character and potential of such social forces in the South in a historical moment when belief in the paramount role of the Leninist party and its sociological foundation, the 'organized working class', is no longer viable. This, then, is one extension, among others, of Brus's reference to different starting points and different conditions of struggle (cited above). Other examples of its applications include serious engagement with the ideas and practices, in all their diversity, of 'anti-globalization movements' (not the same as either sweeping endorsement or dismissal of their analyses and claims); the scope of popular nationalist politics in opposition to both imperialism and domestic reaction – e.g. the powerful essays on South Asia by Aijaz Ahmad (2000); and debate about redistributive land reform driven by politics 'from below', rather than by programmes of (bourgeois) 'modernization' and the World Bank (e.g. Bernstein 2004; Moyo and Yeros, 2005).

I am aware of the prescriptive tenor of how I have sketched these three aspects of Marxist intellectual work on development, and by extension on contemporary imperialism, in current conditions, and – by the same token? – how this has moved away from some of the specific issues concerning development studies proposed earlier. What, then, of issues of practicality? Of development studies as applied knowledge, and its 'room for manoeuvre' when the spaces once provided by more progressive regimes in the South (and governments in the North), and by intellectually and ideologically more sympathetic elements in aid agencies, are so reduced? One response presents a different kind of paradox: the extent to which critical intellectual work of any substance on development – Marxist and other – requires a greater *distance* from the agendas of official development discourse and practice and their 'knowledge-power regimes'. The paradox is that this is to reinstate a classically 'liberal' theme of intellectual work, namely the necessity of its independence from established centres of power, privilege and patronage. That independence in development studies in British universities is now subject to the combined pressure of neo-liberal development doctrine and a higher education policy for competitive performance in the market for research funding with its conceptions of ostensibly beneficial knowledge 'output'.

This is not to be judgemental about those, Marxists and others, who undertake applied research and consultancy on behalf of government and other aid agencies, and may do so in the quest for 'room for manoeuvre' and/or for other purposes. It is simply to recommend that they do so without illusion; a self-conscious cynicism may be less harmful existentially than delusion of self and others. There is a final point to be made about 'practicality' – or, in more grandiose terms, about utopia and reality. The most identifiable criterion of 'practicality', and in that sense of professional success as well as 'realism', for many academics in development studies is the demand for their services as experts by aid agencies. This is far less elusive than any measure or assessment of the effects of such activity in accelerating economic growth and/or reducing poverty, as part of the mission of those agencies. The formulation of that mission – as 'pro-poor' (capitalist) development, or (in the terms I have suggested) as a global project of extending bourgeois civilization to those denied its benefits – is, I suggest, no less utopian, no more 'practical' or 'realistic', than the fantasies of socialism once entertained by many Marxists.[32]

Conclusion

This essay has emerged in more idiosyncratic fashion than envisioned, which perhaps reflects personal experience, with all its attendant tensions (and worse?), of many years of employment as an academic social scientist concerned with issues of development and intellectually committed to Marxism. That element of biography, even without the confessional mode of several contributions to the first part of this book, no doubt manifests itself in ways I failed to anticipate. Nevertheless, it seems right to conclude with some brief observations on the intellectual power and promise of a Marxist approach to processes of development, as distinct from the issues that confront Marxists who may be employed in development studies in its restrictive or institutional sense.

The most salient feature that is most directly relevant is the breadth and depth of Marxist analysis of the political economy of capitalism, which is unparalleled in the other great traditions of social science enquiry. This is a form of analysis centred on social relations, their historical formation, contradictions and changing forms, above all but not exclusively relations of class. Indeed, as hinted earlier, analytical class 'purism' remains a major obstacle to the renewal and development of Marxist investigation, and the knowledge it can yield of how (global) capitalism works, with all its Northern and Southern variants *and* with all its manifold contradictions: across social relations of gender, ethnicity and generation, of mental and manual labour, countryside and town, and other divisions inscribed in its social divisions of labour – as well as, and intimately connected with, those of class. What makes capitalism dynamic, and the effects of its uneven development for different regions and social groups within its international structure, remain central preoccupations, the exploration of which today requires the labour of innovative empirical research and analysis as much as (more than?) that of theoretical elaboration.[33] At the same time, this requires engagement with other approaches capable of generating questions, and sometimes concepts and methods, that can be assimilated to and reformulated by a Marxist intellectual agenda to its benefit.

The vital question of a viable Marxist political project – the future of socialism – in current and foreseeable conditions remains as problematic as ever, and even more unanswerable. An element of solace in this is that the contributions of academics to the making of revolutionary or transformational politics are, in any case, negligible, and recognition of this may help to avoid the seductions of *amour-propre* that professional intellectuals are prone to. Awareness of the limits of one's conditions of social existence can enhance a fitting modesty, and also the nature and quality of intellectual production possible within those limits – better that that than the hubris of the philosopher-kings of the neo-liberal ascendancy in development studies.

Notes

1 I am grateful, as always, to my co-worker T. J. Byres for discussion of some of the issues touched on in this essay; responsibility for how those issues are presented remains mine alone. As should be evident, this essay is of a preliminary, hence provisional nature. It was written before I was aware of the stimulating recent work of Michael Burawoy on the sociology of (American) sociology, to which Ben Crow alerted me. The essay would have been enriched had I been able to adapt Burawoy's delineation and uses of professional, critical, policy and public sociologies as intellectual/social practices (e.g. Burawoy 2004) to considering the intellectual and institutional trajectories of development studies. Also missing is any consideration of the magisterial title essay in Leys (1996), which concerns some of the same issues that I comment on here, albeit on a broader intellectual canvas. Finally, I have adapted the title of another essay I admire greatly, that by Mark Harrison (1979), which likewise has resonance for what I attempt here, albeit addressing very different historical circumstances.

2 In France, as one might expect, development research organizations were established by the state, funded from its aid budget and staffed by experts employed as civil servants. The nearest equivalent in Britain was the founding of the Institute of Development Studies (IDS) at the University of Sussex. This was announced in the White Paper of the Labour government elected in 1964 which established the Ministry of Overseas Development, the first time that Britain's foreign aid programme became the responsibility of a full department of state. The first director of IDS was Dudley Seers, a central figure in its founding.

3 In the South, development studies – where it exists – is one expression, among others, of the commitment to national development that typified the moment of political independence and remains a fixture, if somewhat embattled, of the discourses of official politics. Its establishment and profile as a distinct academic entity in the South may have been patchy for a different reason to its relative absence in the USA, namely that national development, and how best to achieve it, was the principal preoccupation across social science departments and institutes in Asian and African universities, as to a large extent in Latin America. To be an economist, say, in India or Tanzania or Chile was, in effect, to be a development economist.

4 The more recent demise of the USSR, as well as the course of decollectivization

and liberalization in China and Vietnam and the dire condition of the Cuban economy, means that today there is no extant version of a state socialist model of development, for better or worse, some effects of which are touched on below.

5 It should be evident that these grand themes also bear on what we now commonly term modernity, with the diverse and fierce debates in the social sciences and cultural studies today which attach to it. It is rare to find all four sets of themes listed synthesized in a single text with much analytical rigour and historical depth. The book by Schwartz (2000) is an unusually impressive attempt to do this; the scale of its ambition and the concentration of its arguments make it a demanding read but by the same token a rewarding one.

6 Two very different books that have done much to stimulate interest in the lineages of ideas about development, and which illuminate their contemporary relevance, are by Kitching (1982) and Cowen and Shenton (1996). The latter is a Marxist account while the former is strongly influenced by its author's long-standing engagement with Marxist ideas. Gavin Kitching (now in Australia) and the late Michael Cowen were notable intellectual figures in development studies in Britain during important parts of their careers, and at one time were colleagues at the Centre for Development Studies, Swansea, while Robert Shenton is an American-born historian of Africa based in Canada. Starting from the eighteenth-century Physiocrats, Kitching provides a lucid and accessible account of populist ideas, their sources, and how and why they are reproduced in the long history of capitalist development in different places at different times, together with a critique of populism based in an 'old orthodoxy' of political economy: the necessity to development of processes of accumulation and industrialization which are inevitably disruptive and painful. Cowen and Shenton's book is highly ambitious and original, and brilliant in parts; it is also, in contrast to Kitching, very long, very eccentric and very reader-unfriendly in its organization and style. (To my knowledge, it is the first work on the history of development ideas to devote a long chapter to the theology of Cardinal Newman – and probably the last.) Their account is grounded in the problem of order disclosed by the disruptions and upheavals of early industrial capitalism and the 'dangerous classes' it generated, especially in relation to labour markets, employment and unemployment; how that problem was constituted as an object of social theory and solutions to it theorized and applied in 'doctrines of development' that prescribe harmonious development under state trusteeship, hence 'intentional' versus 'immanent' development in their terms; and the intrinsic contradictions of such doctrines in both theory and practice, from their early manifestations in Britain and its colonies (including mid-nineteenth-century Australia and Canada) to today's universe of development discourses and interventions.

7 This is explicit in the use of the title International Development by some university departments and centres.

8 The importance of the brief 'developmental' phase towards the end of British and French colonial rule in Africa in the late 1940s and 1950s, and of its legacies, is well established by recent work in modern African history; Cooper (2002, especially ch. 5) argues that the continuities of a state-led development project were more significant in certain respects than the moment of political change from colonial rule to independence in sub-Saharan Africa. I am sceptical that the redeployment of former colonial administrators in the new development agencies of the North contributed much to the *intellectual* framework of development studies. In my own experience the characteristic, and defensive, stance of most such veterans, former district officers and the like, was an ideology of 'practicality' and anti-intellectualism. Interestingly,

Robert Chambers (a contributor to this volume), who appears the most obvious exception to this observation, is best known for his reflections on styles of development practice. With a few noteworthy exceptions, a more explicit theoretical focus on development administration came later with the neo-liberal interest in state reform and efficiency (see below), drawing on developments in neo-classical economics.

9 Its outstanding representative in the formation of development studies in Britain, both intellectually and institutionally, was Dudley Seers (see also note 2 above).

10 A different kind of argument for the 'end of development' as a national, state-led, project – and by extension the end of development studies as originally conceived and practised – is generated by theories of the encompassing power of globalization (e.g. McMichael 1996), usually but not necessarily on the left.

11 For example, two of the largest postgraduate programmes in development studies in Britain today were, in fact, established only in the early 1990s in the University of London, at SOAS (School of Oriental and African Studies) and the LSE (London School of Economics and Political Science). While development studies in the institutional sense appears to flourish still, it can be argued that the centrality to it of a distinct field of development economics, defined by the kinds of concerns noted and with its strong structuralist emphasis, has been undermined: there is now only one (neo-classical) economics, that most dismal of 'sciences'.

12 What needed replacement included the contributions of the Bank and other donors to the debris of that period, produced *inter alia* by the incoherence of aid policies and practices and the frustrations and tensions generated by their results.

13 Which the mostly American social and political theorists of modernization in the 1950s and 1960s were clear about.

14 Wuyts (1992) advocates an analytically more expansive conception of public goods, as shaped by the social and political dynamics of 'public action', in opposition to the restrictive technical definition of public goods in neo-classical economics – a definition which is currently shrinking its sphere of legitimate application in the interests of privatization and market provision.

15 Indeed, it can be argued that notions of development *strategy* of any substantive content are largely absent from the intellectual framework of neo-liberal 'policy science'.

16 And those who fail to play by the rules are *criminalized* by the discourse, in effect; rent-seekers, for example, are associated with corruption, while social actors and practices that disturb the social and political *order* of an emergent global bourgeois civilization exemplify criminal violence. A recent addition to the concerns of development studies – stimulated, funded and steered by aid donors – is the area of state collapse, crisis states, and so on. The connections between development doctrine and global order/security are explored in a stimulating book by Duffield (2001). There are resonances here of the centrality of order to much of the work on political modernization in the 1960s and 1970s, with the particular stimulus at that time of the Vietnam war. Huntington (1968) was a key figure then, as he continues to be with his thesis of the 'clash of civilizations' (2002, first published in 1996). In a recent book review (of Moore 2003), Robert Wade (2004: 150) reports that 'The murderous attacks of September 11 were, of course, very helpful in forging the consensus at Doha [in the WTO, World Trade Organization, meeting], two months later. Moore [then Director-General of the WTO], with US Trade Representative Zoellick and EU Trade Commissioner Lamy, toured developing-country capitals to insist that the new free-trade round would be a blow against Al-Qaeda – and that objectors would be considered as renegades in the war against terror.'

17 This is not to say, of course, that there is not widespread recognition and analysis of processes of struggle and conflict over 'development' in the current period of neo-liberalism, registered politically in anti-globalization sentiments and movements, for example, and intellectually in the wide and diverse array of criticism of structural adjustment models and policies, of the World Bank and the IMF, and so on (see below). My suggestion, however, is that such oppositional thinking thrives *outside* the institutional spheres and practices of development studies rather than contributing to its internal debates, with their increasingly constrained political and intellectual limits.

18 In the case of Britain, this would also entail investigating how changes in the political and institutional framework of universities, including the pressures of government education policy and its funding mechanisms – and how universities handle these changes – affect the character of development studies departments.

19 Along with tendencies to celebrate the 'local' and 'indigenous': the *Gemeinschaftlichkeit* ('community-ness') of the 'natives' once more?

20 If to an insignificant degree compared to commercial consultancy firms, from the big corporates – where the serious money is – to the small independents.

21 Together with the intensity of continuing national liberation struggles in Africa as well as Asia, and of rural guerrilla movements in Latin America.

22 Including the role of communist parties in relation to working-class militancy in the North during the 1960s, with France in 1968 as the near-definitive case.

23 In addition to the impact of Maoism noted, tendencies to 'Third Worldism' were also stimulated by the writings of Frantz Fanon among others. In the output of a burgeoning Fanon industry (stoked by 'post-colonial' cultural studies), the biography by David Macey (2000) is a deeply sensitive and illuminating account of the experiences that stimulated the formation of Fanon's ideas, and hence is the best antidote to the crudity of so many partisan formulations of 'Fanonism' by both its champions and detractors.

24 The concerns of classic Marxism were focused on the problematic of the transition from feudalism to capitalism, in both its western European heartlands and the adjacent zones of incomplete transition/'backwardness' (what would later be called 'underdevelopment') in southern and eastern Europe, and Ireland. Also highly influential, however, were the importance of analyses of imperialism by Lenin and others to subsequent work on development/underdevelopment in the peripheries of imperialism. For example, Rosa Luxemburg's *The Accumulation of Capital* (1963, first published 1913) was an important influence on the formulation, in the 1960s and 1970s, of the articulation of modes of production to explain specific forms of underdevelopment, and their reproduction, in the conditions of capitalist imperialism. As with so much else at the time, the foremost theorists of the articulation of modes of production were French Marxists, in particular two formidable scholars of Africa: Claude Meillassoux and Pierre-Philippe Rey.

25 A companion volume by the same three authors was titled simply *For Mao: Essays in Historical Materialism* (1979), a reference to Louis Althusser's seminal *For Marx* (1970, first published in France 1965).

26 Also at this time there were fewer dedicated development studies journals and other publication media.

27 With its intellectually formidable planning apparatus which attracted such European Marxist luminaries as Charles Bettelheim and Maurice Dobb (on whom see further, note 29).

28 In several of these cases there was an influx of expertise from the Soviet bloc as well as a range of Marxists from other countries, some of them Communist Party members but many without party affiliations. The encounters of experts of such different provenance – with each other, and with the political and administrative structures and cadres of the countries they worked in – would make for a fascinating ethnography of one type of situation of development practice. A more recent example – and perhaps the last for the foreseeable future – of international mobilization of expertise on the left was *Making Democracy Work: A Framework for Macroeconomic Policy for South Africa*, produced by a team of progressive South African and foreign economists, some of them Marxists, during the transition from apartheid in the early 1990s (MERG 1993) – and which sank with barely a trace under South African governments from 1994.

29 Writing of Maurice Dobb – 'undoubtedly one of the outstanding political economists' of the twentieth century – Amartya Sen (1990: 141, 146) notes Dobb's contribution as 'a major bridge-builder between Marxist and non-Marxist economic traditions'.

30 Although the purchase of 'political religion' – in the Arab and wider Muslim world, in India ('Hindu fascism') and in Latin America (evangelical Protestantism) – challenges, to varying degrees, the popular bases of socialist, as of secular nationalist, politics.

31 Cooper and Packard (1997: 3) suggest that 'The ultramodernist [by which they mean neo-liberal] and the postmodernist critiques have a lot in common, especially their abstractions from the institutions and structures in which economic action takes place and which shape a power-knowledge regime. The ultramodernists see power only as a removable distortion to an otherwise self-regulating market. The postmodernists locate the power-knowledge regime in a vaguely defined "West" or in the alleged claims of European social science to have found universal categories for understanding and manipulating social life everywhere.'

32 Donald Sassoon (1997: 767) concludes his remarkable survey with the observation that 'In Western Europe, the main achievement of socialism [that is, the politics of the left] in the last hundred years has been the civilizing of capitalism', rather than its replacement. I remain sceptical that there is anything of a civilizing impulse, or any significant 'room for manouevre' to stimulate one, in today's neo-liberal development institutions, discourses and practices applied to the different starting points and conditions of struggle of the South.

33 This is my opinion, or prejudice, perhaps reflecting on what now seems like the inordinate theoreticism of so much Marxist academic debate of the 1960s and 1970s (in which it was followed by subsequent deconstructionisms: blame the French in both cases?!). Solid empirical research always has a utility, unlike theoretical elaboration for its own sake which remains detached from concrete enquiry.

References

Ahmad, A. (2000) *Lineages of the Present: Ideology and Politics in Contemporary South Asia*, London: Verso

Althusser, L. (1970) *For Marx*, New York: Vintage Books

Bernstein, H. (2004) '"Changing before our very eyes": agrarian questions and the politics of land in capitalism today', *Journal of Agrarian Change*, 4(3–4): 190–225 (special issue on *Redistributive Land Reform Today*, ed. T. J. Byres)

Brus, W. (1991) 'Market socialism', in Tom Bottomore (ed.), *A Dictionary of Marxist Thought*, 2nd edn, Oxford: Blackwell

Burawoy, M. (2004) 'Public sociologies: contradictions, dilemmas and possibilities', *Social Forces*, 82(4) 1–16

Cooper, F. (2002) *Africa since 1940: The Past of the Present*, Cambridge: Cambridge University Press

Cooper, F. and R. Packard (eds) (1997) 'Introduction', in *International Development and the Social Sciences: Essays on the History and Politics of Knowledge*, Berkeley: University of California Press

Corrigan, P., H. Ramsay and D. Sayer (1978) *Socialist Construction and Marxist Theory: Bolshevism and Its Critique*, London: Macmillan

— (1979) *For Mao: Essays in Historical Materialism*, London: Macmillan

Cowen, M. P. and R. W. Shenton (1996) *Doctrines of Development*, London: Routledge

Duffield, M. (2001) *Global Governance and the New Wars: The Merging of Development and Security*, London: Zed Books

Ferguson, J. (1990) *The Anti-politics Machine: 'Development', Depoliticization and Bureaucratic Power in Lesotho*, Cambridge: Cambridge University Press

Fine, B. (1997) 'The new revolution in economics', *Capital and Class*, 61: 143–8

— (2001) *Social Capital versus Social Theory: Political Economy and Social Science at the Turn of the Millennium*, London: Routledge

Harrison, M. (1979) 'Chayanov and the Marxists', *Journal of Peasant Studies*, 7(1): 86–100

Harriss, J. (2001) *Depoliticizing Development: The World Bank and Social Capital*, London: Anthem Press

Huntington, S. P. (1968) *Political Order in Changing Societies*, New Haven, CT: Yale University Press

— (2002) *The Clash of Civilizations and the Remaking of World Order*, London: Simon and Schuster

Kitching, G. (1982) *Development and Underdevelopment in Historical Perspective: Populism, Nationalism and Industrialization*, London: Methuen

Leys, C. (1996) *The Rise and Fall of Development Theory*, Oxford: James Currey

Luxemburg, R. (1963) *The Accumulation of Capital*, London: Routledge & Kegan Paul

Macey, D. (2000) *Frantz Fanon: A Life*, London: Granta Books

Mackintosh, M. (1992) 'Questioning the state', in M. Wuyts, M. Mackintosh and T. Hewitt (eds), *Development Policy and Public Action*, Oxford: Oxford University Press

McMichael, P. (1996) *Development and Social Change: A Global Perspective*, Thousand Oaks, CA: Pine Forge Press

Marx, K. (1976) *Capital, a Critique of Political Economy*, vol. 1, Harmondsworth: Penguin

MERG (Macroeconomic Research Group) (1993) *Making Democracy Work: A Framework for Macroeconomic Policy in South Africa*, Bellville: University of the Western Cape

Moore, M. (2003) *A World without Walls: Freedom, Development, Free Trade and Global Governance*, Cambridge: Cambridge University Press

Moyo, S. and P. Yeros (eds) (2005) *Reclaiming the Land: The Resurgence of Rural Movements in Africa, Asia and Latin America*, London: Zed Books

Rostow, W. W. (1960) *The Stages of Economic Growth: A Non-Communist Manifesto*, Cambridge: Cambridge University Press

Sassoon, D. (1997) *One Hundred Years of Socialism: The West European Left in the Twentieth Century*, London: Fontana Press

Schwartz, H. M. (2000) *States Versus Markets: The Emergence of a Global Economy*, 2nd edn, London: Palgrave

Seers, D. (1969) 'The meaning of development', *International Development Review*, 11(4): 2–6

Sen, A. (1990) 'Maurice Herbert Dobb', in J. Eatwell, M. Milgate and P. Newman (eds), *The New Palgrave Marxian Economics*, London: Macmillan

Wade, R. (2004) 'The ringmaster of Doha', *New Left Review*, 25: 146–52

Warren, B. (1980) *Imperialism: Pioneer of Capitalism*, London: Verso

Wuyts, M. (1992) 'Deprivation and public need', in M. Wuyts, M. Mackintosh and T. Hewitt (eds), *Development Policy and Public Action*, Oxford: Oxford University Press

7 | Journeying in radical development studies: a reflection on thirty years of researching pro-poor development

JOHN CAMERON

This piece describes my research journey from 1973 to 2003. It is intended to inform the reader about the shifts that have taken place in development studies over those thirty years as seen through my eyes. In that time, I have been privileged to have worked for significant periods in South Asia, the smaller South Pacific island countries and Ethiopia, and for briefer stretches of time in East and West Asia and other parts of sub-Saharan Africa. I have always been to the left in politics and get terribly angry about poverty, so I make no claims to have achieved, or even attempted to achieve, objective universality in this reflection. The epistemological virtues, if any, of this piece lie in being ontologically explicit, respectful of logic and sceptical of empirical claims to incontrovertible evidence.

The underlying theme is how poverty has been understood as a vital distinguishing feature of development studies as an area of research. It attempts an archaeology of the concept of poverty through digging down through the strata of my writing, though the presentation starts at the lowest strata. The archaeology reveals both change and continuity, though the emphasis here is on a cumulative continuity. There is much in the debates between liberals and radicals over basic needs in the 1970s that is recognizable today, both by aid technologists attempting to reach the Millennium Development Goals (MDGs) and Maoist guerrillas in the hills of Nepal. But there have been changes. The rise of neo-liberalism has touched everyone's lives and poverty, like everything else, will never be quite the same again. But to reflect further here would be to end a voyage before it has started. So, let us journey back in time when development studies and I were much younger.

This chapter traces a personal journey that has a public face. It aims to show the changes in both analysis and observation that I have undergone over thirty years of researching poverty and how these are reflected in my publications. But the journey proves to be more about add-ons than reversals, a process enriching the understanding of poverty.

The original context

Understanding change in the human condition in the early 1970s when I started field research in development studies can now be seen retrospectively as standing at a crossroads in a journey from post-Second World War optimism to millennial pessimism in terms of prospects for eradicating poverty. On the positive side, rational small farmers had been discovered in the 1960s and the informal sector was being explored in the mid-1970s, both of which discoveries gave greater respect to poorer people. In the mid-1970s, 'basic needs' was to acquire strategic status as a development concept. Unfortunately, the 1970s also saw the massive rise in international debt that would change the whole development debate in the 1980s.

Developmentally, the global economic 'long boom' between 1945 and 1970 ended with an economic whimper as the USA de-linked its currency from gold and a political bang as it faced military defeat in Vietnam. In poverty terms, statistics reported at the end of the First United Nations Development Decade in the 1960s suggested that the number of people in absolute poverty had actually risen in the previous ten years (Pearson 1969).

The independence 'honeymoon' of the first generation of post-war, former colonial states, notably in South Asia, was coming to a close as hard foreign exchange became scarcer. For mainstream development economists, a new era was opening with Social Cost–Benefit Analysis (SCBA) offering micro-economics methods for technically rationing resources (Little and Mirlees 1969). SCBA was capable of including poverty indirectly through giving labour a low shadow wage rate with implications for the location of more labour-intensive economic activities in areas of labour abundance and choice of labour-intensive techniques for all activities. More boldly, SCBA in radical hands could directly give added weight to costs and benefits attributed to the poor. But an element of judgement was required, and this was generally rejected by positivist economists.

Any inclusion of poverty in economics analysis was welcome as mainstream neo-classical economics was notoriously poverty-blind (Cameron 1992). But for wider development studies, the question was not so much how poverty could be included in analysis, but why so many people were poor. Importantly, the answers to this question were seen to lie in political economy and not in economics.

Political economy questioned the mainstream development research claim to be the apolitical technical handmaiden of post-colonial developmental states. A generation of radical researchers with no direct experience of colonial regimes was emerging in the West. They were strongly influenced by

Latin American experience of more than a century of 'flag' independence with continuing mass poverty. The 1959 Cuban revolution was seen as a potent claim against this history (Huberman and Sweezy 1961). Also, the more positive accounts of China's Cultural Revolution were giving a new lease of life to intellectual Marxism-Leninism for radicals in a generation that had been distanced from the Soviet Union by Hungary in 1956 and Czechoslovakia in 1968 (Robinson 1970).

It was in this intellectual atmosphere, though also equipped with the dry, rigorous tools of neo-classical economic analysis, and full of determination and with some trepidation, that I set off for Nepal with partner and child on New Year's Day 1974. The challenges and opportunities of being a member of a small, multi-disciplinary team on a well-funded, two-year research project lay ahead.

The mid-1970s: Marxian modes of production analysis

The aim of this section is to demonstrate the contribution that Marxian thought has made to development studies. Marxian methodology insists we look at how people are brought together in processes of production as an ontological foundation. Epistemologically, Marxian theorizing is dialectical in seeking out tensions and rejecting models of equilibrium. Marx claimed to have logically deduced that widespread poverty, seen in terms of insufficient consumption to reproduce a healthy human life, is intrinsic to the reproduction of the capitalist system as a mode of production. As the system is now global, that widespread poverty is now distributed globally. Interest in Marxian analysis in development studies peaked in the 1970s, but the principles described in this section still have relevance today, although the structuralism and associated lack of human agency have been tempered.

Neo-Marxian thought on political economy had a growing influence on development economics from 1955 to the late 1970s. Key texts included Paul Baran's political economy of growth (Baran 1968) and Gunder Frank's development of underdevelopment (Frank 1969). Other related thinkers could be found in South Asia and western Europe, including those of French Althusserianism, the UK New Left and the Frankfurt School and the Monthly Review school in the USA (Alavi 1972; Blackburn 1972, 1977; Braverman 1974; Godelier 1972; Marcuse 1964; Sweezy and Bettelheim 1971).

Marx bequeathed a rich set of texts on how to understand one particular mode of production – the capitalist mode of production. At the core was a logical model building up from the concept of the commodity relationship, through labour power as a commodity in relation to capital, economic exploitation and the relationship between capitals to a tendency towards systemic crisis in which class struggle could play a crucial political role. Supporting the logical model was a dense historical description of how capitalism came into ascendancy in the UK and how the interests of capital were moulding cultural and political institutions that would support the extended reproduction of capitalist relationships despite the tendency to crises (Marx 1954, 1964; Hilton 1976).

Marx also suggested a historical progression in which modes of production succeeded each other as their developmental potential was exhausted (Marx 1970). Transitions between modes of production were not rigorously described, but the idea gave a much-needed dynamic to the application of the modes of production model to Nepal, where capitalist development was very patchy and rural society tended to be seen in terms of a customary equilibrium as documented by cultural anthropology. In Nepal, with its limited experience of colonialism and numerous examples of non-capitalist economic practices, it was easy to think that a process of transition to capitalism was still taking place.

Confidence in neo-Marxian modes of production and transitions analysis underpinned two papers published in 1979 (Cameron 1979a, 1979b). These papers are the mere single-authored tip of an iceberg of continuing substantial co-authored writings that have resulted from twenty-five years of team research on Nepalese underdevelopment. Two of the original co-authored texts have been republished in South Asia after a gap of twenty years, suggesting some continuing relevance of the original neo-Marxian theoretical approach (Blaikie et al. 2002).

The 1979 papers use a modes of production/transition to capitalism analytical framework and organize both qualitative and quantitative empirical data to place two groups of unambiguously poor people – agricultural labourers and highway construction labourers – in the context of a late transition to capitalism. The style of analysis owes much to the writings of E. P. Thompson on an earlier transition to capitalism (Thompson 1968).

The papers attempt to describe people's economic experiences as complex combinations of feudal extraction, primitive capitalist accumulation and capitalist exploitation with the Nepalese state treated as playing a significant role in causing underdevelopment. The epistemological appeals are to rigorous logic and careful observation, plus recording 'voices' of the otherwise unheard experiences of these people. There is an element of forecasting in the papers, though this is very much in a radical pessimism vein of the long-term historical inevitability of oppressive and exploitative continuity, rather than potential immediate action, by the people themselves, to produce change.

Generally, modes of production and transitions analysis as an approach to poverty fell from grace in western European development studies in the late 1970s (later in South Asia). The foundations of the analysis were torn apart by a tendency to go into totally obscure abstraction or into naive empiricist description (Foster-Carter 1978). The 1979 papers can therefore claim to meet the specific and peculiar epistemological standards of modes of production analysis as a particular way of looking at processes of change. But more importantly they attempt to capture the lived political economy of being exploited and oppressed agricultural or highway construction labourers in Nepal in the mid-1970s, thus providing a historical account of lived experiences of poverty for which there is a very limited written record.

It is difficult for me to stand back from these papers in terms of their representation of lived lives, even after twenty-five years. The intellectual position is one of commitment, with a clear indignation that these people and their offspring would continue in poverty as a consequence of processes of underdevelopment in peripheral capitalism. In terms of predictive accuracy, the radical pessimism proved unfortunately accurate over the following twenty years (Cameron et al. 1998). The rise of a Maoist movement across Nepal in the following five years utilizes the same Marxian understanding of poverty that I used in the 1970s, though with much greater confidence in the agency of the poor.

The early 1980s: engaging with a potentially developmentalist state

The convention in development studies up until 1980 was to invest the state with a virtual monopoly of developmental agency. While the rest of society could be structurally analysed, the over-arching aim of research was to inform the present government or some more developmental future government on what it should do, notably to reduce poverty. This section describes such an engagement with a state that seemed to have genuine developmental potential, highlights the approach to development studies research implicit in such activity and explores the conditions needed for it to be effective and ethical. Development studies researchers still frequently engage with informing and advising governments, and why such engagement should be critical and have an exit option is examined in the following section.

Mainstream development studies has had a strong, if naive, tendency to treat the state as an effective anti-poverty agency. Cameron (1985b), writing on poverty in Fiji, can be seen as following that convention – although arguably more politically radical and historically sensitive. The article also follows the spirit of the Brandt Report in claiming to set a social democratic developmental, anti-poverty agenda (Brandt 1980).

In terms of a potentially benign, developmental role, the state in Fiji appeared more promising than most in the early 1980s. The country had received 'flag' independence in 1970 and the colonial inheritance had left a balanced external trading position with a reasonably sound government revenue base. The self-acknowledged primary task of the post-independence government was to reduce the greater inequities of colonial spending priorities. In 1982, when I arrived in Fiji to work as an EEC-funded consultant in the Central Planning Office, the economy had middle-income status globally and was still fiscally sound. Also, a mixture of prudence and good fortune (given the behaviour of world sugar market prices in the 1970s and access to the EEC market) meant that the economy was not heavily internationally indebted and had been little affected by the global hike in real interest rates in 1980.

Politically, Fiji had conducted general elections regularly since independence and there were active mass media, a trade union movement and customary institutions as indicators of a healthy civil society. Thus, the developmental challenges for the Fiji state were being widely discussed internally. A central debate involved the future of the schooling sector, where the tensions were apparent between advocates for education for labour market flexibility, planned 'manpower' requirements and effective citizenship (Cameron 1985a). A comparative approach was used to clarify the issues involved and show that the debate could not be resolved through 'technical' expertise but that wide public debate was necessary to seek a consensus (Cameron 2000b).

Poverty was a developmental issue in Fiji, though less widely debated as absolute poverty was virtually absent. A paper written in 1985 (Cameron 1985b) is my contribution to the poverty debate in Fiji for an academic audience. The paper shows the existence of poverty in Fiji at that time, even on the basis of a relatively 'generous' poverty line, and its policy manageability. Both quantitative survey evidence and more qualitative insights from policy records were used to demonstrate that the colonial inheritance in terms of welfare policy was proving less and less adequate in meeting equity-justifiable claims for public assistance. Technical economics and discursive techniques were also combined in an effort to bring authority and understanding to policy processes.

Understanding the role of ethnicity is vital to any research in Fiji. The 1970 constitution had embedded ethnic difference deeply in the political system by making it a formal factor in the electoral system. Cameron (1987a), in an explicit attempt to contribute to greater ethnic understanding, applied the type of production analysis that underpinned the Nepalese writing (though less explicitly than in the papers on Nepalese agricultural and highway building labourers). The paper shows how a distinctive Fiji-Indian/Indo-Fijian society,

143

worthy of respect as an indigenous creation, had lifted itself out of poverty in the 1920s and 1930s. The socio-economic form of production and pattern of life that were a consequence of their specific experiences in Fiji further legiti-mized their claim to national identity.

In an attempt to contribute to conceptualizations of development and pov-erty as a whole-life experience, I combined demographic and economic status data with Active Life Profiles to indicate societies' developmental status across time and space (Cameron 1987b). These profiles were intended to be an alter-native, or at least a supplement, to GNP per capita as a developmental indica-tor. They also lent themselves to ethnic and gender comparisons, both of which were important to Fiji's development debates, and allowed comparisons to be made internationally and within Fiji. As with more direct poverty analysis, the results suggested that the ethnic groups had different experiences, but were not simply rankable in terms of inequality. They also suggested that lived lives in Fiji for ethnic groups and genders were different from lives in Hong Kong and Malaysia, with their own merits and weaknesses. As with the other papers in this period, the argument was not seeking a technical closure of debate, but a contribution to better-informed debate in a lively, open polity.

Together these four papers represent efforts to bridge academic epistemo-logical standards and policy processes in discussing poverty. But this was at a time when the intellectual iceberg of global neo-liberalism was drifting closer to the islands and threatening to freeze all meaningful debate on poverty and inequality. They can be academically criticized as being too engaged with, and one-sided on, the ongoing policy debates in Fiji, but both the data and their analysis have proven sufficiently resilient to be acceptable as a basis of a more recent publication (Cameron 2000c).

Later 1980s: malign external hands and neo-liberal resource allocation priorities

In many circumstances, development studies, with its focus on poverty, must recognize that it faces a situation where effective agency lies beyond the national, let alone the local, level, and damage to people's lives is being done at such a distance that accountability has lost any meaning. The global order has never been a Westphalian system of sovereign states meeting on level ground. In the last fifty years, state sovereignty has become even more a relative, rather than absolute, quality. The papers in this section place the cause of poverty, and a national inability to do anything about it, in the global domain. The analysis is not about lack of 'aid' – in one case there was arguably too much 'aid' – but instead focuses on political judgements in the interests of an outside agency. In such circumstances, understanding the situation of the poor and vulnerable of one country requires engagement with decisions over which they would have no control, even under a democratic national system of politics. The relevance of this form of analysis to the current global situation should not need further explanation.

The process of debating poverty and inequality in Fiji was fundamentally changed by two military coups in 1987. Elsewhere in the Pacific region at almost the same moment, the Federated States of Micronesia (FSM) were coming to 'flag' independence after a forty-year period of UN trusteeship under the USA. In the following few years in South Asia, Pakistan returned to full electoral politics at the same time as it ceased to be a cold war front-line state with the withdrawal of the USSR's troops from Afghanistan.

In all three cases, developmental research on poverty was being strongly influenced by external agencies. The context for conducting research was not being left to national governments, whether formally more democratic or more authoritarian. The willingness of the Bretton Woods institutions (hereafter IFIs) to intervene in national macro-development strategy and micro-policy decisions grew in the 1980s and has been widely documented (Banuri 1991; Mosley et al. 1991; Petras 1997). The IFIs were directing economies down a one-way street of liberalization and deprioritizing poverty analysis, and international indebtedness was a vital element in their capacity to influence policy in most cases.

Neither FSM nor Fiji was particularly indebted. Even Pakistan, which was heavily foreign-debt-exposed in the early 1980s and had signed a sequence of structural adjustment agreements with the IFIs, came under real pressure to fully implement these only after the withdrawal of Soviet troops from Afghanistan in 1989. In all three cases, the process of liberalization was not simply an economic process but had implications for wider debates on multi-dimensional deprivation and vulnerability.

Cameron (1993a) analyses the background to the Fiji coups of 1987 using conventional tools of political economy in terms of class analysis. The elite post-colonial political inheritors were becoming increasingly exposed to criticism as being uncaring and corrupt. Therefore, the emergence of a new opposition party, the Fiji Labour Party, building on the trade union movement, had a historical logic, and its alternative economic strategy, entitled 'clean and caring', included a greater concern with deprivation and inequality. The 1987 general election, however, which the Labour Party-led opposition won, was too close in terms of votes, and perhaps too early in terms of the political development of the party, to give a clear mandate for an alternative economic development strategy. The IFIs had been pushing the Fiji government towards liberalization with some success in the mid-1980s, but their leverage had proved relatively weak. More ominously for the new government, however, the year 1987 was a peak year for the Reagan regime in the USA in terms of both liberalizing economics and cold war politics.

The new Fiji government was committed both to more economic intervention and a non-nuclear South Pacific. In the Pentagon model of the world at that time, there were only 'ours' and 'theirs' and the newly elected Fiji government was not unproblematically 'ours'. The leader of the first military coup was rapidly recognized by the USA as Fiji's legitimate political leader with no disturbance to bilateral economic and political relations. I argue (Cameron 1993a) that these anti-democratic forces had to usurp state power as they were losing the rational debate with their deceptions/corruption unmasked and the only remaining option was conspiratorial coercion and violence. In summary, the exploration of an alternative pro-poor development path in Fiji was overridden by a combination of internal and external anti-democratic forces, and a development studies researcher concerned with poverty had no place in the new order.

In an article in 1991 I describe the creation of FSM as a complex process from late colonization to decolonization in which conspiracy is seen as playing only a minor role – more an unintended, developmental disaster. The sideswipes of other people's agendas, notably post-Second World War confusion over cultural 'modernization' and the 'Great Society' experiment in the USA in the 1960s, washed over the islands, drowning autonomous economic, cultural and political developmental potential, although welfarism meant that absolute poverty was absent. United Nations indignation finally brought FSM into existence in 1987 as a by-product of a more general agenda of late decolonization. The underdevelopment of FSM was unmasked at the moment of independence, and the only clear option to escape long-term, structural poverty lay in mass migration to the USA. Understanding the relationship between continuing poverty and migration became a feature of development studies in the 1990s. Indeed, in FSM it was the risk of descent into poverty as a consequence of loss of superpower patronage which shaped the relationship.

Cameron (1997a) engages with another national development disaster in the shape of Pakistan, where absolute poverty is rife. The paper suggests that in every developmental dimension Pakistan is either a well-documented failure or the statistics suggesting non-failure are dubious.

While Pakistan was a front-line cold war state with Soviet troops in Afghanistan, the West was willing to accept the corruption and violence that were blighting so many people's lives in Pakistan. This relationship has now been given new life under the slogan of the 'war against terrorism'. Structural adjustment agreements were signed with the IFIs, but poor implementation was forgiven and 'Official Development Assistance' ensured there was sufficient foreign exchange to maintain Pakistan's military spending. With the Soviet Union out of Afghanistan and then imploding, the IFIs were given more room to insist that structural adjustment conditionalities were implemented.

The paper argues that a consequent concentration on privatization has diverted developmental priorities and energy away from anti-poverty policies. The high profile given to privatization is due to its relative convenience for both the IFIs and the national government as an institutional gambit that can be isolated from more difficult, delicate matters. It has also proved conveniently corruptible for powerful private interests in Pakistan, giving much opportunity for Byzantine relationships with transnational corporations (TNCs) in which the interests of the mass of the population in Pakistan, especially the vast majority of women, are at best sidelined, at worst damaged.

The early 1990s: thinking development anew, ancient and postmodern

This section reflects on the ideology that has underpinned the view that poverty should not be a subject for serious research since the advent of social Darwinism in the mid-nineteenth century. The argument varies from the claim that the poor are economically (and socially and politically) inadequate to the position that poverty is a normative concept inaccessible to positivist science. Development studies has given little credibility to such views, but it ignores these arguments at its intellectual peril, especially when they are advanced by people in power. Despite the claim that the Washington consensus of the IFIs has ended and hence neo-liberalism is no longer hegemonic in these institutions, there is a continuing need to confront those who dismiss poverty as a valid field of research.

Neo-liberalism is an ideological force upon which every development studies researcher has had to reflect since the 1980s. Much effort has gone into denying neo-liberalism's claim to have arrived at 'the end of history' (Fukuyama 1992) and, with that, the end of poverty by allowing market forces to determine the distribution of everything. Every less developed economy has experienced increasing inequality despite the end-of-transition promise of neo-liberalism, and its attendant neo-classical economics, to abolish poverty. This promise is not based on careful empirical studies, but emerges logically from ontological claims drawn from philosophy and economics. Only once these claims are critiqued and exposed can a space be created for alternatives to be proposed.

The following discussion focuses on articles that attempt to meet neo-liberalism on its own ideological territory.

Cameron (1992) starts from the basic premises of neo-classical economics and connects them to the wider philosophical propositions of liberal individualism in order to demonstrate the ideological foundations of neo-liberalism and the subsequent formulation of structural adjustment policy packages. The paper argues that this philosophically holistic neo-liberal model is a formidable, but nevertheless relativistic, intellectual position. It can claim to be rational (in the sense of logically rigorous), realistic (in terms of empirical non-falsification and some appeal to describe positive and negative experiences), and regulatory (clear policy recommendations) but it cannot claim to be universal in any of these dimensions.

Therefore, a major challenge for those who feel uncomfortable with the neo-liberal position is to construct an alternative intellectual reality that is equally comprehensive in its rationality, realism and regulatory dimensions. This argument suggests that the Adjustment with a Human Face (AHF) position associated with UNICEF (Cornia et al. 1987), though laudable in intention, falls short of meeting this challenge. AHF concentrates on the realism dimension by marshalling empirical evidence that children have failed to thrive under structural adjustment regimes. This was an embarrassment for the neo-liberal position, but not deeply intellectually damaging. The AHF case is therefore vulnerable to being reduced to a temporary qualification to the neo-liberal position. Arguably AHF in practice took the form of add-on compensatory social dimensions to structural adjustment packages.

Cameron (1992) suggests that a full alternative to neo-liberalism needs to start from a clear alternative ontological position. It proposes a modification to the Kantian categorical imperative of a universal right to non-deception and non-coercion as such a rigorous alternative. From this perspective, the greatest obstacles to reducing poverty arise from deception and coercion in any of their many guises. For instance, corruption and threats to security not only ruin lives in themselves, but also undermine confidence and close routes to escape poverty. Poverty decreases in a society when the degree of deception and coercion experienced by people decreases. Neo-liberal claims that the more a society is based on market principles the less poverty there will be can then be assessed in terms of whether people feel confident in their day-to-day lives as well as their levels of consumption. These ideas are worked upon further in a later paper (Cameron 1999b).

The intended effect of these papers is to undermine neo-liberal claims to be the universal development theory and neo-classical economics a value-neutral, scientific approach to resource allocation and to restore a concern with poverty as a central intellectual issue.

The mid-1990s: closely observing poverty

This section is concerned with the empirics of poverty. Poverty is multi-dimensional and impossible to capture with a single indicator. In addition, many of the indicators advanced for estimating poverty are either difficult to observe or liable to substantial inaccuracies in observation. The papers in this section offer positive ways forward to observe poverty without falling into the quantitative versus qualitative debates or 'magic bullet' choices that have bedevilled choices of methodologies.

Poverty is a complex concept that opens up a wide potential for observation. The intention to know poverty from direct observation drove my research in Nepal in the mid-1970s. The opportunity to collect and, where necessary, re-gather large amounts of primary data over an eighteen-month period resulted in an appreciation of the information cycle from variable conceptualization and sampling design through collection, processing, analysis and reporting. The potential for errors and inaccuracies at each stage in the cycle, and how earlier errors can feed through to later stages, was learned the hard way at first hand. Conventional statistical concerns with significance in relation to sampling error were discovered to be only one form of error, and often relatively unimportant. Therefore the data, interpretations and conclusions were self-critically and reflectively sieved for possible errors and inaccuracies and subjected to tests of robustness.

The immediate responses to AHF after 1987 were social policy add-ons to structural adjustment programmes, provided they could be justified in terms of poverty and/or gender impact. But such evidence was hard to find given the erosion of standardized national survey and livelihoods data collection in the 1980s and demands for data on fiscal matters and financial flows rather than for poverty measurements. Alongside increasing quantitative survey data, however, there was a revival of interest in ethnographic methods (encouraged by increasing academic interest in gender analysis and postmodernism). This revival of theoretical interest in qualitative data was of special interest to NGOs. They were particularly interested in using Participatory Rural Appraisal as an approach to understanding the lives of poorer people in a more empathetic, locally sensitive manner.

Cameron (1993b) was a general reflection on these issues and Cameron (1996) represents an attempt to resolve some of these issues in practice in Bangladesh, building upon similar, but more extended, research in Pakistan

(Cameron and Irfan 1991). The study of Bangladesh combines quantitative, large-scale, standard Labour Force Survey data with more qualitative data. The tabulated survey data are adapted to provide more sensitive insights into time use and gender issues and make them more compatible with local, qualitative data.

The difficulties of combining limited quantitative and qualitative data under great time pressure to monitor and understand processes of change and observe and evaluate the impact of development agency interventions are a continuing challenge in poverty analysis. Keeping a healthy tension between rigorous thinking and careful observing is a fundamental epistemological challenge in pro-poor research.

The late 1990s: back to basics

In this section I trace responses to the re-emergence of concern with chronic human vulnerabilty in the 1990s. The emergence of HIV/Aids as a developmental challenge was paralleled by increasing existentialist concern with mortality as a developmental as well as a philosophical issue (Lyotard 1991). One direction of response is into relativism; another leads to social theorizing on unifying basics of human material existence – time, energy and space, and reproduction, morbidity and mortality.

Therefore some of the papers written between 1994 and 2000 (Cameron 1994, 1997b, 1998 and 2000c) can be seen as fundamentally concerned with people's bodies in terms of accessing sources of energy and ways of understanding use of time and energy in economic activity. This concern can be understood in the post-cold war historical conjuncture of the late 1980s and early 1990s, with its image of an 'impasse' in development studies (Booth 1985) and the rise of anti-development thinking (Escobar 1995). The 'back to basics' element found in these publications was also present in much of my consultancy work at this time, including famine prevention in Ethiopia and human reproduction interventions in Ghana and Pakistan. In similar vein, I was responsible for closing an ILO project in Burma/Myanmar in response to evidence of widespread physiological abuse by agents of the government. Thus, development studies and development policies appeared to be increasingly concerned with dealing with people whose very existence was under threat.

In 1998 I re-engaged with the fundamentals of absolute poverty in terms of chronic food insecurity and returned to Nepal. I worked as an FAO-funded poverty and food insecurity consultant contributing to the Asian Development Bank-funded Agricultural Perspective Plan (APP), looking forward fifteen years to 2010. The underlying approach was to combine water and transport infrastructure development with neo-liberal confidence in open market forces and small farmer short-term profit-seeking. Poorer households and women were to benefit from the trickle-down of supply side and demand side linkages, as described by Mellor (1976). Unfortunately for the APP and most people in Nepal, the evidence of the twenty years since my first fieldwork in rural Nepal in the 1970s did not suggest significant changes in rural lives, especially in poorer households and for women (Cameron et al. 1998). Consequently I described an alternative model of change, and continuity, in rural Nepal and made the case for direct action to reduce poverty and food insecurity and conserve the physical environment (Cameron 1998).

In Cameron (2000c) I returned to my work on poverty in Fiji in the 1980s, whose continuing relevance was reflected by being cited in a report on poverty in the late 1990s (UNDP and Government of Fiji 1997), and adopted neo-Kantian thinking on violence and deception as a conceptual basis for understanding poverty. The management of cross-ethnic relationships is put forward as a basic development challenge in Fiji, requiring resources to be prioritized for social policy if social tension, with its negative effects on the psychological quality of life and threat to the physiological quality of life, is to be reduced.

This focus on improved health and concern with management of the state of the human body has postmodernist resonance (e.g. in the works of Foucault). The critical pressure from environmentalists on the great developmental meta-narrative of modernism and its theme of inevitable progress has forced theorization of development studies back towards the physical and human physiology with its vulnerability to damage and death. Ensuring environmental conditions for better human health is a valid poverty focus and arguably should be at the centre of development thinking and practice. But such prioritization runs the risk of reducing the development discourse to technocratic management of the physical environment and human bodies. Basing development thinking on the care and maintenance of the human body has to take into account that poor people possess self-awareness and a capacity for choice as agents, albeit in the face of much uncertainty.

The present looking to the future

The journey described so far can be summarized as follows:

- a starting point in neo-Marxist modes of production analysis with an explicit concern with the concept of a structurally exploited, poorer class in an uncertain transition to capitalism with a developmentally ineffective regime;

- working in the context of a complex economy with the concept of poverty to inform a developmentally more effective regime with a potential for further reform;
- critiquing external interventions when they are either masquerading as technical economic advice or claiming to defend individual liberty as an ultimate universal developmental 'good' and decentring poverty as a conceptual and policy concern;
- challenging the neo-classical economics foundations of neo-liberalism/ structural adjustment to reveal its non-universalist nature and the possibility of a rational alternative with poverty as a central concern;
- meeting the methodological/empirical challenges of data shortages and fragmentation with respect to poverty;
- drawing a universalist physiological bottom line to poverty under the wider development discourse as a partial response to postmodern relativism.

Although each step in this journey has its own distinctive identity, there is also a cumulative fundamental continuity in the relationship between development studies and poverty research. This is based on the continuity of positive and normative ontological stances, teleology, observation and ethics.

Positive or normative ontological positions are distinguished by the degree of the researcher's detachment or commitment to a specific ideological position. Research on poverty is shaped by wider development policy processes, commitments and conditions set by funding and implementing agencies. For example, a researcher needs resources for fieldwork and, in development research, these resources rarely come without implicit or explicit judgements on what constitutes poverty in the human condition. It is possible to maintain a consistent ontological stance, however. My own resarch has been committed to the improvement in the quality of life of specific groups of people and is consistently sceptical of the proposition that open market forces are the sole means to diminish poverty.

There is a continuing concern not to specify development processes in terms of a closed future that is analytically inevitable or evaluatively desirable. Although the papers presented here are not particularly teleological in vision, they do tend to be pessimistic and most do allow room for human agency. For example, the continuing influence of Marxism in my work has been more concerned with the crisis-ridden uncertainty of capitalism than the inevitability of socialism.

In terms of observations of poverty, the quantitative data in my research acknowledge that likely total errors of plus or minus 20 per cent would leave the conclusions largely intact. The continuing sympathy to denser, local, more ethnographic methodologies originated in my early Nepalese fieldwork, which involved careful local observation and listening to people in villages. Efforts to combine quantitative and qualitative methodologies are evident in much of the research as is a scepticism of the accuracy of large-scale surveys and the representativeness of larger populations in small scale studies.

Another continuing concern has been with research ethics. In Nepal in the 1970s, respondents had to be protected from the state. I argue that poverty research must always be concerned with the vulnerabilities of the people who are being researched. Later this was extended to the right not to be deceived as part of the Kantian categorical imperative applied to research data collection and use.

As to the future of poverty research in development studies, Amartya Sen raises issues of valuation of well-being in a wide-ranging development ethics framework. He also resists epistemological closure of debates arguing that the responsibility of research is to inform debate, not offer solutions (Cameron 2000b). The New Institutional Economics combines analysis of collective agency, acting under conditions of uncertainty, with useful models of the costs that give historical continuity, including that of the reproduction of poverty (Cameron 1999a; Cameron and Ndhlovu 1999; Cameron 2000a). Livelihoods analysis at its best attempts to grasp the totality of lived lives, including a civil society and social wealth dimension (Cameron 1999a), though this last point is not without its critics (Fine 1999).

The unifying principles acknowledge the importance of seeing human beings in poverty as constrained agents collectively making history, not necessarily under conditions of their own choosing. The future for an even more intellectually inclusive discourse on poverty in development studies may be found in further adding on to previous thinking and observing of poverty. The journey continues.

References

Alavi, H. (1972) 'The state in postcolonial societies: Pakistan and Bangladesh', *New Left Review*, 74

Banuri, B. T. (1991) 'Introduction', in T. Banuri (ed.), *Economic Liberalization: No Panacea: The Experiences of Latin America and Asia*, Oxford: Clarendon Press

Baran, P. (1968) *The Political Economy of Growth*, New York: Monthly Review Press

Blackburn, R. (ed.) (1972) *Ideology in Social Science*, London: Fontana

— (ed.) (1977) *Revolution and Class Struggle*, London: Fontana

Blaikie, P. M., J. Cameron and J. D. Seddon (2002) 'Understanding 20 years of change in West-Central Nepal: continuity and change in lives and ideas', *World Development*, 30(7): 1255–69

Booth, D. (1985) 'Marxism and development sociology: interpreting the impasse', *World Development*, 13(7): 761–87

Brandt, W. (1980) *North–South: A Programme for Survival*, London: Pan

Braverman, H. (1974) *Labour and Monopoly Capital*, London and New York: Monthly Review Press

Cameron, J. (1979a) 'Agricultural labourers', in J. D. Seddon (ed.), *Peasants and Workers in Nepal*, Warminster: Aris and Phillips, pp. 105–26

— (1979b) 'Highway construction labourers', in J. D. Seddon (ed.), *Peasants and Workers in Nepal*, Warminster: Aris and Phillips, pp. 127–44

— (1985a) 'The nature of, and reponses to, growing unemployment among young people in Fiji', in R. Fiddy (ed.), *Sixteen Years to Life: National Strategies for Youth Unemployment*, Brighton: Falmer Press, pp. 194–204

— (1985b) 'Destitute allowance vs family assistance: conflict over welfare labels in Fiji', *Development and Change*, 16: 485–502

— (1987a) 'A note on the history of the sugar sector in Fiji: "peasantization under capitalism"', *Peasant Studies*, 14(3): 211–19

— (1987b) 'Assessing the quality of life for women and men in Fiji using Active Life Profile Analysis', *Journal of Pacific Studies*, 13: 80–93

— (1991) 'Economic development options for the Federated States of Micronesia at independence', *Pacific Studies*, 14(4): 35–69

— (1992) 'Adjusting Structural Adjustment: getting beyond the UNICEF compromise', in P. Mosley (ed.), *Development Finance and Policy Reform*, Basingstoke: Macmillan, pp. 291–309

— (1993a) 'A political economy of market-led Structural Adjustment, a case-study of Fiji', *Journal of International Development*, 5(2): 123–33

— (1993b) 'The challenges for M&E in the 1990s', *Project Appraisal*, 8(2): 91–6

— (1994) 'A policy framework for enabling productive employment in Pakistan in the 1990s', in J. Cameron et al. (eds), *Poverty and Power: The Role of Institutions and the Market in Development*, Delhi: Oxford University Press, pp. 227–44

— (1995a) 'The impact of IMF and World Bank policy stances on the economic planning debates in India', *Pakistan Journal of Applied Economics*, XI(1&2): 153–65

— (1995b) 'Development thought and discourse analysis: a case-study of Nepal', in K. Bahadur and M. P. Lama (eds), *New Perspectives on India–Nepal Relations*, New Delhi: Har-Anand, pp. 215–23

— (1996) 'The challenge of combining quantitative and qualitative methods in labour force and livelihoods analysis: a case-study of Bangladesh', *Journal of International Development*, 8(5): 625–53

— (1997a) 'Privatization and the real economic development problems of Pakistan', *Journal of Asia Pacific Economy*, 2(2): 239–49

— (1997b) 'Public policy for a better nourished, healthier South Pacific population consistent with sustainable environments', in B. Burt (ed.), *Environment and Development in the Pacific Islands*, Australia: National Centre for Development Studies and University of Papua New Guinea Press, pp. 218–38

— (1998) 'The Agriculture Perspective Plan: the need for debate', *Himalayan Research Bulletin*, XVIII(2): 11–14

— (1999a) *Trivial Pursuits: Reconciling Sustainable Rural Development and the Global Economic Institutions*, London: IIED/DFID

— (1999b) 'Kant's categorical imperative as a foundation for development studies and action', *European Journal of Development Research* 11(2): 23–43

— (2000a) 'Development economics, the new institutional economics and NGOs', *Third World Quarterly*, 21(4): 627–35

— (2000b) 'Amartya Sen on economic inequality: the need for an explicit critique of opulence', *Journal of International Development*, 12: 15

— (2000c) 'Confronting social policy challenges in Fiji', in A. H. Akram-Lodhi (ed.), *Confronting Fiji Futures*, Canberra: Asia Pacific Press, pp. 133–51

Cameron, J. and M. Irfan (1991) *Enabling People to Help Themselves: An Employment and Human Resources Strategy for Pakistan in the 1990s*, Geneva: ILO-ARTEP/World Employment Programme

Cameron, J. and T. P. Ndhlovu (1999) 'Keynes and the distribution of uncertainty: lessons from the Lancashire spinning industry and the General Theory', *Review of Social Economy*, LVII(1): 99–123

Cameron, J. with P. M. Blaikie and J. D. Seddon (1998) 'Patterns of change in Western Nepal: rural households of the 1970s and 1990s compared', *Himalayan Research Bulletin*, XVIII(2): 15–21

Cornia, G., R. Jolly and F. Stewart (1987) *Adjustment with a Human Face*, vols 1 and 2, *Protecting the Vulnerable* and *Promoting Growth*, Oxford: Clarendon Press

Escobar, A. (1995) *Encountering Development: The Making and Unmaking of the Third World*, Princeton, NJ: Princeton University Press

Fine, B. (1999) 'The developmental state is dead – long live social capital?', *Development and Change*, 30: 1–19

Foster-Carter, A. (1978) 'The modes of production debate', *New Left Review*, 107: 7–78

Frank, A. G. (1969) *Capitalism and Underdevelopment in Latin America*, London and New York: Monthly Review Press

Fukuyama, F. (1992) *The End of History and the Last Man*, New York: Free Press

Godelier, M. (1972) *Rationality and Irrationality in Economics*, London: New Left Books (New York: Monthly Review Press, 1975)

Hilton, R. (ed.) (1976) *The Transition from Feudalism to Capitalism*, London: New Left Books (New York: Schocken Books, 1977)

Huberman, L. and P. M. Sweezy (1961) *Cuba: Anatomy of a Revolution*, New York: Monthly Review Press

Little, I. M. D. and J. Mirlees (1969) *Manual of Industrial Project Analysis in Developing Economies: Social Cost–Benefit Analysis*, Paris: OECD

Lyotard, J. (1991) *Inhuman*, New York: Polity Press

Marcuse, H. (1964) *One Dimensional Man*, London: Routledge & Kegan Paul (Boston, MA: Beacon Press, 1964)

Marx, K. (1954) *Capital*, London: Lawrence & Wishart

— (1964) *Pre-capitalist Economic Formations*, London: Lawrence and Wishart

— (1970) *A Contribution to the Critique of Political Economy*, Moscow: Progress Publishers (New York: International Publishers' Co., 1971)

Mellor, J. (1976) *The New Economics of Growth*, Ithaca, NY: Cornell University Press

Mosley, P., J. Harrigan and J. Toye (eds) (1991) *Aid and Power: The World Bank and Policy-based Lending*, vol. 1, *Analysis and Policy Proposals*, London: Routledge

Pearson, L. (1969) *Partners in Development*, London: Praeger

Petras, J. (1997) 'Alternatives to neoliberalism in Latin America', *Latin American Perspectives*, 24(1): 80–91

Robinson, J. (1970) *The Cultural Revolution in China*, Harmondsworth: Penguin

Sweezy, P. M. and C. Bettelheim (1971) *On the Transition to Socialism*, New York and London: Monthly Review Press

Thompson, E. P. (1968) *The Making of the English Working Class*, Harmondsworth: Penguin (New York: Random House, 1966)

UNDP and Government of Fiji (1997) *Fiji Poverty Report*, Suva: Government Printer

8 | The rise and rise of gender and development

RUTH PEARSON

Few would doubt the success of 'gender and development' both as an intellectual project and as a lens for viewing development analysis and practice. Gender talk is everywhere – mainstreaming gender into all development policy and practice, targeting women's practical and strategic needs, developing gender-participatory budgets, celebrating the high participation of women in micro-credit initiatives, lamenting women's susceptibility to the HIV/Aids pandemic, celebrating women's key role in population policies and family planning, foregrounding women's rights in the new development turn to a rights-based development approach. The success of gender and development is also reflected within the academic and other institutions that provide student courses and qualifications both at masters level and in terms of professional training. In addition gender and development research activities have mushroomed in recent years with increasing numbers of academics (the vast majority women researchers) being employed in the research institutes and development studies centres in the UK, western Europe, sub-Saharan Africa, Asia and Latin America, and to some extent in North America also. In the UK the Institute for Development Studies' (IDS) pioneering MA in gender and development established in 1986 was followed by the postgraduate gender programme at the University of East Anglia in 1991. Since that date a number of other development studies institutions at, for example, the London School of Economics (LSE), Manchester, Leeds, Wolverhampton, Warwick, Swansea, Reading and Wolverhampton have run postgraduate courses and/or shorter professional training courses in the area of gender and development (see Development Association Guide, <www.dsa.org.uk>).

Given this exponential growth in the area we can argue that, in many ways, gender and development has 'arrived'. In its beginnings some thirty or more years ago, gender issues were seen as a feminist diversion from the real issues of poverty and modernization which preoccupied development planning and thinking. As in the social analysis and policy of Northern countries, there was an ongoing struggle to include women's experiences, interests and marginalization as central issues for analysis rather than specialist minority interests for feminists and fanatics. And while the parallel examination of men's gender identities and interests is still in its infancy (see White 1993) the inclusion of the study of men and masculinity is increasing even if it has yet to claim a lot of mainstream (male) attention (Pearson 2000).

Just as the development world has had to accept the inevitable collision/collusion with 'globalization' as an analytical category or an (un)welcome prescriptive policy, the role of women in the production of internationally traded goods and services, from non-traditional agricultural exports to garments and electronics goods as well as computer-related services such as data entry and call centre operations, has become undeniable (Pearson 1998). And although football, the ultimate global phenomenon, has not yet become gender equitable, women's contribution to the manufacturing of sports clothing and footwear (trainers) highlights the pivotal role of women in the global economy (Oxfam 2004). From a marginal positionality which had initially to argue the case for visibility and inclusion, the central role of women in the world economy as well as the development process has been established beyond doubt.

This chapter will trace the trajectory of gender and development from its institutional and academic beginnings to its ubiquitous positioning in development studies at the present time. It will trace the intellectual journey of gender and development from critical intervention to mainstream policy. It will then problematize some of the difficulties in moving gender and development studies forward within the context of both the postmodern post-development turn in (some) academic writing in the field as well as the institutional pressures to dissolve gender within a more generalized category of (in)equality. And finally, the chapter will draw attention to the ways in which radical gender analysis has yet to be acknowledged in key sites of development analysis and policy within the global context of development, in spite of its apparent success in terms of institutional development practice.

The birth of gender

From when can we date the history (radical or otherwise) of gender and development? The general consensus places the birth of gender and development in 1970 with the publication of Ester Boserup's path-breaking volume on 'Women's Role in Economic Development' (1970) (see Pearson 1992 for further discussion on origins). While the voluminous literature in the field since that date has revealed this book as over-general and not informed by anthropological or local research, it remains emblematic because it placed women – as new subjects – into development, and heralded the development of a new field of both research and activity in the years of the UN's first development decade and beyond (Emerij et al. 2001).

From the point of view of feminist scholarship the concern of gender analysts engaging with the analytical and policy arenas of the burgeoning development institutions of the time was to insist that, first, women were beneficiaries and participants in the modernist development cooperation that was the optimistic order of the day. This desire, which was characterized as the 'WID' (Women in Development) position, was fuelled by a number of different, and perhaps parallel, political influences. First, there were the anti-colonial struggles in the global South which were supported by, and echoed in, the anti-imperialist movements in the North, linked to the opposition to the Vietnam war during the late 1960s and the first half of the 1970s. Second, there were the student uprisings of 1968, which mobilized a whole generation of young people who had benefited from the expansion of tertiary education in the boom years of the post-war period, and who were anxious to assert their political as well as economic independence from their parents' generation. Third, there was the civil rights movement, in the United States and in Ireland, which claimed the right of self-determination and freedom from discrimination for currently suppressed minorities and marginal groups. And last but not least these were the years of the renascent second wave of feminism, which was sweeping both politically radical women and young professional women into its sway, demanding equality of opportunity with men as well as support from the state for women to accomplish their dual roles in production and reproduction.

Given the heady times, it is not surprising that the politicization of educated youth and the renaissance of feminism should have provoked a reaction among those committed to pursuing development assistance in the poorer parts of the world. Women in the global North, both professional women working in development agencies as well as academics and researchers, were influenced by one or more of these factors. The more politically radical chose activism in anti-imperialist/solidarity movements of the burgeoning non-governmental organizations (NGOs), and/or combined their radicalism with academic writing and research. This wing of the gender and development movement was intrinsically committed to ongoing solidarity and cooperation with their counterparts, organizations and academics, in the South. It was no accident that the first UK-based international conference on gender and development, which was organized by the SOW (Subordination of Women) collective at the Institute for Development Studies in September 1978, comprised sixty international feminists of whom UK-based individuals were restricted to 25 per cent of the total (Whitehead 1979). This followed what was perhaps the first international academic meeting on gender and development organized in the North, which took place at Wellesley in 1976 (Wellesley Editorial

Committee 1977). Interestingly the two conferences reflected different political approaches; the Wellesley meeting was under the title of 'Women and National Development', very much reflecting the post-liberation struggles of the 1960s and 1970s, whereas the later one at the University of Sussex was focused on the tension within gender and international development policy and analysis between the 'particular and the universal in terms of unequal gender relations', in opposition to the universal and inaccurate use of 'patriarchy' that was more widespread at the time (Pearson et al. 1984: x).

Those who aspired to a career, or at least a job, in the UN multilateral or the increasing number of bilateral development agencies tended to adopt a more equality-based position, arguing that women should get a fair share of development assistance, preferably in ring-fenced funding for women-targeted projects. An early and unreplicated expression of this position was the Percy Amendment of 1973. Senator Percy, a Republican representative, sponsored an amendment of the US Foreign Assistance Act of 1961. The amendment required US bilateral assistance to 'integrate women into the economies of developing countries'. The USAID later formulated a specific WID policy in 1982 which mandates that country strategies, programmes, projects and reporting documents explicitly involve women; identify benefits and impediments to participation; establish sex-disaggregated benchmarks to measure women's participation and benefits from development; and ensure that contractors address gender issues in their work for USAID (Tinker 1990).

Integrating gender into development analysis and planning

The technical or equality-based approach to women's participation or integration into development activities, described above, continues to characterize many development agency approaches to gender issues. Initially most of the gender and development interventions undertaken by development agencies concerned economic participation and/or income generation for women. While WID has been reclothed as 'GAD', gender analysis in development, reflecting the analytical insistence that women's gender position is a relational one (in comparison with men's) as well as a concrete condition reflecting the reality of being female in a poverty and underdeveloped situation (see Young 1988), the priority of 'integrating women into development' has remained the objective of development agencies. They have accepted the centrality of women's contribution to development activity and the desirability of enhancing both the potential of women's productive activity and the benefits to women and their reproductive responsibilities of development expenditure and progress.

The political dynamic behind the integration of gender into development planning meant that technical staff of development agencies welcomed a translation of what might be seen as quite conceptual and complicated gender analysis into terms and frameworks that could be applied to gender-focused development activities. This is why the gender interests framework developed by Molyneux (1985) was transformed by Moser into a gender needs framework (Moser 1989, 1993), which became widely disseminated during the 1990s.

Molyneux's contribution to understanding the parallel and complex policy and political arenas into which gender equity and feminist analysis were being applied was to deconstruct a general notion of gender issues. She conceptualized the gender interests of women and men in terms of two categories: practical gender interests and strategic gender interests. In terms of this distinction, the practical gender interests of poor women frequently translated into the desire for resources, services and infrastructure to support their role in reproductive activities, such as clean water, access to primary health facilities, occupation-related training, adequate housing and a safe local environment. This distinction, formulated in terms of analysing the ways in which women had been mobilized in support of the Nicaraguan revolution, which Molyneux claimed had not addressed issues of inequality, still holds good today. A recent study of remote rural villages in Bolivia, for example, reports that women living in households mainly dependent on natural resources and agriculture prioritized the provision of drinking water systems (where men rarely carry water) and laundry facilities for washing clothes and cooking utensils, whereas men emphasized the importance of investment in improved roads and transportation links as contributions to increased agricultural production and income (Luyckx 2004).

Practical gender interests therefore correspond to changes and investments required to address women's disadvantage in terms of poverty and deprivation – akin to Young's conception of women's condition discussed above. On the other hand the issues related to strategic gender interests concerned the desire to address women's relative disadvantage vis-à-vis men, in terms, for example, of representation in local or national political bodies, inequalities in wages or non-waged benefits and social protection, access to different levels of education, social sanctioning of freedom of mobility, expressions of sexuality, the reversal of son preference and undervaluation of the girl child, renegotiation of unfair divisions of domestic labour, and freedom from gender-based physical and sexual violence. All these are aspects of life which add to the vulnerability and suffering of poor women; all these are issues which, if addressed, could contribute to the improvement in women's life experiences and life chances.

Moser (1989) set out to provide a guide for what she called 'Gender Planning' which would meet the practical and strategic needs of women. Using the Molyneux distinction as a starting point she proposed that practical gender needs are generally a response to women's immediate perceived necessity formulated by women in terms of their gendered responsibilities for household survival. This could then be interpreted as a demand for training and resources for income generation, often within traditional female occupations, the provision of housing and utilities to provide shelter and services for poor families, appropriate transport that matches women's journey patterns, and adequate health and education facilities for children and other household members. Strategic needs were identified as being more explicitly 'feminist' – for example, policies on the redistribution of domestic work, and public legislation and institutional reform to give women equity in the field of wages, political representation, reproductive rights and protection from gender-based violence.

Moser added to this the widely adopted formulation of 'women's triple roles', referring to productive (income-generating), reproductive (i.e. unpaid domestic) and community management roles, which challenges both the invisibility of women's economic participation and the centrality of reproductive work at the household and community level, which was prevalent in most policy formulations of the time (ibid.: 86). This was the basis of a schematic historicized formulation that set out a five-stage sequence of the changes in 'policy approaches to low income Third World women and gender planning', namely the welfare, equity, anti-poverty efficiency and empowerment approach. According to Moser, these reflected different historical moments in the development of international policy towards developing countries. The welfare approach corresponded with the colonial practice of 'civilizing' the public and private practices of more primitive societies by directing resources to the improvement of household management, nutrition and child-rearing practices. The equity approach of the 1970s reflected the political impetus of second wave feminism mentioned earlier. The anti-poverty approach corresponded with the growing realization that 'Redistribution with Growth' was not going to achieve vast improvements in the living standards of most Third World countries, so a focus on the basic needs of poor households, and thus women, was preferable, hence the proliferation in aid circles of that time of women's income-generation projects. The new realism of the 1980s, however, which led to the 'Washington Consensus' and structural adjustment and stabilization policies of the period, required an increase in women's market-oriented production, hence the stress on women as an overlooked but productive resource for increasing efficiency and competitiveness either in import-substituting activities or in export sectors, including cash crops and labour-intensive goods (e.g. garments and shoes) for the consumer markets of the North. These were all distinguished from the so-called empowerment approach, which Moser claimed was still unaccepted in mainstream policy circles. The empowerment approach, it was argued, derived from the mobilization of women's groups in developing countries and focused on increasing women's capacity for 'their own self reliance and internal strength' (ibid.: 107). It claimed legitimacy for women's role from the DAWN analysis of global redistribution and social valuation, as well as other initiatives against domestic violence, economic exclusion and poverty placing the emphasis on the capacity of Third World women to form innovative organizational structures that would fight for collective empowerment. This formulation might well be seen as a stake in pursuing women's strategic gender needs and was influenced by the Dutch feminist conceptualization of 'autonomy' which was also supported by leading Latin American analysts (see Meynen and Vargas 1994).

From equality to empowerment

Since the 1990s empowerment has become the new liberation. The way in which gender, or rather the specific disadvantage of women, has been deployed in the policy and research debates about micro-credit, for example, illustrates the seductiveness of the empowerment goal as the preference for women borrowers in credit-based anti-poverty programmes has been elevated into a win-win strategy that will also deliver women's empowerment. This also highlights how feminist notions of autonomy have become, in an increasingly post-structuralist, postmodern and post-development world, interpreted in terms of individual actions and satisfactions. Linda Mayoux (2001) argues that the notion of feminist empowerment in the context of micro-credit interventions is intended to encompass the transformation of power relations throughout society and requires the development of self-sustaining participatory women's organizations linked to a 'wider women's movement for transformation of gender relations' (ibid.: 247). She contrasts this with the concept of 'individual economic empowerment', which assumes, in simplistic terms, that women's access to financially sustainable micro-finance programmes will enable women to increase their incomes through micro-enterprise. Women's enhanced economic power, mediated through what Sen (1990) designated as 'perceived contributions' in his cooperative conflict model, will then be translated into improvements in women's and children's well-being and enable women to initiate the social and political changes required for development as well as for women's self-fulfilment.

This is a different debate from the one initiated by Goetz and Sen Gupta (1996), who proposed as a measure of women's empowerment the extent to which the businesses supported by women's micro-loans were controlled and/or operated by women themselves, or whether their husbands utilized the additional financial resources to invest in joint or male-owned business. Kabeer (2000) has since demonstrated that women's well-being, particularly in South Asia, is more firmly linked to the economic flourishing of the household, and the management and control of the actual businesses does not necessarily demonstrate the potential for individual women to benefit. The transformations promised in terms of empowerment and changes in gender inequality are not, however, central to either side of this debate, though there is (conflicting) evidence about reductions in domestic violence, the enhanced role of women in household decision-making and implications for female children. In terms of strategic changes such as a renegotiation of domestic burdens, son preference and public participation are more strongly recognized in the experience of self-help groups for which micro-finance and savings are only a small part of the raft of activities aimed at collective organization and advancement (Fisher and Sriram 2002).

Micro-credit, then, is part of a gender and development initiative because women have come to be the majority of borrowers in such schemes for a variety of reasons, including their higher propensity to repay and to conform with the terms and timing of loans. It should be stressed, however, that initially micro-credit in the Grameen bank formulation was primarily aimed at men.

This has some parallels with the reality of the rapid incorporation of women into export labour forces as more and more of the rich world's consumer goods are sourced from cheap labour economies in the global South. It took some time for policy-makers, as opposed to feminist economists, to recognize that women were the largest part of this new labour force (Elson and Pearson 1981; Joekes 1987) from the 1970s to the present day. But while micro-credit might legitimately be seen to be part of a clearly delineated development initiative and policy, aimed at making the working poor's labour more productive in the absence of waged employment and/or social safety nets, it is only recently that development agencies have turned their attention to the situation of women export workers.

This is partly because of the dominance of the Englian myth that holds dearly the proposition that women's liberation lies in the path of wage labour exploitation, which can dissolve the differences between men's and women's position in capitalist societies (real economies; Sayers 1980). For many decades development policy concentrated on celebrating women's entry into the 'modern' sectors of export industrialization, including the fast-growing and clean electronics industries, as it was generally assumed that waged work would be in women's interests. As Joan Robinson was reported to have declared, there is only one thing that is worse than being exploited by capital, and that is not being exploited by capital. It was left to feminist researchers to stress the contradictions involved in this new form of women's employment and the possibilities of intensification and reconstruction of patriarchal systems of women's subordination, as well as the scope for deconstruction and achievement of personal and collective freedoms (Pearson 1998). In more recent times the plight of women export workers has been taken up more widely by bilateral agencies including the Department for International Development (DfID) (White Paper on 'Making the Poor Work for Globalization') and Oxfam as well as the Ethical Trade Initiative (ETI), which has furthered the interest in the working conditions of a range of export sectors, including non-traditional agricultural exports as well as manufacturing and services (Barrientos and Perrons 1999). This concern has been orchestrated by the demise of the international regulation of Transnational Corporations (TNCs) and their suppliers and the growth of Voluntary Codes of Conduct in their place (Jenkins 2002). The representation of the interests of women workers in these concerns has had to be fought for as labour organizations, as noted above, have traditionally misunderstood the interrelation of capital and gender relations in terms of women's priorities. It is interesting to note, however, that while many of the concerns women emphasize, including protection from violence and harassment, security of income and humane treatment at work, reflect the issues identified earlier as strategic gender issues, the route to their achievement has been via private non-binding agreements rather than state action and international policy (Pearson and Seyfang 2001). Indeed, much of the impetus for change has come from consumer and activist campaigns, such as the Clean Clothes Campaign and Homeworkers Worldwide – that is, from internationalist-minded socialist feminists rather than from within the gender and development community itself (see Pearson 2004).

So the balance sheet on integrating women in development is complex. This is not to deny that it is an honourable activity and has achieved many positive outcomes. Indeed, the recognition of women's contribution to household and national economies, the inclusion of women's work in national statistics, the challenging of unequal pay for women and men engaged in similar work, for example, have been an important contribution to raising the profile of gender and development and ensuring its widespread acceptance and dissemination. The intellectual histories of gender and development often connect its growing reach to the dynamics of gender-equity-focused development activity, which has achieved the transformation of a clear WID approach (Women in Development) to a GAD approach – so called because of the recognition that gender is a social relation, and issues of inequality need to address the relationships between men and women and not focus exclusively on women, which means that women's relative as well as absolute disadvantage in development terms must be addressed (see Pearson 2000). Indeed, recent years have witnessed a distinctly masculinist turn in gender and development to make room for the critique, perceptions and activism of men committed to gender equity, as well as to redress the grievances of those who argue that a true gender approach should target men as well as women (see IDS Bulletin 2000; Jackson 2000).

Mainstreaming gender in international development

The ways in which gender has been incorporated into global development targets illustrate both the success and the problems with what has come to be known as the 'mainstreaming debate'. From the first UN Conference on Women held in Mexico City in 1975 through the UN's Decade for Women (1976–85), the Nairobi Conference on Women which produced the Forward Looking Strategies through to the Fourth World Conference on Women held in Beijing in 1995, there has been an increased visibility and reach of women's organizational, analytical and policy-related activity on an international scale. Interestingly, though, most accounts of the international conferences omit the mid-decade conference held in Copenhagen in 1980. This conference, unlike its predecessor and the subsequent ones, emphasized international inequality and imperialism as the backdrop, with its theme equality, development and peace. It took place at a time of cold war conflict which was increasingly being fought by surrogate states in the developing world, and the beginning of the rise of neo-conservative ideology and governments. One of the key events in my memory of this meeting was the demonstration against the military coup in Bolivia, led by Domitilia de Changara, the leader of the Miners' Wives Committee, whose struggle against imperialism and patriarchy had been disseminated in her autobiography (Barrios de Chungara with Viezzer 1978). The Copenhagen conference was also notable for its success in persuading the UN to include on its agenda of the UN the issue of domestic violence and violence against women, which paved the way for the women's tribune and subsequent changes at the UN Conference on Human Rights in Vienna. But most accounts of the 1980 conference tend to focus on the fact that a plan for the second half of the development decade was produced, which provided the basis for the Forward Looking Strategies produced and adopted in Nairobi in 1995.

The success of the international feminist movements in terms, however, of bringing women to the agenda of United Nations international conferences, which increased in number and energy throughout the 1980s and 1990s, has led in some ways to a very bureaucratic response to the issue of mainstreaming. All kinds of organizations within the UN system, as well as bilaterals, NGOs and national state bureaucracies, have claimed that they have mainstreamed gender into their operations. Although it can be claimed, however, that mainstreaming has a number of elements that imply changing policies, design and delivery of implementation of public policies and development projects, and changing administrative systems so that gender bias is removed and the development agenda directly addresses women's relative and absolute disadvantage, this has not been the experience to date. Rather, organizations have tended to insert gender-sensitive declarations and aspirations into their mission statements and policy documents with an absence of effective structures to ensure compliance and accountability. For instance, the International Labour Organization (ILO), like other international bodies, has attempted to mainstream gender into their institutional bureaucracy, policies and practices (see Razavi and Miller 1995). Their website indicates that the ILO has adopted a gender focus, established a gender coordination union, set up a network of gender focal points and tasked the various parts of the structure with the responsibility of ensuring that gender equity issues are incorporated in all training, programme design and implementation activities (see <www.ilo.org>). There is a lot of detail about what mainstreaming means and how administrative reorganization and new practices will forward the mainstreaming agenda.

The major way in which the ILO has forwarded the agenda of mainstreaming gender issues into its activities, however, is not bureaucratic but thematic. In the late 1990s the ILO overcame the limitations of its tripartite structure, which represented states, employers and employees, to take on issues concerning decent work in the informal economy. This has placed on the ILO's agenda issues central to gender equality, given that the majority of the world's working poor seek their living in the informal economy, and that women are over-represented in the growing informal sector. There is still extensive and sometimes quite tense discussion about who might be the institutional representatives of the informal economy's workforce, with a strong case to be made that traditional trade unions have ill represented women's interests even within the regulated labour market, and that there are a range of other organizations including women's groups and community associations which have more claim to legitimacy in terms of representing women's interests in the informal economy. But the placing of the informal economy at the heart of the ILO's agenda, rather than the incorporation of gender intentions and responsibilities into the structures and documentation of the organization, surely has greater claims in terms of mainstreaming gender interests in the world of work. We must also acknowledge that although there has been considerable pressure from feminist organizations insisting that the ILO take on issues pertaining to informal sector women workers, including social safety nets, health and safety insurance, maternity issues and pensions (see <www. wiego.org>), the main drivers for this policy shift have been radical elements of the international trade union movement, and (male-led) labour organizations from the global South.

What is the development agenda that needs gendering?

Although gender and development did indeed have its origins in the plans for economic restructuring and growth that were formulated in the second half of the twentieth century, this agenda has itself widened in recent years.

Indeed, so convincing has been the case for integrating gender analysis in development policy that by the end of the twentieth century gender and development had moved firmly into the mainstream. All bilateral and multilateral agencies now have policies, and in many cases dedicated staffing and units, dedicated to gender issues. NGOs, particularly big international NGOs such as Oxfam, Care International and Save the Children, have mainstreamed gender issues into their overall mission and remit. In addition to specialized courses and programmes on gender and development, academic development studies programmes routinely include modules on gender and development within their programmes and students are encouraged to bring women's perspectives and gender issues into the general analysis of development theories and strategies. The Millennium Development Goals (MDGs), which the UN system is pledged to achieve by 2015, are aimed at eradicating extreme poverty and hunger, achieving universal primary education, reducing child mortality, improving maternal health, combating HIV/Aids and other communicable diseases, ensuring environmental sustainability and developing a global partnership for development. And goal number two is 'Promoting gender equity and empowerment of women'. Not only has gender equity and women's empowerment earned a high place on the list of internationally recognized development objectives but, as the World Bank (2003) argues, there are strong linkages between gender equality and all the MDGs. Gender equality, it is argued, is central to cutting extreme poverty because it requires investment in the human capital of women and in education and health services to raise labour productivity. Investment in physical infrastructure will diminish time poverty, which is related to inequitable gender-based divisions of labour; including women in the potentials of the digital highway offered by information communication technologies will offer income-enhancing opportunities to a wide range of women micro-entrepreneurs. Success in these areas will eliminate malnutrition and food insecurity.

Similar analyses are made concerning the centrality of gender equity for the other MDGs. There is widespread consensus that achieving equality in different areas of development activity, such as education, training, literacy, access to health services, and elimination of communicable diseases, will achieve linked targets in terms of reducing maternal and child mortality, increasing women's income-earning potential and poverty reduction (Kabeer 2003).

One issue that was absent from development discourses in earlier years was that of conflict and wars. In recent decades, however, the proliferation of armed conflict within and between countries in the developing world has placed 'conflict', including the causes, consequences and nature of humanitarian relief and development efforts, firmly on the agenda. This has widened the debates about development and its role in the contemporary world. Although some argue that humanitarian assistance even with the best of intentions exacerbates existing fault lines in post-colonial political systems (see Duffield 2001), bilateral and multilateral development agencies are claiming a central role in post-conflict reconstruction and development. The UK government's Department for International Development, for example, has a Conflict Reduction and Humanitarian Assistance Department, which funds a range of relief and development interventions related to conflict and complex political emergences (see <www.dfid.gov.uk/aboutDfID/files/conflict>). The department claims to cover a range of humanitarian interventions, including rapid and gradual disaster response, complex political, technological or natural disasters, disaster preparedness, prevention and mitigation, post-disaster repair and rehabilitation, conflict preparedness, prevention and reduction, policy and institutional development, and training and research on all these areas. While DfID has claimed on different historical occasions, however, to have mainstreamed gender across its policies, it makes only one mention of gender issues in a seven-page document on conflict, and that to assert that the reversal of gender inequalities is essential (p. 2). In none of the other parts of the document, which include 'Conflict and Poverty', 'Responding to Conflict', 'Conflict Reduction Strategies', 'Humanitarian Response' and 'DfID's Principles for a New Humanitarianism', is there any hint of gender awareness or gender analysis. The gendered nature of conflict, the ways in which gender identities are deployed in the dynamics that switch potential disputes to armed conflict, the ways in which masculinities in conflict coalesce around essentialized hegemonic versions which increase gender inequalities, the ways in which sexuality, and especially women's sexuality, is constructed as a strategy of conflict or a resource in armed struggle, are not problematized. When there is evidence that armed participants, whether they are UN troops or Coalition services, use sexual violence against prisoners or civilians, governments and international organizations are shocked. They have ignored evidence from countless conflicts about the significance of gender relations in the dynamics of pre-, during and post-conflict situations (e.g. Bangladesh 1972; Chile 1973; Argentina 1976; Rwanda 1984). In spite of claims to have mainstreamed gender across their policy remit, they appear to have ignored many of the insights of courageous feminist scholars who have sought to highlight the significance of this aspect (BRIDGE 2003; El Bushra et al. 2002).

The failure of humanitarian agencies involved in conflict management prevention and reconciliation to internalize the important insights from gender analysis reflects what has been happening in the academic field of international relations, which is the theoretical basis of conflict analysis. Although in many disciplines feminists have been involved in deconstructing, and to a lesser extent reconstructing, the discipline, specific gender blind spots and the ongoing gender blindness of conflict management stand in contrast to other areas of development studies (Reimann 2002). The ungendered nature of the categories of analysis, including people, perpetrators, victims and indeed the generic notions of violence and security, has ignored feminist understandings of the gendered power inequalities that imbue differential meaning and experience of conflict, violence and security on men and women. The private sphere and the local, national and international sphere of international conflict are assumed to be gender-neutral spaces, so the precise importance and effects on the roles and position of women and men in society are not central to this analysis (ibid.: 103). While silence about gender issues can be traced to realist, pluralist and transformative conflict approaches, it can also be attributed to 'academic machismo'. The majority of male academics seem unclear as to how gender analysis will 'add value' to the field, and certainly there has been no rush to deconstruct the hegemonic masculinities of theorists and practitioners, and the exclusion of gender becomes self-reinforcing.

Reimann's point about the failure of mainstream international relations/conflict theorists to understand the value-added of gender analysis strikes a chord in the understanding of the specific forms of institutionalization of gender analysis in the development field. The ways in which gender analysis of structural adjustment policies proceeded is a case in point. The first and most trenchant critique of the effects of structural adjustment on those less successful in responding to a more market-oriented economic system came from UNICEF. Cornia et al. (1987) argued that structural adjustment should be given a human face; country programmes should have a parallel social assistance package so that 'vulnerable groups' (i.e. women and children) do not suffer unduly from their relative inferior market participation skills. The Commonwealth Secretariat at that time employed an able and forward-looking feminist who assembled a group of feminist economists and others who wrote a number of briefing papers about gender and structural adjustment (Elson 1988). But times and staffing changed. The feminist departed and the Commonwealth Secretariat convened an 'Expert Group' from which the original UK feminist economists were excluded. Their publication 'Engendering Adjustment for the 1990s' was an influential document, but significantly its analysis confined itself to exploring the 'impact' of economic crisis and adjustment on women, and emphasizing the social dimensions of adjustment, in much the same manner as UNICEF had done previously. No references were made to the earlier feminist analysis.

Feminist analysis of structural adjustment has continued (see Afshar and Dennis 1992; Elson 1995) but such texts rarely find a place on the reading lists of mainstream development courses. Instead the Word Bank has taken up the analysis in an instrumental way. The World Bank's embracement of gender analysis in the context of understanding the efficacy of its neo-liberal economic reforms, particularly in the agricultural sector, bore the revealing title of 'Paradigm postponed: gender analysis and structural adjustment in sub-Saharan Africa' (Blackden and Morris-Hughes 1993). This paper drew heavily on Elson's analysis of 'male bias' – retermed gender bias – which focuses on the gender bias of macroeconomic models that ignore the gender division of labour between the paid economy and the non-paid economy, gender divisions within each labour activity and the non-elasticity of women's labour, which is being stretched between its triple roles (Elson 1991). The Bank's interpretation, however, was and continues to be purely instrumental. The conclusion is not that women's unpaid work should be valued; that gender divisions of labour should be challenged; that women's empowerment and autonomy, education and training should be strengthened and macroeconomic policy should be modified – instead the Bank's position is that parallel investment in some social services should be instigated in order to free women to work more effectively in the market economy.

So can we really claim that the rise of gender and development has been successful in terms of internalizing gender critiques and analysis in all development institutions and initiatives? Indeed, many claim that gender has been significantly and successfully mainstreamed and it is therefore not necessary to devote resources to ensuring gender equality in development programmes. In the restructuring of a range of government and non-governmental development programmes gender is so twentieth century. Recently, for example, Save the Children Fund (UK) abolished the post of gender adviser, in spite of the salience of gender differences in terms of the exploitative work female and male children are carrying out in different parts of the developing world, and despite the documented increase in sex tourism and trafficking involving young girls, the vulnerability of young women to early marriage, adverse 'traditional' practices such as genital mutilation and the gender inequalities that give women the responsibility for the survival and care of their children while at the same time blocking employment and other sources of resources with which to carry out those responsibilities. These are gender issues that are germane to the mission of Save the Children and yet, in the name of mainstreaming and in the name of the success of the gender and development project over the years, Save the Children has seen fit to eliminate its capacity in terms of gender equity, preferring the more diffuse and general notion of diversity. Furthermore, it would appear that in the NGO sector this is not an isolated case and many other organizations have downgraded and downsized their gender capacity on the grounds that gender is a cross-cutting issue and therefore should be mainstreamed across the organization and its programmes.

Of course, the reduction of gender capacity is not just because of claims of successful mainstreaming. It also reflects a more general tendency in the UK and beyond to institutionally view different kinds of 'difference', aka 'disadvantage', such as race, sexuality, religion, disability and gender, as disadvantages that need to be treated holistically – hence the UK government's decision to create a single Commission for Equality and Human Rights (CEHR) 'to deliver a step change in how we promote, enforce and deliver equality and human rights' (UK government 2004). Transcending disadvantage to achieve equality of opportunity is translated into removing unfair barriers in terms of access to information, employment, public services and the private sector, as well as encouraging the respect for difference. This development in part mirrors the debates within feminism and other parts of academic philosophy on deconstructing meta-notions of identity, arguing that the category of 'women' is so conditioned by other aspects of identity and location, including age, class, geographical location, environment, household position, sexuality, maternity, race and ethnicity, that it is a meaningless category. But since public policy has to formulate policies for all dimensions of difference/disadvantage, this has been translated into an integrated body that will serve and protect individuals and communities, speaking with a single clear voice on equality and human rights matters. So the Equal Opportunities Commission, the Race Equality Council and the newly established Disability Commission are all being merged into the new CEHR even though the pieces of legislation and regulation pertinent to each 'community of disadvantage' in the UK are not parallel or cross-cutting.

Within development institutions the drive for mainstreaming, and thus for the dismantling of the gender machinery, is propelled by similar kinds of reasoning. First, the 'Rights Based Approach to Development' (RBA), which draws on the UN Declaration on the 'Right to Development', proclaims that 'the right to development is an inalienable human right by virtue of which every human person and all peoples are entitled to participate in, contribute to and enjoy economic, social, cultural and political development in which all human rights and fundamental freedoms can be fully realized'. It calls upon states to ensure that all sustained action for rapid development is implemented, and that all violations of human rights are eliminated. It affirms (Article 6) that 'all states should cooperate with a view to promoting, encouraging and strengthening universal respect for and observance of all human rights and fundamental freedoms for all without any distinction as to race, sex, language or religion'.

The RBA has been taken up enthusiastically by development agencies since it seems to offer a non-conflictual and inclusive statement of entitlement of all to development benefits. Potential conflicts of interest, however, between, for example, individuals and 'peoples' in the field of customary disadvantage against women are ignored. Many gender and development practitioners argue that little has changed apart from the language used, and that the 'new' approach has been imposed by donors on grassroots organizations and partners. Moreover a rights-based approach will leave all gender and development organizations and activities vulnerable to being 'mainstreamed', thus reducing the capacity to advocate, organize and intervene in terms of gender and class-based disadvantages. As one leading authority in the field has put it,

> Women's rights has a new level of expectations. In the past much work with women has been about educating women about their rights. But how is it going to done? How will a rights based approach which is not a treaty or document help us to deal with the problems of class and gender? Or to understand intra household relations? How will we avoid being used instrumentally for national development outcomes rather than being able to fight for gender equality objectives. (Tsikata 2003).

So how do we interpret the success of gender advocates in achieving such widespread and official recognition that gender equity is central to the whole development exercise? Does this represent a triumph for feminist analysis and political consciousness? Does it mean that we have converted our colleagues from their scepticism in the 1970s to a wholehearted acknowledgement that gender is central to all development activities, from international economic and trade policies, national economic strategies such as structural adjustment and poverty reduction strategies, through to sector-based approaches to health and education and project-level community-based development activities? Can we confidently say that all development analysts and practitioners are effectively feminist, in the sense that they all buy into gender equity as the key to success in other areas?

In some senses, of course, the answer is yes. But if we examine these arguments more closely there are two things that need to be emphasized. The first is that many of the key development programmes and actors in fact only pay lip-service to the importance of gender issues, rarely going beyond an exhortation that women and gender equity should be considered in agricultural productivity initiatives, or health service reform programmes. A telling indicator of the limited extent of the internalization of gender analysis in mainstream (male) development literature is the fact that many writers scarcely include gender advocates' perspectives and publications in their writing and policy papers.

The second important point is that even when there is a more thorough incorporation of women's disadvantage into development policy and discourse, this generally represents an instrumental approach to gender and development; that is, an acknowledgement that gender is a primary issue or entry point in development policy and strategy not because it is a desirable end in itself, but because it represents a route by which to achieve other objectives. This observation, which is consistent with the current endorsement of the centrality of gender in the achievement of all the Millennium Development Goals, has been a constant factor throughout the whole history of the gender and development project; for instance, the way in which 'reproductive rights' has been incorporated into the population and development area has, it is argued by many feminists, been largely intended to facilitate higher acceptance of contraceptive practices by Third World women, rather than a genuine commitment to furthering women's autonomy and choice in terms of reproduction and sexuality (Smyth 1996).

In many ways this instrumentalist approach can be linked to some of the WID policy identified by Moser (discussed above). The anti-poverty approach

174

sees women's poverty and disadvantage as a direct consequence of the lack of development in the global South, rather than engaging with any kind of gender-based discrimination (see Jackson 2000). This is differentiated from the efficiency approach, which berates the failure of development policy to mobilize women's productive potential to increase productivity and output and thus improve the material standards of living for the working poor, a position that is both assumed in the structural adjustment/liberalization policies of the 1980s and 1990s and replicated in the contemporary discussion on Millennium Development Goals. If women's inequality is not addressed then overriding development targets will not be achieved and paradigms will be postponed. This is why the World Bank can justifiably argue that although only one of the MGDs explicitly deals with gender equity and empowerment, the need to address women's disadvantage is implicit in all the others. That is, in order to efficiently use all potential resources for development, women's health, education and productive capacity both in the productive world of labour markets and paid work and the reproductive economy of care and social reproduction must be fully utilized.

Is it better to travel hopefully than to arrive?

The history of gender and development within development studies and policies is therefore one in which we can discern an increasing incorporation of economic rationality (in terms of maximizing the potential of limited productive resources) as much as any direct concern for the consequences and suffering occasioned by women's subordination both in developing societies and in development policies. Some have even gone so far as to argue that the 'naturalness' of women's subordinate and domestic role has been so internalized by development planners from Northern countries that there was little acknowledgement of the consequences of relegating women to a separate and invisible role (Rogers 1980). The burgeoning recognition in the 1980s, the decade of the Washington Consensus, that women's activities outside and inside the home were central to the development strategies based on the extension of market relations to wider aspects of Southern economies, such as diverting subsistence food production to commercial products, or imposing charges for education or health services and supplies, does indeed represent an important shift from the earlier position and acknowledges the fundamental role of women's work in rural and urban societies in developing countries. But does it represent a triumph for feminist commitment to achieving equality *between* women and men?

Certainly the commitment to addressing gender disadvantage has mainly been translated in terms of practical gender needs. In the increasingly market-based approach to poverty alleviation (e.g. micro-financial services for the poor, increase of cash crops and wage labour), planners and development agencies will give priority to meeting women's practical needs in the name of gendering development policies. Initially there was evidence that they felt uncomfortable with interventions that would upset the local gender order, such as preference for boys' schooling over girls, pre-puberty marriage practices or lack of political representation of women in decision-making, arguing that local 'cultures' should not be disturbed by external notions of equality and participation. As the MDGs indicate, however, we have travelled a long way from that situation, and, as we have seen, equity in terms of literacy and access to education is central to the overall strategy.

But the evidence suggests that the acceptance of gender needs that were previously characterized as strategic, and therefore by some as 'feminist', has taken place for instrumental reasons rather than through a political commitment to equality. While gender and development is on everyone's lips, if not their word processors, the feminist commitment to political struggle and change has in many ways been decoupled from both the postmodernist deconstruction of women as an analytical category and the technical implementation of gender mainstreaming in development policy. As an academic realm of study, gender and development has been successful in generating a vast amount of data, research and information over the last thirty years. Although in terms of the academy and of the increasing number of development practitioners it appears to be on the wane, this in the end might prove to be the best route to repoliticizing gender and development and returning it to its radical roots.

References

Afshar, H. and C. Dennis (eds) (1992) *Women and Adjustment in the Third World*, Basingstoke: Macmillan

Barrientos. S. and D. Perrons (1999) 'Gender and the global food chain', in H. Afshar and S. Barrientos (eds), *Women, Globalization and Fragmentation in the Developing World*, Basingstoke: Macmillan, pp. 150–73

Barrios de Chungara, D. with M. Viezzer (1978) *Let Me Speak!: Testimony of Domitilia, a Woman of the Bolivian Mines*, New York: Monthly Review Press

Blackden, M. and E. Morris-Hughes (1993) 'Paradigm postponed: gender analysis and structural adjustment in sub-Saharan Africa', *World Bank*, AFTHR Technical Note, no. 13, August

BRIDGE (2003) *Report on Gender and Armed Conflict*, <www.ids.ac.uk/bridge>

Commonwealth Secretariat (1989) 'Engendering adjustment for the 1990s: report of a Commonwealth Expert Group', London

Cornia, G., R. Jolly and F. Stewart (1987) *Adjustment with a Human Face*, vols 1 and 2, *Protecting the Vulnerable* and *Promoting Growth*, Oxford: Clarendon Press

Duffield, M. (2001) *Global Governance and the New Wars: The Merging of Development and Security*, London: Zed Books

El Bushra, J., A. El Karib and A. Hadjipateras (2002) 'Gender sensitive programme design and planning in conflict situations', RESCOR Research Project Report R 7501

Elson, D. (1988) 'Gender aware policy making for structural adjustment', unpublished report for the Commonwealth Secretariat

— (1991) *Male Bias in the Development Process*, Manchester: Manchester University Press

— (1995) (ed., special issue) 'Gender, adjustment and macroeconomics', *World Development*

Elson, D. and R. Pearson (1981) 'The subordination of women and the internationalisation of factory production', in Young et al. (1994), pp. 18–40

Emerij, L., R. Jolly and T. Weiss (2001) *Ahead of the Curve: UN Ideas and Global Challenges*, Bloomington and Indianapolis: Indiana Press

Fisher, T. and M. S. Sriram (eds) (2002) *Beyond Micro-Credit: Putting Development Back into Micro-Finance*, Oxford and New Delhi: Oxfam and Vistaar Publications

Goetz, A. M. and R. Sen Gupta (1996) 'Who takes the credit? Gender, power and control over loan use in Rural Credit Programmes in Bangladesh', *World Development*, 14: 45–63

IDS Bulletin (2000) 'Men, masculinities and development: politics, policies and practice', 31(2) April

Jackson, C. (ed.) (2000) 'Men at work: labour, masculinities and development', special issue, *European Journal of Development Research*, 12(2), December: 1–22

Jenkins, R. (2002) 'The political economy of codes of conduct', in Jenkins et al. (eds), pp. 13–30

Jenkins, R., R. Pearson and G. Seyfang (eds) (2002) *Corporate Responsibility and Labour Rights: Codes of Conduct in the Global Economy*, London: Earthscan

Joekes, S. (1987) *Women in the World Economy*, Oxford: Oxford University Press

Kabeer, N. (2000) *The Power to Choose: Bangladeshi Women and Labour Market Decision in London and Dahka*, London: Verso

— (2003) *Gender, Mainstreaming in Poverty Eradication and the New Millennium Development Goals*, London: Commonwealth Secretariat

Luyckx, K. (2004) 'Land, livelihoods and politics in rural lowland Bolivia: a comparative case study of two indigenous communities', Unpublished PhD thesis, School of Geography, University of Leeds

Mayoux, L. (2001) 'Women's empowerment versus sustainability? Towards a new paradigm in micro-finance programmes', in B. Lemire, R. Pearson and G. Campbell, *Women and Credit: Researching the Past, Refiguring the Future*, Oxford: Berg, pp. 245–70

Meynen, V. and V. Vargas (1994) 'Autonomy as a strategy for development from women's multiple interests', in M. Barrig and A. Wehkamp (eds), *Engendering Development: Experiences in Gender and Development Planning*, The Hague: Novib

Molyneux, M. (1985) 'Mobilization without emancipation: women's interests, state and revolution in Nicaragua', *Feminist Studies*, 11(2): 1019–37

— (1998) 'Analysing women's movements', in C. Jackson and R. Pearson (eds), *Feminist Visions of Development: Gender Analysis and Policy*, London: Routledge, pp. 65–88

Moser, C. O. N. (1989) 'Gender planning in the Third World: meeting practical and strategic gender needs', *World Development*, 17(11): 1799–825

— (1993) *Gender Planning and Development: Theory, Practice and Development*, London: Routledge

Oxfam (2004) *Gender, Development and Trade*, Oxford: Oxfam

Pearson, R. (1992) 'Gender Matters in Development', in T. Allen and A. Thomas (eds), *Poverty and Development in the 1990s*, Oxford: Oxford University Press, pp. 291–31.

— (1998) '"Nimble Fingers" revisited: reflections on women and Third World industrialisation in the late twentieth century', in C. Jackson and R. Pearson (eds), *Feminist Visions of Development: Gender Analysis and Policy*, London: Routledge, pp. 171–88

— (2000) 'Rethinking gender matters in development', in T. Allen and A. Thomas (eds), *Poverty and Development into the 21st Century*, Oxford: Oxford University Press, pp. 383–402

— (2004) 'Organising home-based workers in the global economy: an action-research approach', *Development in Practice*, 14(1–2): 136–48

Pearson, R. and G. Seyfang (2001) 'New hope or false dawn? Codes of conduct and social policy in a globalising world', *Global Social Policy*, 1(1)

Pearson, R., A. Whitehead and K. Young (1984) 'The continuing subordination of women in the development process', Preface to the 2nd edn of Young et al. (1994)

Razavi, S. and C. Miller (1995a) 'Gender mainstreaming: a study of efforts by the UNDP, the World Bank and the ILO to institutionalise gender issues', Occasional Paper Series, Fourth World Conference on Women, Geneva: UNRISD, August

— (1995b) 'From WID to GAD: conceptual shifts in the women and development discourse', Occasional Paper Series, Geneva: UNRISD, February

Reimann, C. (2002) 'Engendering the field of conflict management: why gender does not matter! Thoughts from a theoretical perspective', in M. Braig and S. Wolte (eds), *Common Ground or Mutual Exclusion: Women's Movements and International Relations*, London: Zed Books

Rogers, B. (1980) *The Domestication of Women: Discrimination in Developing Societies*, London: Kogan Page

Sayers, S. (1980) 'Forces of production and relations of production in socialist society', *Radical Philosophy*, 24: 19–26

Sen, A. K. (1990) 'Gender and cooperative conflicts', in I. Tinker (1990b), pp. 123–49

Smyth, I. (1996) 'Gender analysis of family planning: beyond the "feminist vs. population control" debate', *Feminist Economics*, 2(2), summer

Tinker, I. (1990a) 'The making of a field: advocates, practitioners and scholars', in I. Tinker (1990b), pp. 27–53

— (1990b) *Persistent Inequalities*, Oxford: Oxford University Press

Tsikata, D. (2003) 'Is a rights based approach good for gender and development', Paper presented at conference on 'Gender myths and feminist fables: repositioning gender in development policy and practice', IDS, University of Sussex, July

UK Government White Paper (2004) 'Fairness for all: a new commission for equality and human rights', <www.dti.gov.uk/consultations/consultation-1192.html>

Wellesley Editorial Committee (eds) (1977) *Women and National Development: The Complexities of Change*, Chicago, IL: University of Chicago Press

White, S. (1993) 'Making men an issue: gender planning for the "other half"', in M. Macdonald (ed.), *Gender Planning in Development Agencies*, Oxford: Oxfam

Whitehead, A. (1979) 'Some preliminary notes on the subordination of women', *IDS Bulletin*, 10(3)

World Bank (2003) *Sustainable Development in a Dynamic World*, Washington, DC: World Bank

Young, K. (1988) 'Reflections on meeting women's needs', Introduction to K. Young (ed.), *Women and Economic Development: Local, Regional and National Planning Strategies*, Oxford: Berg/UNESCO, pp. 1–30

Young, K., C. Wolkowitz and R. McCullough (1994) *Of Marriage and the Market: Women's Subordination Internationally and Its Lessons*, 2nd edn, London: Routledge & Kegan Paul

9 | Development studies, nature and natural resources: changing narratives and discursive practices

PHIL WOODHOUSE AND ADMOS CHIMHOWU

In a field of study concerned with problems of uneven development, it is to be expected that access to and use of natural resources occupy a central position in the contemporary development discourse. The treatment of natural resources in development studies, however, also manifests the concerns of industrialized society in the twentieth century, and in particular the evolving environmentalist critique of industrialization as a model of development. This chapter charts the interaction between environmentalism and development studies. It argues that, just as environmentalism has been an element of industrial society since its origins in the late eighteenth century, so the growing strength of environmentalist thinking has increasingly imposed itself on debates about what a 'developed' society should be like, opening new spaces for contestation of development under capitalism. In particular, questions of control over natural resources pose challenges in relation to the governance of markets and the allocation and legitimization of property rights.

As in so many other aspects of development studies, current patterns of use and the conditions for access to land, water, forests and other natural resources in most developing countries are rooted in their colonial past and the continuation of such practices after independence. Imperial administration or colonial conquest, especially in the 'settled states', imposed new relationships between colonized people and nature and natural resources. Two key facets of these relationships were the commoditization of production to supply new markets, and an often simultaneous conservation of natural resources as 'reserves' protected against human, primarily indigenous people's, use.

This chapter draws on our combined experience of working in southern and West Africa, regions where environmental and natural resource management concerns loom large in dominant discourses of development. It first identifies the principal elements of the legacy of colonial administration of natural resources. It then considers how this legacy influenced the early years of development studies, and particularly the prevailing modernization model of development, during the last decades of colonial administration and the early post-independence years. The chapter goes on to examine the interaction between the crisis of modernization and the mounting perception of environmental crisis during the 1970s and 1980s, and the emergence of new narratives: neo-liberalism in development studies, and a constructivist approach to the study of nature which undermined positivist science as the sole basis for decisions on managing nature. The chapter concludes by charting the rise in political ecology during the 1990s and explores its impact on development studies at the end of the twentieth century.

Colonial administration and the management of nature

A writer on French colonial interests in Africa once commented, 'if colonies, the foundation of which nearly always costs the metropolis so much money and sacrifices and which exposes them to such great risks, were not made to serve those metropoles, they would have no *raison d'être*' (Harmond 1912, quoted in Young 1994: 97). While it is fair to say that, as this quote suggests, the motivation for colonial occupation centred mainly on a quest for raw materials (particularly mineral, timber and agricultural commodities) needed for developing the 'mother' country, it must be recognized that this was accompanied by other, sometimes contradictory, concerns to conserve and protect 'nature'. Such concerns, while evident, did not necessarily alter the overriding agenda of colonial administration, but they prompted debates that continued to resurface in development discourse throughout the twentieth century.

Such debates were largely absent, however, in the period of early European colonial expansion from the sixteenth to eighteenth centuries, in which the conquest of nature included the subordination of human populations that the colonizers encountered. A simple utilitarianism guided the appropriation of minerals, land and labour in the form of a plantation economy underpinned by slavery. In the nineteenth century, industrialization of the principal colonial powers brought with it an intensification of demand for 'raw materials' from the colonies, such as rubber, palm oil, cotton and cocoa. Troup (1940), for example, suggests that colonial forestry policy in Asia derived from the fact that Britain imported up to 80 per cent of timber requirements for the shipbuilding industry. Imperial strategic interests therefore informed natural resources policy in the colonies. In addition, local wood biomass needs, particularly for strategic industries such as mining and tobacco farming, also influenced how natural resource policy evolved. It is not surprising, therefore, that colonial relationship with nature has been characterized by some as 'a destructive, utilitarian and cornucopian view of the feasibility of yoking nature to economic gain' (Adams 2003: 22). By the late nineteenth century, however, this simple utilitarian approach to natural resource use had prompted a set of more strategic concerns to occupy and control territory not only for immediate gain but for future exploitation and to deny access to competing colonial projects. The 'scramble for Africa' by European colonial powers in the final years of the nineteenth century meant that colonial administration was established in some areas of Africa where there was little or no immediate economic rationale in the form of exploitable minerals or agricultural production to serve European industry. In such cases of 'hegemony on a shoestring', the imperative for colonial authorities was, therefore, to find ways to intensify natural resource exploitation not simply to satisfy demand from metropolitan industry, but also to fund the colonial administration itself. In such situations, unlike in the Americas, where European expansion had largely displaced existing populations, colonial administration needed to make African societies work for the colonial project. The resulting 'compromises', which included indirect rule through reconstituted customary African authorities, commoditization of production by small-scale farmers, and the creation of areas reserved for wildlife and pastoralists, shaped the discourses on environment and natural resource management during the late colonial period and subsequently in the post-independence field of development studies. A key feature of these discourses is the contradictions between the prevailing pursuit of modernity in the industrial society of the colonial metropoles and the maintenance of 'traditional' society, albeit one fully engaged in the service of the colonial economy, in the African colonies (Cowen and Shenton 1991, 1996; Mamdani 1996). This produced further tensions in the terms of access to, and control over, natural resources.

First, colonial occupation introduced new forms of commoditization of natural resources (Berry 1993). Colonial occupation, particularly in 'settled' states, always involved the introduction of new forms of relationships to nature (Adams 2003; Neuman 1997; Grove 1987a, 1987b). While limited local markets for natural resource produce existed before colonization, what changed was the scale and range of resources involved once the export market to the 'mother' countries was established. Apart from the pressure on resources, this often meant a modification of property laws and restrictions of access to some resources by indigenous groups. In southern Africa the introduction of private property regimes reserved for Europeans often involved relocation of indigenous populations and intervention in native agricultural production, often in the name of conserving those resources (Beinart 1984). A colonial legacy often included, therefore, unequal access to and control of natural resources, often weighted in favour of a minority of privileged settler communities and local political and bureaucratic elites.

While institutions of private property and market exchange for land were considered a necessary element of the expropriation of land for European settlement or the plantation economy, the development of markets in land and other natural resources among Africans was actively suppressed by colonial authorities (Chanock 1991), even where commoditized production among African farmers arose in response to new market opportunities (see Hill 1963; Berry 1993). Further, where commercial agricultural production by Africans competed with colonial priorities for African labour, as was often the case, particularly in the settler colonies of southern Africa, Africans were prohibited from access to land markets, excluded from markets for cash crops and had only restricted access to land within designated reserves (Bundy 1979), where land use was to be governed by 'traditional' or 'native' institutions reconstituted as the lowest rung of colonial administration (Mamdani 1996).

This African colonial context was not unique, as indeed similar processes of incorporation and exclusion were often seen in parts of Latin America. It did, however, produce an extreme contrast between the 'modernity' of colonial industrial societies and a consciously maintained non-modern model of colonized societies and, by extension, of non-modern natural resource management. This juxtaposition of modern and non-modern visions of society and nature produced two opposing discourses in the late colonial period. First, a 'modernist' narrative that viewed 'traditional' African land use (i.e. that which was allowed under colonial administration) as backward and sought to find ways to modernize it; and a second, 'populist' narrative that saw in 'traditional' social forms a cohesion and solidarity, and above all an absence of class formation, that provided favourable contrasts to the processes of dislocation and conflict characteristic of industrial society. Below we explore these two narratives in turn.

Modernist and populist narratives

The early-twentieth-century colonial administrations sought to modernize Africans' land use only in so far as it was needed to serve market demand. Hence they focused on introducing new types of crops or animals, and providing marketing and processing infrastructure, but simultaneously maintaining a 'traditional' character of political and social control. Science was deployed to improve crop and soil productivity and animal health, while maintaining social organization (and order) through a model of African society as essentially rural, where individuals' access to land, water, pasture or forest was determined by membership of a community whose claims to those resources were legitimized through ancestral occupation and use. The tension inherent in this mix of social conservatism and modern scientific approaches to managing nature surfaced following environmental concerns about land use in farming which emerged in industrial societies during the 1930s, as a consequence of the dust bowls in the United States. These concerns were raised by scientists in many African colonies, in relation to low levels of farming productivity and the deteriorating living conditions of people on 'native reserves' in southern Africa. Attempts to introduce to African farmers scientifically based soil conservation measures developed in the USA, however, soon encountered problems. The techniques developed for large-scale mechanized farming of the USA were often incompatible with the small-scale, often hand-cultivated, fields in Africa. Similar problems confronted attempts to improve range management. One commission of inquiry observed that:

> ... the efforts of government are being frustrated by the Natives themselves. Once a water supply is provided, the natives, without regard to the capabilities of the veld, congregate their flocks and herds around it. The grass and other edible vegetable is soon eaten or trampled under foot and the surface soil is reduced to powder. The first heavy rains sweep away the powder and if there are any dams in the catchment area, they soon become silted up. (Colony of Southern Rhodesia 1939: 30)

The response was that not only did the technical basis of African farming need modernizing, but the 'traditional' social basis of access to land was a barrier to the adoption of more productive technology. This modernist narrative, therefore, generated proposals for the reorganization of land use by Africans by government planners, as in the Betterment schemes in South Africa in the 1950s, and the Swynnerton Plan in Kenya's Central Province following the armed rebellion of the Mau Mau. These schemes were marked by a belief that 'traditional' land tenure needed to be replaced by more 'modern' forms of individualized tenure. This was nowhere more apparent than in policies to conserve nature, for which the colonies adapted and introduced legislation relating to wildlife and other natural resources from the colonial metropoles. In the case of British colonies the legislation was modelled around the principles of the London Convention for the Preservation of Fauna of the Empire which a number of colonies had agreed to. According to McGregor (1991), movement of technical staff from the mother country to the colonies facilitated such policy transfers. The prevailing narrative of these policies was uncompromisingly modernist towards indigenous populations and their use of resources. Concern was largely with 'the intention to develop the African up to a civilised state in his own areas' (NRB 1944: 3). This 'native' stereotyping accompanied tightening controls on resource use since 'it seems very doubtful whether recommending any course of action to natives, unaccompanied by any sanction for disobedience will ever be effective' (ibid.: 7).

In contrast to the modernist narrative, populist narratives drew together a number of disparate strands that had in common their opposition to the model of large-scale industrial production, and a belief in the merits of small-scale individual production as the basis for a more equitable and fair society. As such, populist discourse supplied a critique of both agrarian and industrial capitalism from their inception. In the early decades of the twentieth century, populism was intellectually reinforced by Chayanov's model of peasant production, developed to challenge the collectivization of farming in the newly established Soviet Union. To populists, the maintenance of a 'traditional' African society under colonial administration promised the survival of a moral economy of social solidarity, a view that meshed with other sets of environmental concerns stemming from nineteenth-century romanticism which perceived an authenticity of both nature and the human experience in 'wilderness' areas. From this 'environmentalist' standpoint, not only was it desirable to maintain agrarian, traditional society in preference to industrialization, but Africa presented possibilities of wilderness and natural experience, a veritable Eden, unobtainable in Europe.

The key difference between the modernist and populist narratives identified above was on the one hand the perception of African natural resource users as 'backward' and in need of modernization, and on the other hand as custodians of social values, often extended to include less destructive relationships with nature, that had been lost to industrial society. Our purpose here is to identify these narratives in the colonial period as precursors to debates that recur subsequently in development studies. This is not to say that the two narratives were mutually exclusive, or even opposed under all circumstances. Similarly, the practice of environmental management did not necessarily conform with the scientific principles from which it was derived. Where policies for checking resource degradation existed, it was not uncommon for this to be waived in the name of pushing the wilderness frontier forward. For example, a native commissioner in the then colony of southern Rhodesia wrote in his annual report that 'many visiting teams and individual "conservationists" are on occasion alarmed at the local river bank cultivation with no regard to the legal 200 foot from the river bank rule. They are apt to lose sight of the fact that wild fly country has to be tamed to make it suitable for human habitation' (District Native Commissioner for Binga 1961: 4).

Nature and modernization: 1950s and 1960s The intellectual field of development studies emerged at the moment when colonial empires had become politically unsustainable and independence was being granted to many colonial territories in Africa and Asia. Not only did development studies' concern with uneven development reflect the politics of this period of independence for colonial territories, however, it also reflected the modernization narratives that characterized the late colonial administrations of the 1940s and 1950s. While the formal genesis of modernization bore the imprint of the cold war (Rostow 1960), serving to define the role of the developmental state to foster human progress through private enterprise, rather than state or social ownership, no such opposition confronted the modernist narrative of natural resource management. Throughout West and East Africa, the years immediately preceding and following independence witnessed the high point of state support for modernizing African land use by small-scale farmers through the application of science to identifying appropriate seed varieties, fertilizer and pesticide treatments, and through financing and delivering these inputs, and marketing and processing the harvest. Confidence in this science-based farming development was underpinned by the rapid increases in farm productivity achieved in Europe and, through green revolution technologies, in Mexico and India. A feature of this period of state-sponsored development of small-scale farming in Africa was the assertion of state ownership of natural resources in principle, and in designated development projects in particular. In the latter, typically irrigation schemes such as the Gezira in Sudan, or resettlement areas such as the groundnut scheme in Tanganyika, state provision of infrastructure was associated with extinction of existing land rights and farmers became effectively tenants of the state. Outside these development projects, however, only in rare instances, notably in Kenya, did the state attempt to modernize the social and political basis of access to land through the introduction of individualized freehold land titles.

For development studies, the continuation of these 'traditional' farming patterns generated two sets of debates. The first of these, derived both from anthropology and from political economy (see Meillassoux 1964; Haswell 1963; Hill 1963), sought to understand the political and economic dynamics of the persistence of small-scale commodity production under conditions of capitalist development. The second, inspired more by environmentalist concerns, perceived the continuation of non-modern 'communal' forms of access to natural resources, such as land, pastures and forest, as destined to destroy those resources, hence the thesis of a 'tragedy of the commons' (Hardin 1968). This perceived non-viability of existing African institutions of resource access provided further impetus to post-independence efforts to modernize natural resource management, through individualized land tenure, enclosure of grazing areas for management as 'group ranches', or through state controls of resources such as forests. Hardin's metaphor gained particular strength because it tapped into environmental concerns in the industrial societies of Europe and North America, which were generated by the long post-war period of economic growth and rapid technological change. Echoing a similar phenomenon in the early years of nineteenth-century industrial growth, memorably portrayed in Mary Shelley's *Frankenstein*, in the 1950s and 1960s the impact of technology (such as nuclear power and pesticides), and the question of how much growth was possible, were sources of insecurity in an era otherwise dominated by scientific optimism. For development studies, the tragedy of the commons, and its modernist agenda, set a challenge that provoked divergent responses that essentially shaped debates about natural resource management for the remainder of the twentieth century. These debates assumed immediate significance, especially for Africa, during the decades of economic and environmental crisis in the 1970s and 1980s.

We can see that from the formative stages of development studies as a discipline, its preoccupation with former colonies meant that it had to engage with these notions of nature and natural resource governance, which still bore a very colonial imprint. More crucial was the fact that it inherited certain discourses of nature that largely remained a core part of theory and practice until the 1970s, when the burgeoning environmental movements began to question the use of resources. In the next section we locate what we term strategic deconstruction of colonial narratives within the development studies discourse that characterized the period beginning in the late 1970s and culminated in the emergence of social and political ecology as an emerging area within development studies.

The crisis of modernization and the rise of populist environmentalism: the 1970s and 1980s

The economic recession that followed the increase in oil prices in the 1970s ended post-war economic expansion, and prompted a collapse in prices for primary commodities and of the African economies that depended upon them. The economic crisis was also accompanied by growing environmental concerns about the impacts of continued growth of production and consumption in industrial society (Meadows et al. 1972), and of population in developing countries. The neo-Malthusian narrative of agrarian populations growing faster than the production of food appeared to be supported by famines in the Sahel and Ethiopia in the 1970s and in Ethiopia and southern Africa in the 1980s. The 'Sahel effect' on both the discourse of development and discursive practices had echoes of the 1930s dust bowls of Arkansas that influenced African farming practices, in spite of the vast differences in the ecological setting.

Within development studies the most far-reaching consequences were the questioning of the effectiveness of the state as the organizing force for development, and the neo-liberal assertion of the need for market-based principles of resource allocation. Neo-liberal principles quickly extended to natural resource management, with the development of environmental economics (Pearce et al. 1990) supplying the framework for market-based management of natural resources as a basis for environmental conservation. Although the neo-liberal challenge focused more on the means of delivery (the state) rather than the implicit end-point of a process of modernization (industrial society), its emphasis on comparative advantage could be regarded as consistent with non-industrial futures for societies with no comparative advantage for manufacturing. In this sense, at least, neo-liberal perspectives were compatible with new thinking on natural resource management which emerged to challenge the modernist narrative of the preceding decades. Primarily populist in inspiration, and based on detailed empirical fieldwork, this new work mounted an assault on (colonial and post-independence) scientific interpretations of natural resources. A series of research movements arising from agronomy and microeconomics (farming systems research: Byerlee et al. 1982), ecology and anthropology ('Farmer First': Chambers et al. 1989; Scoones and Thompson 1994), and ecology and physical geography (the 'new ecology': Scoones 1999; Botkin 1990) argued that colonial science had not only misunderstood the biophysical dynamics of tropical ecologies (Ford 1971; Richards, 1983, 1985; Thomas and Middleton 1994; Fairhead and Leach 1996; Hecht and Cockburn 1990; Kjekshus 1996), but had also misunderstood both the technical and the economic rationale for 'native' or 'indigenous' natural resource management. A more radical critique and re-evaluation of some long-held 'rational and scientific' analysis upon which colonial narratives were based occurred in the 1980s. For example, approaches to the analysis of soil erosion began to transcend the 'pressure of population on resources' thesis as focus shifted towards approaches that combined the study of physical and of social processes in the political economy of soil erosion (Blaikie 1985). This was in contrast to the earlier approaches that blamed the victims (such as indigenous groups causing soil erosion through their production practices). Land degradation under this revisionist approach was now seen as a 'rational response of poor households to changes in the physical, economic and social circumstances in which they define their survival strategies' (de Janvry and Garcia 1988: 3).

Four influential texts on similar themes deserve particular mention here as they embody this revisionist theme. Richards' (1985) work on attempts to modernize indigenous agriculture brought to the fore the failure of the modern scientific establishment to respect local knowledge and provided examples where the rational science got it wrong. Blaikie's (1985) publication on *The Political Economy of Soil Erosion in Developing Countries* produced a new framework for analysis of resource degradation which did not blame the peasants but sought to understand their production environment. Similarly Tiffen et al.'s (1994) arguments in *More People, Less Erosion*, showing how communities adapt to changing local environmental and demographic conditions, provided further evidence that the 'pressure of population on resources' narrative was seriously flawed. Their work highlighted that it was not always the case that a fivefold increase in population between the 1930s and the 1990s led to more degradation, revealing how population increases brought on new local technologies to make the land more productive. In *The Lie of the Land*, Leach and Mearns (1996) provide further evidence that what was once seen as rational scientific judgement on African environments was based on a misunderstanding of local environments.

Much of this work emphasized the power relations inherent in scientific discourse, and argued that colonial efforts to systematically replace indigenous local agricultural and natural resources knowledge systems and practices, often in the name of modernization (ibid.; Plumwood 2003), was frequently misplaced and ineffective as 'African environmental management practices reflected sets of conditions and constraints with which scientists trained in Europe were unfamiliar' (Richards 1985: 13). This supplanting of local knowledge systems with 'modern' scientific knowledge under colonialism was linked with the prevailing perception that the failure of development in Africa, evidenced by famine and insecurity, was rooted in a failure in natural resource management (Timberlake 1985). The logic of this analysis was that improvement in environmental management, and therefore development, could be sought in the rediscovery of pre-colonial systems of managing nature. Thus, within development studies from the mid-1980s onwards there was considerable interest in 'appropriate technology' and 'indigenous technical knowledge' (see, for example, Brokensha et al. 1980; Richards 1985; Warren et al. 1995; Chambers et al. 1989).

The pursuit of scientific modernization was thereby subordinated to the goal of understanding indigenous technical knowledge, and the economic rationale of small-scale users of resources. A key feature of this approach was inter-disciplinarity across the natural and social sciences. Nowhere is this demonstrated better than in the debate on carrying capacity and its attendant narrative, often called the 'pressure of population on resources' view. The concept of carrying capacity was based on the thinking that the natural ecological setting can only support a fixed population under given technological practices. Exceeding this threshold was seen to lead to resource depletion. Discursive practices based on it produced policies that sought to limit both human and livestock populations to the predetermined carrying capacity (Leach and Mearns 1996; Potts 2000). A key characteristic of this work, apart from the re-evaluation of knowledge, is the emergence of methodological pluralism to understand the human nature relationship. In assembling an alternative understanding of relationships between demography and ecology, a critical approach was developed to both the measurement and interpretation of environmental phenomena (Thomas and Middleton 1994), quantitative analysis of photographic evidence, written records, early travellers' accounts, oral and life histories, and also to the investigation of 'participatory' approaches to understanding the rationale of resource users (Scoones 1994; Scoones and Thompson 1994).

Above all, this new populist discourse decisively shifted the locus of management of natural resources away from the state and towards rural communities of cultivators, pastoralists and other resource users. This shift was given further impetus by Ostrom's (1990) empirical work, which concluded that long-term productivity of 'commons', natural resources owned collectively, was sustainable, so long as access (effectively, property rights) was restricted to a defined social group. Hardin's 1968 thesis on 'The tragedy of the commons' was argued to be an example of failure to understand indigenous resource management systems, particularly the difference between open access and common property resources (Roe 1994).

By the end of the 1980s, a discourse based in a radical reinterpretation of ecological dynamics and the privileging of both local knowledge and local property rights had achieved a considerable sway within development studies, providing, through community-based natural resource management, a populist alternative to challenge 'centralized' state-led efforts to manage the environmental crisis through large-scale science-based management (such as large dams and forest reserves) and private property. An added advantage of this discourse was that it was consistent with prevailing neo-liberal prescriptions to reduce the involvement of the state in resource allocation, if less comfortable with the neo-liberal emphasis on market-based access to natural resources.

The impact of the discourse of 'community-based natural resource management' was considerable, not only within development studies, but also within development policy, where it meshed with wider movements to decentralize government in developing countries (Mawhood 1993; Ribot 2003). It was also the main discourse of opposition to modernist environmental discourse which argued the tragedy of the commons increasingly in global terms, with a scale of science-based intervention to match. Ever-increasing areas of nature were reserved for conservation or rational exploitation and protected from local people, whose growing population and destructive resource use (typically 'shifting cultivation') were perceived to constitute the main threat of environmental degradation. In this respect, the political significance of 'community-based natural resource management' in real-life struggles (for example, Amazonian rubber tappers and South-East Asian forest dwellers) should not be ignored. In particular, the populist environmental narrative ensured that reducing poverty, and especially rural poverty, through more secure livelihoods for those dependent on using natural resources was identified as a key to reducing environmental degradation. This linkage of poverty reduction and environmental management was the guiding principle of the Bruntland Commission's conclusions (WCED 1987) and underpinned the World Conference on Environment and Development organized by the UN in Rio de Janeiro in 1992.

Despite these significant impacts, however, the populist focus on the local meant that linkage to wider processes of social and economic change was weak. Indeed, in common with earlier populist discourse, there was an implication that (rural) society would not, or should not, change its underlying social and economic structure. Where the 'political economy' of natural resource use was addressed within the literature on environment in developing countries (see Blaikie 1985; Blaikie and Brookfield 1987; Conroy and Litvinoff 1988), the problem of environmental degradation was seen in terms of the 'marginalization' of local resource users by disruption of local regulatory institutions by outside forces: usually colonial or post-independence government, or markets. Resource degradation was argued to be a cause and function of social marginality and pressure of capitalist commodity markets that force individuals with access to a resource to overuse it (de Janvry and Garcia 1988). In treating the primary cause of 'marginalization' as being outside the 'rural community', however, the populist-environmentalist literature in the 1970s and 1980s contrasts sharply with the political economy literature on agrarian change (Byres 1982; Watts 1983a; Mackintosh 1989), which explicitly addressed processes of social and economic differentiation and change within rural society. The difference between the populist and political economy arguments was perhaps most clearly set out in Michael Watts' (1983b) commentary on Paul Richards' (1983) paper 'Ecological change and the politics of African land use', and summarized in Watts' quote from Kitching that the central weakness of a populist agenda is that 'it is unable to provide any coherent account of how a continuing process of rising material productivity and living standards is compatible with the maintenance of an economy in which peasant producers are the dominant social force' (Kitching, quoted in Watts 1983b: 81). A major implication of the political economy view of rural society is that processes of social and economic differentiation will be accompanied by processes of competition, differential control and conflict over natural resources *within* communities, as well as between 'local' people and outsiders. On the rising tide of environmentalism in the 1980s, however, such concerns tended to be marginalized by the struggle between modernist and populist environmental discourse in development studies.

By the end of the 1980s, environmentalist narratives of development had gained sufficient influence for the United Nations to seek international agreement on the need for 'sustainable development' that did not damage natural resources in ways that would prejudice their usefulness to future generations (WCED 1987). This amounted to an acknowledgement that industrialization in general, and its highly uneven social and economic impacts under capitalism, were creating environmental problems on a scale that required a reassessment of industrial urban society – modernization – as an unproblematic model for a developed economy. International consensus on the need for sustainable development therefore significantly shifted the terms of debate within development studies. In the next section we review the principal axes of that debate in relation to natural resource management.

'Incorporated environmentalism' and political ecology: the 1990s

The World Conference on Environment and Development (WCED) in some ways marked the high point of environmental populism in the 1990s. It represented a triumph for the many organizations that had lobbied for decades to have environmental matters considered as part of development policy. It also marked the realignment of much of the scientific establishment in favour of international efforts to manage environmental change, in the wake of confirmation of polar depletion of the ozone layer of the earth's atmosphere and growing concern about climate change due to increased atmospheric concentration of carbon dioxide. The collapse of the Soviet Union and the end of the cold war also opened up the field of international politics, and one observer commented that the WCED 'was not a conference about the environment at all, it concerned the world's economy and how the environment affects it ... [T]his was the first meeting of world leaders since the end of the Cold War. The old East/West agenda is dead, attention is now focused on North and South' (Sandbrook 1992: 16).

It is at least arguable that the international consensus on the need for 'sustainable development' manifested at the WCED marked the demise of modernization as a model for development, since it called into question so many of the science-based technologies (notably the consumption of energy from fossil fuels, and the production of food using agrochemicals) on which the industrialization model of modern society had been based. In development studies 'sustainable development' quickly became established as a new field of contested interpretations. A neo-liberal interpretation stressed environmental management through neo-classical market mechanisms, made possible through the valuation and pricing of natural resources, or 'environmental services', to reflect supply and demand. Sustainable development would thus be achieved by 'getting the prices right'. A variant on this approach focused on game theory as the basis of understanding institutional behaviour in the management of shared resources.

While these economic paradigms significantly influenced the development of environmental policy, such as emissions trading schemes, in development studies they were keenly contested by 'community-based natural resource management' paradigms that had emerged in the 1980s. From the perspective of such populist narratives, neo-liberal prescriptions of environmental management through market mechanisms merely reinforced existing international power relations – a 'reformist' environmentalism, incorporated into an agenda of continued capitalist growth. Despite the continued political prominence of populist environmentalist opposition to the emergence of a neo-liberal 'global governance' (as, for example, in Seattle in 1999), by the mid-1990s the political economy critique (see above) of populist environmental narratives was becoming more widely aired in development studies (Leach and Mearns 1996). This not only opened up the possibility for environmental narratives to address issues of control over resources but also raised questions of social change and development: nature is now seen as 'socially constructed – no longer just an exploitable domain' (Escobar 1996: 47). The emergence of 'political ecology' in the 1990s represented a confluence of political economy approaches to the analysis of resource use and environmental conservation (Peet and Watts 1996: 2) with constructivist approaches that drew on the 'indigenous knowledge' research of the 1980s to understand how competing discourses of nature represented not just competing understandings of nature but also different ideas about how decisions should be taken about nature, and by whom (Forsyth 2003). Peet and Watts (2004) have identified two principal streams of work within political ecology.

The first focuses on the power relations inherent in the construction of knowledge about 'nature'. This draws on the populist-inspired narratives of indigenous technical knowledge, and the critique of colonial science of the 1980s, which itself can be traced back to earlier populist narratives of the colonial period. Despite these antecedents, however, arguments within political ecology on the construction of knowledge about nature identify both science and its alternative (for example, indigenous knowledge) as inherently political processes (Forsyth 2003). This strand of political ecology draws heavily upon post-structuralist approaches to knowledge and overlaps significantly with science and technology studies on the social and political aspects of scientific explanation, particularly in relation to environmental issues such as risk.

This line of analysis offers not only a means to investigate current development policy, but also suggests a reinterpretation of colonial experience, whereby, if solutions did not work, this was often put down to the entrenched conservatism of the indigenous populations. Rational science and 'facts' obtained and interpreted within the scope of the scientists' own knowledge setting were relied upon to make decisions often at the expense of the social and political context in which the knowledge was used (Beinart 1984; Richards 1985; Roe 1994). For development studies this colonial legacy and the continued dominance of Western over indigenous knowledge systems still provide a front where discourses of knowledge and its use are related to what others still see as imperial dominance without colonialism (Said 1994).

The second main strand of political ecology is concerned with governance, justice and control over natural resources. It draws on the perception that many of the 'environmental' movements in developing countries are concerned with asserting control over those resources in the face of government or commercial claims to exploit or conserve them. This 'environmentalism of the poor' (Martinez-Alier 2003) shows clear continuity with the populist environmental narrative of the 1980s, but is more alert to the processes of struggle within 'local' communities rather than seeing the locus of struggle as being essentially between the 'local' and the 'non-local'. Peet and Watts (2004) observe that local 'environmental' struggles over natural resources are the means through which 'globalization' is mediated or created in each locale. They argue that environmental discourse, including the criteria and process by which sustainability is to be assessed, essentially defines a preferred choice of development, and, in that sense, is a key area of contestation over alternative visions of development.

The emergence of participatory resource governance as a theme in development studies has meant that since the early 1990s there has been a renewed focus on studies investigating the creation of local spaces for the expression of resource governance interests. While this may be a logical attempt by the discipline to force a renegotiation of the post-colonial resource use turf, it has also meant that emerging discourses on natural resource use are driven by practice following experiences of local actors and other animators. It is instructive to note, for example, that in the case of community-based natural resources management, although its emergence in the late 1980s to early 1990s signified a radical paradigm shift in discursive regional practices on the management of natural resources, especially in Africa, there has been no attempt to create or generate grand theory. Rather the interest has been to treat the discourse as perennially nascent and therefore still in need of documentation before grand theory-building can begin. A possible reason for the absence of empirically derived grand theory in the current discourse stems in part from a desire to purge itself of the modernist influences of the scientism of the immediate post-war period that was (ab)used by colonial empires in effecting resource alienation. Further, the nature of the discipline as a bridge between a variety of disparate areas of study that have no common conceptualization of nature or natural resource use makes theory-building that much more difficult. Alternatively, it may well be that there is no current need for grand theory as current practice in resource use is adequately explained by existing knowledge. But as Watts (1999) observes, there is still a need for a grand theory if the discipline is to have coherence, binding together our understanding of the place of natural resources in the development discourse.

Conclusion

We have briefly reviewed the impact of colonialism, and the narratives about natural resource use associated with it, on the emerging field of development studies in the 1950s and 1960s. As some have observed, 'the end of direct political control might have been expected to open the way for more independent thinking about the relationship between society and nature perhaps based on non-western traditions and cultural fashions' (Adams 2003: 11). We have argued that colonial discourse on nature, whether to modernize along utilitarian lines and according to scientific principles, or to protect nature, and/or natives, from industrialization, continues to influence environmental policy-making. The crisis of modernization since the 1970s, however, and the rise of environmentalism that culminated in international consensus on the need for sustainable development in the 1990s, has opened spaces for anti-modernist discourse. Initially these drew heavily on 'communitarian' populist narratives that failed to address processes of social difference and change, but have increasingly incorporated political economic analysis of struggles over natural resources and post-structuralist approaches to understanding the political dimensions of production of knowledge about natural resources and their 'degradation'. The emerging field of political ecology thus offers to development studies an important new avenue through which to understand competing agendas not only of natural resource use but, through them, agendas of social and economic change.

References

Adams, W. M. (2003) 'Nature and the colonial mind', in W. Adams and M. Mullighan (eds), *Decolonising Nature. Strategies for Conservation in a Post-colonial Era*, London: Earthscan

Beinart, W. (1984) 'Soil erosion, conservation and ideas about development: a southern African exploration, 1900–1960', *Journal of Southern African Studies*, 11(1): 52–83

Berry, S. (1993) *No Condition Is Permanent: The Social Dynamics of Agrarian Change in Sub-Saharan Africa*, Madison: University of Wisconsin Press

Blaikie, P. (1985) *The Political Economy of Soil Erosion in Developing Countries*, London: Longman

Blaikie, P. and H. Brookfield (1987) *Land Degradation and Society*, London: Methuen

Botkin, D. (1990) *Discordant Harmonies*, New York: Oxford University Press

Brokensha, D., D. M. Warren and O. Werner (1980) *Indigenous Knowledge Systems and Development*, Washington, DC: University Press of America

Bundy, C. (1979) *The Rise and Fall of the South African Peasantry*, London: Heinemann

Byerlee, D., L. Harrington and D. Winkelmann (1982) 'Farming systems research: issues in research strategy and technology design', *American Journal of Agricultural Economics*, 64(5): 897–904

Byres, T. (1982) 'Agrarian transition and the agrarian question', in J. Harris (ed.), *Rural Development*, London: Hutchinson

Chambers, R., A. Pacey and L. A. Thrupp (1989) (eds) *Farmer First. Farmer Innovation and Agricultural Research*, London: Intermediate Technology Publications

Chanock, M. (1991) 'Paradigms, policies and property: a review of the customary law of land tenure', in K. Mann and R. Roberts (eds), *Law in Colonial Africa*, London: James Currey

Colony of Southern Rhodesia (1930) *Official Year Book of the Colony of Southern Rhodesia 1924–1928*, Salisbury: Rhodesia Printing and Publishing Company

— (1939) *Report of the Commission to Enquire into the Preservation, etc., of the Natural Resources of the Colony*, Salisbury: Rhodesia Printing and Publishing Company

Conroy, C. and M. Litvinoff (1988) *The Greening of Aid: Sustainable Livelihoods in Practice*, London: Earthscan

Cowen, M. P. and R. W. Shenton (1991) 'The origin and course of Fabian colonialism in Africa', *Journal of Historical Sociology*, 4(2): 143–74

— (1996) *Doctrines of Development*, London: Routledge

De Janvry, A. and R. Garcia (1988) *Rural Poverty and Environmental Degradation in Latin America: Causes, Effects and Alternative Solutions*, Rome: IFAD

District Native Commissioner for Binga (1961), Unpublished Annual Report of the District Native Commissioner for Binga District, Harare: National Archives of Zimbabwe

Escobar, A. (1996) 'Constructing nature; elements of a post-structuralist political ecology', in R. Peet and M. Watts (eds), *Liberation Ecologies: Environment, Development, Social Movements*, London: Routledge

Fairhead, J. and M. Leach (1996) *Misreading the African Landscape: Society and Ecology in a Forest Savannah Land*, Cambridge: Cambridge University Press

Ford, J. (1971) *The Role of Trypanonosomiasis in African Ecology. A Study of the Tsetse Fly Problem*, Oxford: Clarendon Press

Forsyth, T. (2003) *Critical Political Ecology*, London: Routledge

Grove, R. H. (1987a) 'Early themes in African conservation: the Cape in the 19th century', in D. Anderson and R. Grove, *Conservation in Africa. People, Policies and Practice*, Cambridge: Cambridge University Press

— (1987b) 'Colonial conservation, ecological hegemony and popular resistance: towards a global synthesis', in J. M. MacKenzie (ed.), *Imperialism and the Natural World*, Manchester: Manchester University Press

— (1989) 'Scottish missionaries, evangelical discourse and the origins of conservation thinking in southern Africa, 1820–1900', *Journal of Southern African Studies*, 15(2)

Hardin, G. (1968) 'The tragedy of the commons', *Science*, 162: 1243–8

Harriss, J. (ed.) (1982) *Rural Development*, London: Hutchinson

Haswell, M. (1963) *The Changing Pattern of Economic Activity in a Gambia Village*, London: HMSO

Hecht, S. and A. Cockburn (1990) *The Fate of the Forest*, London: Penguin

Hill, P. (1963) *The Migrant Cocoa Farmers of Southern Ghana*, Cambridge: Cambridge University Press

Kjekshus, H. (1996) *Ecology Control and Economic Development in East African History*, London: James Currey

Leach, M. and R. Mearns (1996) *The Lie of the Land: Challenging Received Wisdom on the African Environment*, London: James Currey

McGregor, J. (1991) *Woodland Resources: Ecology, Policy and Ideology*, Unpublished PhD thesis, Loughborough: Loughborough University of Technology

Mackintosh, M. (1989) *Gender, Class and Rural Transition*, London: Zed Books

Mamdani, M. (1996) *Citizen and Subject. Contemporary Africa and the Legacy of Late Colonialism*, Oxford: James Currey

Martinez-Alier, J. (2003) *The Environmentalism of the Poor: A Study of Ecological Conflicts and Valuation*, Cheltenham: Edward Elgar

Mawhood, P. (1993) *Local Government in the Third World: Experience of Decentralization in Tropical Africa*, Pretoria: Africa Institute of South Africa

Meadows, D. H., D. L. Meadows, J. Randers and W. Behrens III (1972) *The Limits to Growth*, London: Earth Island Ltd

Meillassoux, C. (1964) *Femmes, Greniers et Capitaux*, Paris: Maspero

Metcalfe, C., H. Johnston and F. P. Mennell (1916) 'The development of Rhodesia from a geographical standpoint: discussion', *Geographical Journal*, 48(4): 305–10

Neuman, R. P. (1997) 'Primitive ideas: protected area buffer zones and the politics of land in Africa', *Development and Change*, 28(4): 559–82

NRB (Natural Resources Board of Rhodesia) *Annual Reports*, 1944, 1945, 1946, 1955, 1969, 1979, 1982, 1992

Ostrom, E. (1990) *Managing the Commons*, New York: Cambridge University Press

Pearce, D., E. Barbier and A. Markandya (1990) *Sustainable Development: Economics and environment in the third world*, London: Earthscan

Peet, R. and M. Watts (eds) (1996) *Liberation Ecologies: Environment, Development and Social Movements*, 2nd edn, London: Routledge

— (eds) (2004) *Liberation Ecologies: Environment, Development, Social Movements*, 2nd edn, London: Routledge

Pieterse, J. N. (2000) 'After post development', *Third World Quarterly*, 21(2): 175–91

Plumwood, V. (2003) 'Decolonising relationships with nature', in W. Adams and M. Mullighan (eds), *Decolonising Nature. Strategies for Conservation in a Post-colonial Era*, London: Earthscan

Potts, D. (2000) 'Environmental myths and narratives. Case studies from Zimbabwe', in P. Stott and S. Sullivan (eds), *Political Ecology: Science, Myth and Power*, London: Arnold

Ribot, J. (2003) 'Democratic decentralisation of natural resources: institutional choice and discretionary power transfers in sub-Saharan Africa', *Public Administration and Development*, 23(1): 53–65

Richards, P. (1983) 'Ecological change and the politics of African land use', *African Studies Review*, 26(2): 1–72

— (1985) *Indigenous Agricultural Revolution: Ecology and Food Production in West Africa*, London: Hutchinson

Roe, E. (1994) 'New framework for an old tragedy of the commons and an ageing common property resource management', *Agriculture and Human Values*, 11(1): 29–36

Rostow, W. W. (1960) *The Stages of Economic Growth: A Non-Communist Manifesto*, Cambridge: Cambridge University Press

Said, E. (1994) *Culture and Imperialism*, New York: Knopf

Sandbrook, R. (1992) 'From Stockholm to Rio', in J. Quarrie (ed.), *Earth Summit*, London: Regency Press Corporation

Scoones, I. (1994) *Living with Uncertainty: New Directions in Pastoral Development in Africa*, London: Intermediate Technology Publications

— (1999) 'New ecology and the social sciences: what prospects for a fruitful engagement?', *Annual Review of Anthropology*, 28: 479–507

Scoones, I. and J. Thompson (1994) *Beyond Farmer First*, London: Intermediate Technology Publications

Scoones, I., C. Chibudu, S. Chikura, P. Jeranyama, D. Machaka, W. Machanja, B. Mavedzenge, B. Mombeshora, M. Mudhara, C. Mudziwo, F. Murimbarimba and B. Zirereza (1996) *Hazards and Opportunities. Farming Livelihoods in Dryland Africa: Lessons from Zimbabwe*, London: Zed Books

Thomas, D. and N. Middleton (1994) *Desertification: Exploding the Myth*, Chichester: Wiley

Tiffen, M., M. Mortimore and F. Gichuki (1994) *More People, Less Erosion. Environmental Recovery in Kenya*, Chichester: Wiley

Timberlake, L. (1985) *Africa in Crisis: The Causes and Cures of Environmental Bankruptcy*, London: Earthscan

Troup, R. S. (1940) *Colonial Forest Administration*, Oxford: Oxford University Press

Warren, D., L. Michael, J. Slikkerveer and D. Brokensha (eds) (1995) *The Cultural Dimension of Development: Indigenous Knowledge Systems*, London: Intermediate Technology Publications (Indigenous Knowledge and Development series)

Watts, M. (1983a) *Silent Violence. Food Famine and the Peasantry in Northern Nigeria*, Berkeley: University of California Press

— (1983b) 'Good try, Mr Paul: populism and the politics of African land use', *African Studies Review*, 26(2): 73–83

— (1999) 'Collective wish images: geographical imaginaries and the crisis of development', in J. Allen and D. Massey (eds), *Human Geography Today*, Cambridge: Polity Press

WCED (World Commission on Environment and Development) (1987) *Our Common Future*, Oxford: Oxford University Press

Young, C. (1994) *The African Colonial State in Comparative Perspective*, New Haven, CT: Yale University Press

10 | Individuals, organizations and public action: trajectories of the 'non-governmental' in development studies

DAVID LEWIS

This chapter traces the emergence of the 'non-governmental' as a category of research in development studies during the past two decades and seeks to analyse the reasons for this growth of interest. The piece begins with a brief personal review of the growth of writings on non-governmental organizations (NGOs) which took place in the 1980s. It then goes on to examine explanations for the growth of 'non-governmentalism' within some sections of development studies, finding them in the increased numbers and profiles of NGOs and the emergence of new opportunities for applied research. Both of these were loosely associated with the ascendancy of neo-liberalism at this time, which brought a disillusionment with states and state-led development, strategies of privatization, an expansion of academic consultancy opportunities and an emerging set of new agendas of 'alternative development'.

NGOs were not, however, new, and the chapter then goes on to, first, uncover some of the hidden history of the non-governmental sector, and then investigate some of the reasons for the 'remembering' of the non-governmental which took place within development studies from the late 1980s onwards. Some of the main problems associated with the academic literature on NGOs are then discussed. It is argued that many of these shortcomings resulted from the conditions under which much of this NGO literature was produced, including normative bias, a sense of parochialism, predominantly non-theoretical content and a strong emphasis on managerialism. Finally, some pointers for productive ways forward for NGO research are briefly outlined.

Encountering the non-governmental

The narrative of the growing preoccupation with NGOs among some sections of development researchers to some extent coincides with my own professional career trajectory within development studies. I therefore begin with some personal, somewhat autobiographical, reflections on this theme. During my years as a social anthropology undergraduate in the early 1980s (having selected as many development-related courses as possible), and subsequently as a one-year postgraduate development studies student, the subject never came up. I do not recall ever coming across the term 'NGO', or indeed discussion about the existence or roles of such organizations, within research literature on either the theory or practice of development during those years. If I return now to some of the texts concerned with development policy and practice that I can remember reading and identifying with at that time, such as Sandy Robertson's *People and the State* (1984), Norman Long's *An Introduction to the Sociology of Rural Development* (1977) or Lucy Mair's *Anthropology and Development* (1984), I find that this is confirmed. There is simply no mention of such matters in the chapter headings or text, and there is not even an entry for 'NGOs' or 'voluntary organizations' in the index. How and why did all this change?

My first contact with the world of NGOs came with a decision to begin studying for a PhD at the Centre for Development Studies at the University of Bath. It was a personal introduction rather than one encountered through the academic literature. My research, which was funded by the UK Economic and Social Research Council (ESRC), was concerned with the analysis of new agricultural technology and agrarian change in rural Bangladesh. My supervisor, Professor Geoffrey D. Wood, had, over a decade or so of research work in Bangladesh, built up some close personal ties with a number of local activists and emerging development NGO professionals. In particular, Wood had formed a relationship with an organization known as Proshika, a large Bangladeshi NGO that had emerged in the mid-1970s and had gradually scaled up its credit and Freire-inspired social mobilization activities over large areas of the country. The leader of Proshika, Dr Qazi Faruque Ahmed, was, as a result of these links, one of the first people I met in Bangladesh. The organization was in a sense my introduction to the country, helping me with study visits to several possible rural fieldwork locations courtesy not only of their senior management but also their generous and patient field staff. As it turned out, the fieldwork that I eventually undertook in rural Bangladesh was in a part of the country where Proshika did not actually work, and my subsequent PhD research did not in any way engage with the theme of NGOs.

Nevertheless, the experience of undertaking research in Bangladesh had brought me into informal contact with the subject of the 'non-governmental' for the first time. For a variety of reasons, Bangladesh had seen a distinctive and relatively large-scale local NGO sector emerge in the years since liberation from Pakistan in 1971.[1] The country had also become a major area of interest for a new group of international NGO advocates and supporters. For example, I can recall hearing about the work of David Korten, one of the leading writers on NGOs at the time, during this period (1987) when he visited Bangladesh on a consultancy visit for the United States Agency for International Development

(USAID). Bangladesh's Grameen Bank, which had begun as an action research project on rural credit undertaken by Professor Md. Yunus, a professor of economics at Chittagong University, was at that time also beginning to gain an international reputation for its micro-finance work with rural women (see Holcombe 1995). It became clear to me that growing attention was being given to the idea of development NGOs, chiefly as private organizations delivering services, but also in more radical circles for their advocacy and grassroots mobilization possibilities. Indeed, by the late 1980s there was a distinct 'buzz' around the subject in Bangladesh and beyond, much of it coming from the United States, with an emphasis on service delivery and advocacy work, though with some of the Nordic donors and Canada also providing assistance to NGOs engaging in social mobilization work.[2]

In the rural development field in particular, there was growing interest in the role of NGOs as innovators of new technologies and approaches to working with the poor, and in 1990 I became involved as a contract researcher with a large-scale research initiative being undertaken by Dr John Farrington at the Overseas Development Institute (ODI).[3] This project set out to collect a wide range of comparative case studies of rural NGO activity in Africa, Asia and Latin America and to explore evolving relations with government. Initially, I was employed to coordinate the research in Bangladesh, but then later undertook similar work in the Philippines, which was another area where NGOs had been attracting attention for some time. I soon found myself part of a growing community of researchers within development studies, into which many people had stumbled through routes broadly similar to my own (albeit largely 'accidental'), coming into contact with NGOs through other work on broader development themes such as community development, grassroots politics, gender studies and natural resource management and agricultural technology.

When I later decided to seek a full-time academic job in the UK (in early 1995) I was surprised to see that the London School of Economics was recruiting a 'lecturer in non-governmental organizations'. It was to be within this institutional setting that I began more systematically to undertake research and reflection on the NGO theme for the first time. The LSE's interest in NGOs had not come from the direction of development studies but instead from UK social policy.[4] A successful masters programme on organization and policy issues in the British voluntary sector had gradually begun to attract international attention, and small numbers of NGO staff and researchers, particularly from India, had begun to find their way into the MSc programme. The idea for developing specialized research and teaching on the NGO and development theme was then born.[5] As a result of this post, I spent much of the years between 1995 and 2001 working on NGO issues as my primary area of research and teaching at LSE. Perhaps this makes the reflections on NGOs and development studies that I present in this chapter essentially those of the outsider, since they are made from a formal positioning within another discipline.[6] I have, however, remained a member of the Development Studies Association (DSA) and the wider development studies community both at the UK and international levels. I have also worked as part of the 'academic consultant' community, which, as I will argue, has, not always for the best, helped to bring the agenda of NGO research more clearly into focus within development studies. This account is by no means definitive, however, and remains a very personal one: there is no doubt much more to be written about the 'archaeology' of this subject.

NGOs in development studies

The period of relative invisibility of NGOs within development studies ended suddenly with a slew of books and articles which began appearing from the late 1980s onwards.[7] In the United States, the writer and activist David C. Korten's influential 1987 article on NGO 'generations' was followed later by his book *Getting to the 21st Century: Voluntary Action and the Global Agenda* (1990), which set out the case for NGOs, and particularly those of 'the South', as key actors in development. This was a wide-ranging advocacy document which brought together many of Korten's influential papers and articles of recent years alongside many new and emerging ideas. Broadly populist in its orientation, the book combined a theoretical critique of the idea of development as economic growth along with an attack on the conventional institutions and practices of the international development community. Korten advocated instead a 'development as transformation' approach at both the institutional and the personal levels as part of an emerging school of alternative development embodied in the writings of Robert Chambers. While not under any illusion that many NGOs were yet working towards such goals with any real degree of success, the book was confident in its claim that NGOs constituted an important site for potential positive change in development practice. Korten's perspective was therefore both normative and idealistic:

> [NGOs] ... seldom had a clear strategic focus, often lacked technical capability, and seemed reluctant to cooperate with other organisations ... Yet ... the constraints faced by NGOs are largely the self-imposed constraints of their own self-limiting vision. NGOs are capable of shedding these constraints, as many have demonstrated. Their participants need only the courage to embrace a more expansive vision of their roles and potential. (Korten 1990: xiii)

There were similar kinds of publications also emerging from the UK at the end of the 1980s. The first and one of the most influential of these was John Clark's *Democratising Development: The Role of Voluntary Organisations* (1991). This was written by an author with long insider experience at Oxfam, who also saw the potential importance of NGOs, particularly those from the South, as vehicles for transforming development practice. During this period another prominent writer from the UK was Alan Fowler, whose PhD thesis at Sussex University on NGOs in Kenya was one of the first in-depth studies of the new field. His work was widely circulated. Fowler was prolific in his writings on NGOs, which combined academic analysis with more practical material directed at NGO staff and donors.[8] The first academic conference on NGOs in the UK took place in 1992 at the University of Manchester (co-organized with Save the Children Fund UK), and it was from this conference that the widely cited volume *Making a Difference: NGOs and Development in a Changing World*, edited by Mike Edwards and David Hulme, emerged. The three ODI volumes on *NGOs and the State* plus the *Reluctant Partners?* overview volume were published later in 1993 (Farrington and Bebbington 1993; Bebbington and Thiele 1993; Wellard and Copestake 1993; Farrington and Lewis 1993). Within the same crop of NGO publications at that time, Carroll's (1992) book was also influential. Its focus on NGOs and agricultural development in Latin America was more research-focused in tone and structure than many similar studies of the period, and paid close attention to history, context and politics. Carroll's book provided a detailed and systematic comparative study of rural development organizations, which pre-empted many of the NGO debates that would later unfold.

By contrast, a World Bank collection edited by Paul and Israel (1991) drew the NGO work of Korten and others firmly into the emerging policy framework of the period, setting out the reasons for the Bank's decision to begin 'an institution-wide effort to expand its work with NGOs' (Beckman 1991: 134). This decision was based on the recognition that states and markets had limited capacity to reduce poverty while NGOs had distinctive competences such as closeness to the poor, committed leadership and capacity to build access to services for the poor. This was the start of the period of explicit recognition of NGOs from within the unfolding neo-liberal development agenda, which gained confidence rapidly following the end of the cold war. 'Neoliberalism' was a return to the preoccupations of an earlier economic liberalism in the nineteenth century, which privileged the market as 'the proper guiding instrument by which people should organize their economic lives' (MacEwan 1999: 4). While this market-oriented policy agenda brought centre-stage the importance of market competition and theories of comparative advantage, it also shifted ideas about government away from national planning and state services towards markets and the 'non-governmental' actors. It envisaged a new 'enabling' role in which the function of government was to secure the conditions in which markets could operate more fully across a range of areas of social and economic life. For example, the reorganization of wider social service delivery to citizens could be seen in the growth, for example, of non-formal education in Bangladesh and other countries provided predominantly by NGOs. These policies were also highly supportive of the provision of micro-credit aimed at the strengthening of women's incomes. The result was a dramatic explosion in the numbers of micro-credit organizations (mostly in the non-governmental sector) and programmes in both rural and urban areas and the growth of a veritable global micro-finance industry.

Many other policy-level documents on NGOs soon followed, such as the OECD's (1993) *Non-governmental Organizations and Governments: Stakeholders for Development* collection of overviews of donors' NGO policies and the Commonwealth Foundation's (1995) *Non-governmental Organizations: Guidelines for Good Policy and Practice* document. Some emphasized the growing discourse of 'partnership' between NGOs, government and for-profit actors, while others set out guidelines for improving the internal organization of NGOs through improved governance, management capacity and impact assessment. The managerialist language of organizational strengthening, capacity-building, strategic planning and best practice was an essential aspect of this agenda, and much of it began to drift a considerable distance away from the more radical approaches of writers on NGOs such as Korten, Fowler and Clark.

While all this publishing activity created a high profile for the 'new field' within development studies of NGOs and development, and created a potentially useful new interface between activists and researchers, it did not add up to a rigorous or theoretically grounded research literature. Indeed, this was probably not the intention of most of these activist/researcher-writers. Instead, this literature contained much empirical case study material (mostly collected by the organizations concerned), a range of prescriptions concerning new sets of development policy agendas and a tendency for NGOs to serve the purpose of a 'blank screen' on to which reflections and images drawn from the growing movement of ideas and models of 'alternative development' could be projected. For example, Korten's work, which was tinged also with what can perhaps be described as 'utopian managerialism', synthesized emerging ideas about 'organizational learning' and 'strategic management' with strong idealism. Korten drew heavily on his own extensive practical involvement with NGOs, with donors such as USAID and with the new People-centred Development Forum. Korten had extensive field experience and sought practical solutions to real-world problems, but sometimes more personal interests and reflections seemed to tug in a different, more idealistic direction.[9] Clark, on the other hand, was writing as a more pragmatic idealist, concluding his wide-ranging overview of NGO activities within development with a clarion call for NGOs to inform and confront the centres of power in order to shake up prevailing and failing development visions and practices. Soon afterwards, Clark went to the World Bank, where he established its NGO unit, partly as a result of the institution taking him up on the challenge presented by his book.

The gist of this work was broadly positive about the potential of NGOs, and particularly those of the South, to contribute to new ways of thinking about and performing development.[10] Many focused on the ways in which NGOs were being 'held back' in their potential capacity for social transformation, as represented in the debates about 'scaling up', 'capacity-building' and 'partnership' prevalent at that time.[11] There were relatively few doubters among this first crop of writings, though we have noted Tendler's much earlier critique. Dissident voices that were raised at this time from an academic standpoint included Brett's (1993) call for a more rigorous theorization of the comparative advantage and accountability claims made by, and on behalf of, NGOs, while Vivian (1994) questioned the 'magic bullet' philosophy that underpinned a tendency for some pro-NGO writers to construct NGOs primarily as all-purpose solutions to development problems. Interestingly, the strongest voices of dissent came from the activist community within the international humanitarian aid field. Hanlon's (1991) book on Mozambique portrayed international NGOs as a major barrier to post-conflict reconstruction and development. De Waal and Omaar's (1993) work was equally savage in the criticisms made of international NGOs' roles in the Horn of Africa. The lack of ability of humanitarian NGOs to coordinate and cooperate in Sudan during the famine relief operation in 1985 was a major theme of Abdel Ati's (1993).

A second batch of publications began to develop a more critical edge in the mid-1990s, with two more Manchester-edited volumes. The initially optimistic theme of 'making a difference?' had in the ensuing two years shifted to 'beyond the magic bullet?' and 'too close for comfort?', a change that was beginning to reveal a range of anxieties in the minds of the editors and some, though not most, of the contributors, who continued on the whole to present a positive face of NGOs and alternative development. Of the contributors to all three of these volumes, at a rough tally thirty-six were NGO staff or supportive consultants, seventeen were academics in consultancy mode and only fifteen were researchers writing if not entirely working 'outside the aid system'. Other books appearing at this time were Smillie's (1995) *The Alms Bazaar*, a good general critical survey of the emerging perceptions of the world of NGOs. The optimistic strain of writings on NGOs as the main future of development was augmented by books such as J. Fisher's *The Road from Rio* (1993) and *Non-governments* (1998). More theoretical writings on NGOs did not arrive until later in the decade. William Fisher's (1997) piece on NGOs engaged with the context of neo-liberalism, and examined the political implications of NGO discourses. Likewise, Stewart's (1997: 12) paper in the *Review of African Political Economy* commented on the apolitical nature of the new 'NGO management science' on one side and the prevailing ideology of 'NGOs do it cheaper, better, faster' on the other. Outside the more obvious field of writings on and about NGOs, interesting work was beginning to appear in which NGOs were not on the whole the main subject but were important actors that could be analysed within wider institutional landscapes and histories.[12] Clarke's (1998) work on the Philippines was one such study, as was Devine's (2002) research, which critically examined government and donor assumptions about the role of NGOs in the policy process.[13]

Re-remembering hidden histories?

According to Jean and John Comaroff (1999) the resurgence of interest in the concept of civil society around the late-twentieth-century Western world can be best characterized as an act of ideologically triggered 're-remembering' rather than as something qualitatively new. A similar case can be made for NGOs, since there is a long history to the NGO phenomenon which predates their rise to prominence within the development studies discourse.[14] As Sogge (Sogge et al. 1996: 1) puts it: 'After decades of quiet and respectable middle-class existences, private development agencies have come up in the world.'

While NGOs had been present on a small scale for many years, they had rarely troubled the landscape of development researchers or policy-makers. In a lengthy article entitled 'Two centuries of participation', Charnovitz (1997: 185) summarizes a long history of NGO activity at the international level, some of which has remained largely hidden within development studies. He is critical of the ahistoricity of both NGO researchers and supporters: 'Although some observers seem to perceive NGO involvement as a late-twentieth-century phenomenon, in fact it has occurred for over 200 years. Advocates of a more extensive role for NGOs weaken their cause by neglecting this history because it shows a long time custom of governmental interaction with NGOs in the making of international policy.' Charnovitz traces the evolution of NGO roles from 'emergence' in 1775–1918 through to what he terms a current phase of 'empowerment' since the 1992 Rio conference. He begins with the rise of national-level issue-based organizations in the eighteenth century, focused on such issues as the abolition of the slave trade and peace movements, and shows that by the early twentieth century NGOs had built associations to promote their identities at national and international levels. At the 1910 World Congress of International Associations there were 132 associations concerned with issues as varied as transportation, intellectual property rights, narcotics control, public health, agriculture and environmental protection.

After the Second World War, Article 71 of the United Nations Charter provided for NGO involvement in UN activities. Though they were active, however, NGOs' influence was little more than 'nuisance value', since they were hampered by cold war tensions and a weak UN Economic and Social Council (ECOSOC), the body liaising with NGOs. It was only in the 1970s that there was an increased 'intensification' of NGO roles, such as a growing presence at the UN Stockholm Environment Conference in 1972 and the World Population Conference in Bucharest in 1974. NGOs then played a key role in the drafting of the UN Convention on the Rights of the Child. Since 1992, NGO influence has continued to grow, as evidenced by the UN Conference on Environment and Development (UNCED), which saw NGOs active in both its preparation and within the conference itself.

NGO histories can also be recovered from many other parts of the world. In Latin America, the growth of NGOs was influenced by the Catholic Church and the growth of 'liberation theology' in the 1960s, signalled by some sections of the Church's commitment to the poor, and to some extent by the growth of popular Protestantism (Escobar 1997). The political philosophy of the Brazilian educator Paolo Freire, with his ideas about 'education for critical consciousness', were also influential (Blackburn 2000). Peasant movements seeking improved rights to land and against authoritarianism also contributed to the rise of NGOs (Bebbington and Thiele 1993). Sen's (1992) account of NGOs in India highlights the influence of Christian missionaries, the reformist middle classes and Gandhian ideas. In Africa too there is a long history of research on voluntary associations in relation to issues such as urbanization and social integration (Lewis 1999b). Research by Honey and Okafor (1998) on home-town associations in Nigeria shows how community organizations are increasingly important for mediating resources and relationships between local communities and global labour markets, educational opportunities and village resources. Middle-class local and international charitable works, grassroots activism of many kinds and the long-standing activities of missionaries each meant that the non-governmental theme had always been marginally present within development studies research: but it had rarely if ever become explicit.

If NGOs, or the non-governmental more broadly, were not new, then we need to explain the sudden appearance of the NGO agenda within development studies. The growth of writings on NGOs from the late 1980s onwards was largely driven at the level of policy by the privatizing imperatives of neo-liberalism, as we saw in the previous section, both at the intellectual level of ideological recruitment and at the practical level of creating more opportunities for applied research. The crisis of development theory in the 1980s (see Booth 1993, 1994) had contributed to the loss of confidence that development could be produced by the state, and coincided with the rise to prominence of neo-liberal analysis which had long argued that state intervention was the problem rather than the solution. Neo-liberals came to dominate in the international financial institutions, many governments and in significant sections of the development industry. Policies of privatization, market liberalization and administrative reform came to represent the dominant solutions to development problems (Schech and Haggis 2000). All this led to greater levels of funding for NGOs, particularly those engaged in service delivery.[15]

This would not be the first time that research agendas in development studies shifted with the changing priorities of donors. For example, when international donors began to develop bilateral approaches to funding governments in the 1960s there was a tremendous growth of development studies research on the state (Tvedt 2003). Such shifts are in many ways to be applauded, since one might expect a mix of critical and supportive findings (from the donor point of view) to emerge, a blend of applied and theoretical approaches, and a resultant increase in the overall *relevance* of development research (see Bebbington 1994). But in the case of NGO research, four sets of outcomes can be identified, and these are tied up with the ways in which NGOs found their way on to the development studies research agenda. Most of these outcomes have not been particularly positive from the perspective of the strengthening of development studies. These are discussed in the next section.

Problems of NGO research in development studies

While there were strengths to some of this new literature, there have long been criticisms within development studies of the research literature on NGOs. These criticisms can be grouped into four main categories and each is discussed in more detail below. The first is that much of the work has been driven by normative agendas, and characterized as written by people with insufficient distance from their subject of research. The second is that there has been a strong ideological emphasis to much of the work on NGOs, such as the strong tendencies for NGO researchers to be either 'for' or 'against' NGOs in some broad sense, or the influence of managerialism in writings about NGOs. A third set of issues centres on the idealism of many of those writing about NGOs, and the result that expectations have been projected on to NGOs that most are by definition unable to live up to. Finally, work on NGOs has suffered from its perceived location (on the applied side) within wider and persisting debates within development studies about 'applied' versus 'pure' research. Each of these criticisms is related to the routes through which research on the non-governmental has (re-)entered development studies and can be seen as outcomes of these trajectories.

Najam (1999: 143) has contrasted the massive growth of interest in NGOs with the relatively small number of research writings on NGOs that were produced:

> ... our conceptual understanding of this terrain is even more scant than the terrain is expansive ... Despite a few notable exceptions, the broader literature on the subject continues to be restrictive for at least three important reasons. First, the scholarship has been overwhelmingly *descriptive* with little effort to synthesize the wealth of descriptive evidence into analytic frameworks, empirical typologies or holistic conceptual maps of the entire sector as a sector. Second, the focus of the literature is largely *sectarian* in that studies have tended to concentrate on restricted bands of the larger, and much broader, spectrum of activities that these organizations indulge in. Third, much of the literature is *parochial* in that most studies focus exclusively on narrow segments of the sector that they are familiar with (or aware of) with little effort to establish connections with other segments. The result of these chronic deficiencies is a sporadic and temperamental appreciation of the behaviour of this sector, as a sector. (My italics)

There are others who share the view of researchers such as Najam (1996) that overall the research literature on NGOs within development studies is both normative and weak. Tvedt (1998: 3), for example, argues that the whole field lacks conceptual clarity and that 'Definitions have tended to be normative and ideological or so broad as to make discussion and comparison difficult.'

These characteristic weaknesses follow from the conditions under which this literature on NGOs has evolved. The normative dimension is the first outcome of the process described above, since increases in academic consultancy opportunities for financially beleaguered university departments led to a great preponderance of NGO-related evaluation studies and impact assessments which subsequently found their way into published literature.[16] Also contributing to this process was the tendency for those working within NGOs, suddenly presented with the opportunity of an audience within academia, to present accounts of their own organizations and activities in relatively uncritical documented form.

A second outcome was the ideological character of some of what can be termed the 'pro-NGO' literature. In particular, the practical concerns of perceived inefficiency and corruption in the public sector which led many donors to view NGOs as new and alternative channels of funding to government contributed to an at times somewhat virulent strain of anti-state sentiment within the NGO literature. For example, central to Fisher's (1998: 2) upbeat account of the rise of NGOs as 'non-governments' were assumptions about the ' ... increasing inability of the nation-state to muddle through as it confronts the long-term consequences of its own ignorance, corruption and lack of accountability'. This type of thinking led to many accounts of NGOs which took on a strongly functionalist logic. In such accounts, NGOs were often represented as having a set of comparative advantages in relation to public sector agencies such as cost effectiveness, less bureaucratic operating styles, closeness to communities and reduced prevalence to corruption (Cernea 1988).[17] One aspect of the ideology of 'non-governmentalism' was therefore a rather conservative strain of populism in which NGOs were represented as essentially private, non-state protectors of the public interest.

Another manifestation of non-governmentalism was more idealistic, even utopian, in character. This is the third outcome of the 're-remembering of the non-governmental' which occurred in the late 1980s. NGOs became seen by some as a kind of *tabula rasa* on to which could be projected a set of ideas – again, born of the frustration with decades of disappointing development interventions – about issues such as empowerment, participation and new forms of management. David Korten epitomized this line of thinking. His book drew together his ideas about NGOs, citizen action and organizational learning into a potent and readable, if somewhat rose-tinted, blend. Korten's presentation of powerful ideas about new forms of participative 'strategic management' and the evolution of NGOs through several ever more sophisticated organizational 'generations' towards the goal of mobilizing citizens, rather than providing services, was rooted to some extent in his work with some impressive organizations in South and South-East Asia, but they were

211

not always applicable to the 'real world' of NGOs at large, except perhaps as forms of inspirational writing.[18]

Finally, the other outcome that needs to be mentioned here is the tendency among many development researchers to conflate the critique of 'applied research' within development with a dismissal of the NGO research agenda itself. The study of NGOs became strongly associated with what Thomas (2000) has argued is a dominant trend in development thinking which associates the idea of development mainly with 'practice' rather than theory. Perhaps stemming from this tendency is an assumption that most of the people who do research on NGOs must necessarily be people who are broadly in sympathy with NGOs or work for them and are not fully committed academics.[19] This is in part understandable, because much of the increase in consultancy work in development studies during the 1980s was concerned with applied research in relation to NGOs.[20] And it was also the case that many NGOs themselves, as they became more prominent, began to commission research and evaluations from academics in consultancy mode.

But research within development studies which is critical of NGOs has sometimes been more critical of the 'applied origins' of much of the NGO research rather than of NGOs as social phenomena. It is therefore important that a development studies research engagement with the subject of NGOs draws on its own data sources and analyses and not simply on the assertion that all NGO-related research is necessarily 'applied' research. The fact remains that a considerable portion of the applied research being undertaken by members of university departments for development agencies had little to do with NGOs, which, on the whole, have been quite keen to avoid academic scrutiny. Although it has always been difficult to obtain accurate figures, it is estimated that even at the height of NGO funding by donors only around 10–20 per cent of foreign assistance worldwide went through or to NGOs, leaving the vast bulk of foreign aid firmly rooted in bilateral and multilateral government relationships.

The conventional view of the weakness of NGO research, however, which has been argued by several people such as Najam (1999) and Tvedt (1998), is by now to some degree an oversimplification. NGOs have increasingly been subjects for development studies research as much in passing as subjects in themselves. Examples of this type of work include Crewe and Harrison's (1998) study of power and inequality within development encounters in Zambia and Sri Lanka, Hilhorst's (2003) research on local level politics and organization in the Philippines and Fox's (1998) analysis of the cultural practices of development. It can therefore be argued that areas of the 'NGO literature' are also now driven by theoretical interests in such subjects as new social movements, gender and identity and the changing nature of global and local political institutions. This latter type of research seems set to increase as the donor interest in NGOs and civil society has begun to fade as just another policy fashion.

The prospects for future research in relation to NGOs now seem brighter than they have for some time, perhaps precisely because it is becoming possible to separate out more clearly research funding on non-governmental issues from the development donors themselves, who are letting go of their over-heated expectations of NGOs. For example, this year (2004) saw the launch in the UK of a major five-year inter-disciplinary UK ESRC Research Programme which perhaps symbolizes the movement of the subject towards mainstream respectability as an inter-disciplinary research topic in the social sciences. Organized around the wider theme of non-governmental public action rather than focusing simply on NGOs themselves, the programme will structure a portfolio of research projects designed to underpin research which will build theory, generate empirical knowledge and strengthen the relevance of research to both academic and non-academic users. Research can be undertaken at various levels – at the level of global processes and impacts, national and local non-governmental 'sectors' or networks, or at the level of individual organizations themselves. A key challenge for this type of research is the building of links between disciplines on non-governmental themes, as well as the need to connect up research perspectives from both 'industrialized' and 'developing country' contexts to challenge the parallel-worlds problem and to engage more fully with the global and international dimensions of non-governmental action.

NGO-related teaching within development studies still appears to be expanding with courses or options with development studies, development management and social policy attracting considerable interest from students in the UK and from overseas. The challenge for the future within more theoretical perspectives on development studies is to embed the study of NGOs more effectively within courses across major areas of development studies – including the history of development ideas, the economics of state transformations, the changing nature of social services, the workings of the aid industry, and the politics of global development identities and processes. Within more applied development studies teaching NGOs will no doubt remain an important topic, and the main need for the future will be to ensure that teaching focuses not only on NGOs but on their relationships with state, market and other civil society actors.

Looking back at the rise of non-governmentalism

The rise of 'non-governmentalism' in the late 1980s and 1990s can in a sense be seen as a projection of a number of different anxieties about development by both policy-makers and academics. The first was the sense of disillusionment, as Broadhead (1987) points out, with more than two decades of government-centred development initiatives in both North and South and the search for alternatives to government aid and new development practices. In the context of the perceived failure of official aid, the development industry discovered NGOs as a possible solution to various problems, such as a demonstrable lack of impact on poverty, based primarily on the idea that they were 'not government' (Stewart 1997).

The second was the theoretical cul-de-sac that many in development studies acknowledged had been reached by the mid-1980s. As Booth (1993: 49) suggests, this 'impasse' consisted of a loose bundle of different problems. The theoretical debates derived from Marxist approaches which had promised so much had not progressed as far as expected and no longer provided coherent 'guidelines for a continuing research programme'. At the same time, there was a widening gulf between 'academic enquiry and the various spheres of development policy and practice'. In an influential article written in 1989, Michael Edwards, writing from a position from within a UK NGO, developed a polemic on 'the irrelevance of development studies' in which he argued that development studies researchers used predominantly extractive research practices and usually contributed little or nothing to the lives of individuals or communities being researched through direct engagement or indirect policy influence (Edwards 1993). One way out of the impasse for many researchers was to simply focus more on empirical studies of the 'new' non-governmental development actors and emerging alternative approaches to development work.

Following on from the issues raised by Edwards and others, a third reason for the rise of a non-governmentalist discourse within development studies was the attraction among a selection of researchers and practitioners of viewing NGOs as a site for 'working through' some of these troubling researcher–practitioner tensions. Since NGOs had traditionally been concerned mainly with local, small-scale projects, research 'with' NGOs on the new participation and empowerment approaches towards grassroots development became a means of rethinking relationships between researchers and practitioners, and rethinking the ethics and morals of development research and action:

> In contrast to 'pure' science and art history (for example) development studies concerns real, living people and cannot therefore be conducted in the abstract.

This is particularly true for ... NGOs such as my own, for which there is no role in the world without moral discourse. At the very least we need to be about the implications of our work for people's lives, and to declare our beliefs and allegiances openly instead of sheltering behind a spurious 'objectivity'. (ibid.: 81)

Such an approach, however, while positive in many ways, produced only limited understanding of NGOs themselves as development actors. Research *with* NGOs is not necessarily research *about* NGOs, and many NGOs have come to retain a strong vested interest in this status quo, which exists around research.

Finally, this spirit of 'non-governmentalism', which became part of a wider applied development studies, came to dominate some UK university departments as a result of new systems of resource allocation and incentives. Universities in the 1980s did not find themselves immune from the restructuring impulses of neo-liberalism and departments such as development studies and anthropology in particular were in many cases driven farther into the commercial world of academic consultancy. At the same time, the NGO community became more interested in and organized for research, as evidenced by the establishment of the International NGO Research and Training Centre (INTRAC) by NGO staff and academic researchers.

All four of these sets of factors, which are of course interrelated, contributed to the rise of non-governmentalism, which has been both a positive and a negative force within development studies. This chapter has tried to unpack some of the themes and approaches that make up the NGO literature. Yet as we have seen, much of this NGO writing never pretended to be academic research, but simply found its way into development studies as part of the 1990s debates about these wider issues, dilemmas and concerns.

Conclusion

On one level, the subject of NGOs has entered development studies in a relatively haphazard and unstructured way, similar to the trajectory suggested by the personal account of my own encounter with NGOs presented at the start of this chapter. One result of this process has been the difficulty that has been experienced within development studies of building up a solid body of research on NGO themes and issues. Yet on another level the rise of non-governmentalism, while largely undisciplined, has been far from accidental and needs to be viewed against the broader contours of the landscape of neo-liberal ascendancy through which those of us presently mid-career in development studies have lived.

Perhaps the 'moment' of strong interest in NGOs within development studies has now passed.[21] It may be that there is now a recognition that the importance of NGOs was exaggerated during the late 1980s and 1990s, or simply that research has fragmented into a more diverse range of topics relating to a wider concept of 'public action' (see Mackintosh 1992), such as governance, services or rights, in which NGOs play a part but no longer form the central theme. Nevertheless, NGOs remain a dominant force in the contemporary world, in relation to a broad range of areas that include development, globalization, human rights and conflict. NGOs need to be studied both in their own right and as a keyhole into wider processes such as privatization, state transformation and changing gender relations.

Research on NGOs has been important as an entry point into the analysis of neo-liberal policies at local, national and global levels, and as a focus for understanding elements of resistance to those policies. NGOs are also likely to remain a focus for the recurring debates on theory and practice between academics and activists. A new and perhaps more fruitful trajectory for researching the non-governmental will be one that understands NGOs as part of ongoing debates about development as neo-liberalism and globalization, as both instruments of, and sites of, resistance to the transformations of principles and practices within these current paradigms.

Notes

1 There were many reasons for this. These reasons included the post-1971 liberation local and international humanitarian effort, the large quantities of foreign aid that quickly came to dominate the country's institutions and economy, and the problems of state-building in the new nation. For more discussion on this see, for example, Lewis (1993) and White (1999).

2 Perhaps the first significant publishing event that reflected this attention was a 1987 'supplement' volume of *World Development*, edited by A. G. Drabek, which contained twenty-four short articles written mainly, though not exclusively, by consultants, activists and policy-makers. These papers set out an agenda of issues in relation to an emerging vision of NGOs as actors which were beginning to present a set of 'development alternatives'. At the same time, there was at least one strong voice of dissent among the crowd. Tendler's (1982) review of the capacities of a sample of seventy-two US NGOs was scathing in its criticisms of their basic management capacity weaknesses.

3 The ODI project also employed many other researchers, including, from the UK, Anthony Bebbington for Latin America and James Copestake for Africa, and boasted a wide range of links with in-country institutions and researchers, such as Aurea Miclat-Teves at the International Institute for Rural Reconstruction (IIRR) in the Philippines and Satish Kumar at the Administrative Staff College of India.

4 A specialized research and teaching unit known as the Centre for Voluntary Organization (now renamed the Centre for Civil Society) in LSE's Department of Social Policy was established in 1987.

5 The separation of research into work undertaken by social policy researchers on non-governmental organizations in the domestic UK 'voluntary sector' and other work undertaken by development studies academics on non-governmental 'development' organizations in other parts of the world prompted me to write about these two 'parallel worlds' of research and the strange, artificial separation between them. Broadly similar debates about issues such as the accountability of organizations, the privatization of service delivery and the tensions between NGO advocacy and service provision were preoccupations of both development studies NGO researchers and social policy academics working on domestic voluntary organizations in the UK, yet there seemed to be no one connecting up the concerns of these two research communities (Lewis 1999a).

6 It is none the less striking how debates in social policy in relation to the voluntary sector to some extent mirror those in development studies in relation to NGOs. Both are inter-disciplinary fields with similar preoccupations, such as poverty and social and economic change, and both fields are also prone to tensions and soul-searching about the relationships between theory and practice.

7 There were books published on NGOs before this period but these tended to be popular journalistic accounts of agencies such as Oxfam (e.g. Jones 1965) or Voluntary Service Overseas (e.g. Adams 1968).

8 It was not until 1997, however, that Fowler's substantial book on NGOs and development entitled *Striking a Balance* emerged.

9 Korten went on to help found *Yes! – A Journal of Positive Growth*, which focused on issues such as environmental justice, voluntary simplicity and fair trade as well as spiritual growth and 'nurturing your inner wisdom'.

10 Stewart (1997) suggests that in this new discourse NGOs and civil society were frequently spoken of in 'hallowed tones'.

11 The tendency for a 'SNGOs good, NNGOs bad' line of thinking to dominate areas of this literature is another result of this populism, and it was only challenged later in the work of writers such as Lister (2001) and others.

12 This has been one of the intentions of the ODI case study books on NGOs and the state in Africa, Asia and Latin America, and the conceptual framework for the *Reluctant Partners?* overview volume had tried to take important first steps in this direction.

13 Stewart (1997) identified a paradox in much of the NGO literature at the time, namely that the general, theoretical overview writings tended to be positive about NGOs while the large numbers of individual NGO case studies produced tended to come up with empirical findings critical of NGO performance. Why, she asked, did the case studies get ignored while the general overviews were taken as fact?

14 The rise of the 'civil society' and the 'NGOs and development' discourses, while separate, are of course linked in important ways. The focus in this chapter is on NGOs, however. For an overview of the rise of civil society ideas in development in relation to Africa, see Lewis (2002).

15 Among other things, the rise of the 'good governance' agenda of the early 1990s was a tempering of the more extreme approaches towards privatization in favour of a more balanced view of potential synergies between state, market and the non-governmental sector. It led to the funding of NGO activities beyond service delivery to include advocacy. It has also subsequently led donors to move away from favouring NGOs as they did in the early to mid-1990s to, in many cases, a rejection of NGOs in favour of a new discourse of 'civil society'. While there are differences among

donors in the ways this is defined, it generally refers to the idea that NGOs are out of favour and that grassroots membership organizations, business associations, 'faith-based groups' and sometimes even trade unions are 'in'.

16 Since I have sometimes used this route to publication myself, I should mention that there are also some points to be made in its favour! One is that it can generate insider accounts of organizations and processes for which few NGOs would ever grant access to 'formal' academic research. NGOs tend, in the words of Edwards (1993: 81), to be 'often protective, defensive and resistant to criticism'. Another is that relatively up-to-date data can be generated and published through this method.

17 More sophisticated than most work of this kind, Fowler's (1990) discussion of the comparative advantage of NGOs suggested that it was not an innate or automatic characteristic, but needed to be operationalized through a conscious strategy.

18 Some suggested that even in relation to these organizations the ideas were somewhat romantic, particularly as some of the organizations grew ever larger and more bureaucratic and retained single, ever more powerful founder-leader individuals firmly in charge at the top.

19 Apart from the idea that it would be impossible to be committed overall to *an* NGO agenda when there are so many different ones available (from traditional charity approaches to campaigns for radical trade reform), there is an irrationality to the idea that in order to do research on NGOs you have necessarily to have worked for one. As someone who has spent time doing research on NGOs, I have lost count of the number of times I have been asked this question by other academics. I have now taken to responding in kind: for example, if the person asking the question is, say, a researcher on health policy, I now ask them whether they have ever worked in a hospital.

20 It is easy to see how such a perception has arisen. For example, the UK DSA NGO study group has from time to time been made up almost entirely of people from NGOs wanting to talk about their organizations' research rather than wishing to talk about research in relation to NGOs as organizations.

21 Donor reviews of NGO sector funding had by the end of the 1990s started to instil a sense of disappointment that NGOs had not lived up to expectations (e.g. Oakley 1999).

References

Abdel Ati, H. A. (1993) 'The development impact of NGO activities in the Red Sea province of Sudan: a critique', *Development and Change*, 24: 103–30

Adams, M. (1968) *Voluntary Service Overseas: The Story of the First Ten Years*, London: Faber

Bebbington, A. (1994) 'Theory and relevance in indigenous agriculture: knowledge, agency and organization', ch. 8 in D. Booth (ed.), *Rethinking Social Development: Theory, Research and Practice*, London: Longman

Bebbington, A. and G. Thiele (eds) (1993) *Non-governmental Organisations and the State in Latin America: Rethinking Roles in Sustainable Agricultural Development*, London: Routledge

Beckman, D. (1991) 'Recent experience and emerging trends', ch. 5 in S. Paul and A. Israel (eds), *Nongovernmental Organizations and the World Bank: Cooperation for Development*, Washington, DC: World Bank

Blackburn, J. (2000) 'Understanding Paulo Freire: reflections on the origins, concepts and possible pitfalls of his educational approach', *Community Development Journal*, 35(1): 3–15

Booth, D. (1993) 'Development research: from impasse to a new agenda', ch. 2 in F. J. Schuurman (ed.), *Beyond the Impasse: New Directions in Development Theory*, London: Zed Books

— (1994) 'Rethinking social development: an overview', in D. Booth (ed.), *Rethinking Social Development: Theory, Research and Practice*, London: Longman

Brett, E. A. (1993) 'Voluntary agencies as development organisations: theorising the problem of efficiency and accountability', *Development and Change*, 24: 269–303

Broadhead, T. (1987) 'NGOs: "in one year, out the other?"', *World Development* (supplement), 15: 1–6

Carroll, T. F. (1992) *Intermediary NGOs: The Supporting Link in Grassroots Development*, Hartford, CT: Kumarian Press

Cernea, M. M. (1988) 'Non-governmental organisations and local development', World Bank Discussion Papers, Washington, DC: World Bank

Charnovitz, S. (1997) 'Two centuries of participation: NGOs and international governance', *Michigan Journal of International Law*, 18(2): 183–286

Clark, J. (1991) *Democratising Development: The Role of Voluntary Organisations*, London: Earthscan

Clarke, G. (1998) 'Nongovernmental organisations and politics in the developing world', *Political Studies*, XLVI: 36–52

Comaroff, J. L. and J. Comaroff (1999) 'Civil society and the critical imagination in Africa: critical perspectives', Chicago, IL: University of Chicago

Commonwealth Foundation (1995), *Non-governmental Organizations: Guidelines for Good Policy and Practice*, London: Commonwealth Foundation

Crewe, E. and E. Harrison (1998) *Whose Development?: An Ethnography of Aid*, London: Zed Books

Devine, J. (2002) 'Ethnography of a policy process: a case study of land redistribution in Bangladesh', *Public Administration and Development*, 22: 403–14

De Waal, A. and R. Omaar (1993) 'Doing harm by doing good? The international relief effort in Somalia', *Current History*, 92(574): 198–202

Drabek, A. G. (1987) 'Development alternatives: the challenge for NGOs', *World Development* (supplement), 15: ix–xv

Edwards, M. (1993) 'How relevant is development studies?', ch. 3 in F. J. Schuurman (ed.), *Beyond the Impasse: New Directions in Development Theory*, London: Zed Books

Edwards, M. and D. Hulme (eds) (1992) *Making a Difference: NGOs and Development in a Changing World*, London: Earthscan

— (eds) (1995) *Beyond the Magic Bullet: NGO Performance and Accountability in the Post-Cold War World*, London: Macmillan

Escobar, J. S. (1997) 'Religion and social change at the grassroots in Latin America', in J. Fernando and A. Heston (eds), *Annals of the American Academy of Political and Social Science*, 554: 81–103

Farrington, J. and A. Bebbington, with K. Wellard and D. Lewis (1993) *Reluctant Partners?: NGOs, the State and Sustainable Agricultural Development*, London: Routledge

Farrington, J. and D. Lewis, with S. Satish and A. Miclat-Teves (eds) (1993) *NGOs and the State in Asia: Rethinking Roles in Sustainable Agricultural Development*, London: Routledge

Fisher, J. (1993) *The Road from Rio: Sustainable Development and Nongovernmental Movement in the Third World*, New York: Praeger

— (1998) *Nongovernments: NGOs and the Political Development of the Third World*, Hartford, CT: Kumarian Press

Fisher, W. F. (1997) 'Doing good? The politics and anti-politics of NGO practices', *Annual Review of Anthropology*, 26: 439–64

Fowler, A. (1990) 'Doing it better? Where and how do NGOs have a comparative advantage in facilitating development', Agricultural and Rural Development Extension Department, University of Reading, *Bulletin*, 28: 11–20

Fox, J. (1998) 'When does reform policy influence practice? Lessons from the Bank-wide Resettlement Review', in J. Fox and L. David Brown (eds), *The Struggle for Accountability: The World Bank, NGOs and Grassroots Movements*, Cambridge, MA: MIT Press

Hanlon, J. (1991) *Mozambique: Who Calls the Shots?*, London: James Currey

Hilhorst, D. (2003) *The Real World of NGOs: Discourses, Diversity and Development*, London: Zed Books

Holcombe, S. (1995) *Managing to Empower: The Grameen Bank's Experience of Poverty Alleviation*, London: Zed Books

Honey, R. and S. Okafor (1998) *Hometown Associations: Indigenous Knowledge and Development in Nigeria*, London: Intermediate Technology Publications

Hulme, D. and M. Edwards (eds) (1997) *Too Close for Comfort? NGOs, States and Donors*, London: Macmillan

Jones, M. (1965) *Two Ears of Corn: Oxfam in Action*, London: Hodder & Stoughton

Korten, D. (1990) *Getting to the 21st Century: Voluntary Action and the Global Agenda*, Hartford, CT: Kumarian Press

Lewis, D. (1993) 'NGO–government interaction in Bangladesh: overview', in J. Farrington and D. Lewis, with S. Satish and A. Miclat-Teves (eds), *NGOs and the State in Asia: Rethinking Roles in Sustainable Agricultural Development*, London: Routledge

— (1999a) 'Introduction', in D. Lewis (ed.), *International Perspectives on Voluntary Action: Reshaping the Third Sector*, London: Earthscan

— (1999b) 'Revealing, widening, deepening?: a review of the existing and the potential contribution of anthropological approaches to "third sector" research', *Human Organization*, 58(1): 73–81

— (2002) 'Civil society in African contexts: reflections on the "usefulness' of a concept', *Development and Change*, 33(4): 569–86

Lister, S. (2001) 'Consultation as a legitimising practice: a study of British NGOs in Guatemala', Unpublished PhD dissertation, London School of Economics

MacEwan, A. (1999) *Neo-liberalism or Democracy: Economic Strategy, Markets, and Alternatives for the 21st Century*, London: Zed Books

Mackintosh, M. (1992) 'Questioning the state', in M. Wuyts, M. Mackintosh and T. Hewitt (eds), *Development Policy and Public Action*, Milton Keynes/Oxford: Open University/Oxford University Press

Mair, L. (1984) *Anthropology and Development*, Basingstoke: Macmillan

Najam, A. (1996) 'Understanding the third sector: revisiting the Prince, the Merchant and the Citizen', *Nonprofit Management and Leadership*, 7(2): 203–19

— (1999) 'Citizen organisations as policy entrepreneurs', in D. Lewis (ed.), *International Perspectives on Voluntary Action: Reshaping the Third Sector*, London: Earthscan

Oakley, P. (1999) *The Danish NGO Impact Study: A Review of Danish NGO Activities in Developing Countries*, Oxford: International NGO Training and Research Centre (INTRAC)

OECD (1993) *Non-governmental Organizations and Governments: Stakeholders for Development*, Paris: Development Centre of the Organization for Economic Co-operation and Development

Paul, S. and A. Israel (1991) *Nongovernmental Organizations and the World Bank: Co-operation for Development*, Washington, DC: World Bank

Robertson, A. F. (1984) *People and the State: An Anthropology of Planned Development*, Cambridge: Cambridge University Press

Schech, S. and J. Haggis (2000) *Culture and Development: A Critical Introduction*, Oxford: Blackwell

Sen, S. (1992) 'Non-profit organisations in India: historical development and common patterns', *Voluntas*, 3(2): 175–93

Smillie, I. (1995) *The Alms Bazaar: Altruism under Fire – Non-profit Organisations and International Development*, London: Intermediate Technology Publications

Sogge, D., K. Biekart and J. Saxby (eds) (1996) *Compassion and Calculation: The Business of Private Foreign Aid*, London: Pluto Press

Stewart, S. (1997) 'Happy ever after in the marketplace: non-government organisations and uncivil society', *Review of African Political Economy*, 71: 11–34

Tendler, J. (1982) 'Turning private voluntary organisations into development agencies: questions for evaluation', Program Evaluation Discussion Paper 12, Washington, DC: United States Agency for International Development

Thomas, A. (2000) 'Development as practice in a liberal capitalist world', *Journal of International Development*, 12: 773–87

Tvedt, T. (1998) *Angels of Mercy or Development Diplomats? NGOs and Foreign Aid*, Oxford: James Currey

— (2003) 'Development NGOs revisited: a new research agenda', Conference paper presented at workshop on 'Civil Society and the Aid System', University of Bergen, Norway, 30–31 October

Vivian, J. (1994) 'NGOs and sustainable development in Zimbabwe', *Development and Change*, 25: 181–209

Wellard, K and J. Copestake (eds) (1993) *Non-governmental Organisations and the State in Africa: Rethinking Roles in Sustainable Agricultural Development*, London: Routledge

White, S. C. (1999) 'NGOs, civil society, and the state in Bangladesh: the politics of representing the poor', *Development and Change*, 30(3): 307–26

Individuals, organizations and public action

About the contributors

Henry Bernstein is Professor of Development Studies in the University of London at the School of Oriental and African Studies (SOAS). He has long-standing research interests in social theory, the political economy of agrarian change, and the maize economy and issues of land reform in South Africa, on all of which he has published widely. He was co-editor for fifteen years, with Professor T. J. Byres, of the *Journal of Peasant Studies*, and is founding editor, again with Professor Byres, of a new *Journal of Agrarian Change* (2001). He has undertaken consultancy work in Tanzania for the International Labour Office and in Ghana for the UN International Drug Control Programme. Recent publications include 'The Boys from Bothaville, or the Rise and Fall of King Maize: A South African Story' (2004), *Journal of Agrarian Change*, and 'Rural land and land conflicts in sub-Saharan Africa' (2005), in Sam Moyo and Paris Yeros (eds), *Reclaiming the Land: The Resurgence of Rural Movements in Africa, Asia and Latin America* (Zed Books).

John Cameron is a reader in the School of Development Studies at the University of East Anglia, UK. He has been researching and teaching about development and poverty for over thirty years. Initially trained as a neo-classical economist, he is self-educated in political economy and postmodern thinking on development. His applied research interests include livelihoods analysis, population and education/employment planning, public sector reform, food and nutrition planning, and the role of NGOs in poverty alleviation programmes. A strong current research interest is in redefining 'development' from a development ethics perspective.

Robert Chambers is a research associate at the Institute for Development Studies, University of Sussex. His research interests are power and knowledge in development, including perceptions, concepts and realities of poverty and well-being; the development and dissemination of participatory methodologies for workshops and training, and for the empowerment of poor people; and relationships in development, including procedural, institutional and personal change. His publications include *Whose Reality Counts? Putting the First Last* (1997) and *Participatory Workshops: A Sourcebook of 21 Sets of Ideas and Activities* (2002), and he was a co-author of *Voices of the Poor: Crying Out for Change* (2000) (with Deepa Narayan, Meera K. Shah and Patti Petesch).

Admos Chimhowu is a lecturer in Development Studies in the School of Environment and Development, University of Manchester. He is a geographer with research interests in comparative agrarian change and social transformations in rural regions of developing countries. He has carried out research into rural land reform, livelihoods and poverty in Africa and Asia and community-based natural resource management in developing countries. His current research focuses on the nature, form and impact of informal land markets in communal land areas of southern Africa, and the differential impact of redistributive land reforms on livelihoods and rural poverty in southern Africa.

John Harriss is Professor of Development Studies at the London School of Economics, and was the founding Programme Director and later Director of the Development Studies Institute at the LSE. He was previously the Dean of the School of Development Studies at the University of East Anglia, and is a managing editor of the *Journal of Development Studies*. An anthropologist with interests of long standing in the politics and political economy of India, in particular, he is the author (with Stuart Corbridge) of *Reinventing India: Liberalization, Hindu Nationalism and Popular Democracy* (Polity Press, 2000) and, reflecting his current interests in 'new politics', of *Depoliticizing Development: The World Bank and Social Capital* (Anthem Press, 2002), and editor (with Kristian Stokke and Olle Tornquist) of *Politicising Democracy: Local Politics and Democratization in Developing Countries* (Palgrave Macmillan, 2004).

Teresa Hayter has campaigned actively against racism and for refugees and migrants for many years. Her main publications have been books on the World Bank and imperialism, including *Aid as Imperialism* (1971), *The Creation of World Poverty* (1981), *Aid: Rhetoric and Reality* (1985) and *Open Borders: The Case against Immigration Controls* (2004) on migration. Her research has been funded by the World Bank and the Overseas Development Institute, the Social Science Research Council, Friends of the Earth, Oxford University and the University of the South Bank, among others. She worked for the Greater London Council in the early 1980s and wrote about industrial democracy, including a chapter in the post-GLC publication *A Taste of Power: The Politics of Local Economics* (2004), and edited a book on the threatened closure of the car factory in Oxford in the late 1980s, *The Factory and the City* (1994). She continues to write and campaign about refugees and migrants.

Uma Kothari is a senior lecturer in Development Studies at the School of Environment and Development, University of Manchester. She has carried out research in India and Mauritius and her research interests include histories and theories of development, colonial and post-colonial discourse, social development and migration and development. She is currently researching global street pedlars and local networks in European cities, and the global garment industry. She is co-editor of *Participation: The New Tyranny?* (Zed Books, 2001, with B. Cooke) and *Development Theory and Practice: Critical Perspectives* (Palgrave, 2002, with M. Minogue). She has recently published the chapter 'Sweetening Colonialism: A Mauritian Themed Resort' (2003) in M. Lasansky and B. McClaren (eds), *Architecture and Tourism* (Berg, with T. Edensor), edited a special issue of *Journal of International Development* on 'Migration, Staying Put and Poverty' (2003) and published 'Authority and expertise: the professionalisation of international development and the ordering of dissent' in *Antipode* (2005).

David Lewis is Reader in Social Policy at the London School of Economics, University of London. An anthropologist by training, he has worked mostly in South Asia, mainly in Bangladesh, on a range of issues including rural development, NGOs and civil society and development management and policy. He is author of *The Management of Non-Governmental Development Organisations: An Introduction* (2001) and co-author of *Anthropology, Development and the Postmodern Challenge* (1996, with K. Gardner); he recently co-edited *Exploring Civil Society: Political and Cultural Contexts* (2004, with M. Glasius and H. Seckinelgin).

Ruth Pearson is Professor of Development Studies and Director of the Centre for Development Studies, Institute of Politics and International Studies, University of Leeds. Her research interests include gender, globalization and development; social policy, employment and economic and social rights; women organizing in the global economy; and community currencies and social enterprise. She is also interested in North–South development, an exploration of development policies and initiatives that have relevance in both developed and developing countries, including neighbourhood and community development, health and safety issues, violence and security, and the rights of formal and informal sector workers. Her recent publications include *Globalization, Export-oriented Employment and Social Policy: Gendered Connections* (Palgrave, 2004, edited with S. Razavi), *Corporate Responsibility and Labour Rights: Codes of Conduct in the Global Economy* (Earthscan, 2002, edited with R. Jenkins and G. Seyfang), *Women and Credit: Researching the Past and Prefiguring the Future* (Berg, 2002, edited with Beverly Lemire) and 'Organising home based workers in the global economy: an action research approach' (2004) in *Development in Practice*.

Phil Woodhouse is a senior lecturer in Environment and Rural Development at the School of Environment and Development, University of Manchester. He worked as a soil scientist in Mozambique for eight years. For the past eighteen years he has been based in the UK, teaching and undertaking research on institutional aspects of natural resource use in southern and West Africa, and on indicators of resource use sustainability in Africa and Latin America. His recent publications include 'Telling environmental change like it is?: reflections on a study in sub-Saharan Africa' (2001) in *Journal of Agrarian Change* (with H. Bernstein) and 'Constructing a farm level indicator of sustainable agricultural practice' (2001) in *Ecological Economics* (with D. Rigby, T. Young and M. Burton).

Index